Essays by Lewis White Beck

Essays by Lewis White Beck:
Five Decades as a Philosopher

edited by
Predrag Cicovacki

 University of Rochester Press

First published 1998

University of Rochester Press
668 Mt. Hope Avenue
Rochester, NY 14620   USA

and at P.O. Box 9
Woodbridge, Suffolk IP12 3DF
United Kingdom

ISBN 1–58046–042–9

Library of Congress Cataloging-in-Publication Data

Beck, Lewis White.
    [Essays. Selections]
    Essays by Lewis White Beck : five decades as a philosopher /
edited by Predrag Cicovacki.
        p.   cm.
    Includes bibliographical references and index.
    ISBN 1–58046–042–9 (alk. paper)
    1. Philosophy.   I. Cicovacki, Predrag.   II. Title.
B945.B3761C53   1998
191—cd21   98–30651
                                                                                  CIP

British Library Cataloguing-in-Publication Data
A catalogue record for this book is
available from the British Library

Printed in the United States of America
This publication is printed on acid-free paper

*"Du gleichst dem Geist, den du begreifst,
Nicht mir!"*

— Goethe, *Faust*

Contents

Acknowledgments

During his lifetime Lewis White Beck (1913-1997) published two books of his essays—*Studies in the Philosophy of Kant* and *Essays on Kant and Hume*—which deal almost exclusively with different aspects of Kant's philosophy. He also thought about publishing a collection of his essays not so exclusively related to Kant. This volume brings together Beck's essays—from the earliest to the latest—that reflect a variety of his philosophical interests. It includes papers that deal with epistemology, philosophy of science, ethics, aesthetics, philosophy of literature, extra-terrestrials, as well as a few late papers on Kant that were not included in the previous collections. These original and valuable contributions to various philosophical disciplines will provide a more rounded and adequate picture of Beck's philosophical creativity and humanistic orientation. Two more pieces of the puzzle are provided by Beck's own account of how he became a philosopher and by a complete bibliography of his publications.

In the preparation of this volume, I received much help from Ethan Rider, Patrick Tinsley, Mary Cerasuolo, and Kenneth Scott. I am grateful to them, as well as to Sean Culhane, the director of the University of Rochester Press, for his friendly support and valuable editorial advise.

I would also like to thank the following journals and publishing companies for their permission to republish Beck's essays: *The Journal of Philosophy* for "The Synoptic Method," "The Formal Properties of Ethical Wholes," "The Principle of Parsimony," and "Judgments of Meaning in Art;" *Philosophy and Phenomenological Research* for "Psychology and the Norms of Knowledge;" *Synthese* for "Kant on the Uniformity of Nature;" the American Philosophical Association for "Extraterrestrial Intelligent Life;" AMS Press for "World Enough, and Time;" Cornell University Press for "What Have We Learned from Kant?;" Kluwer for "Five Concepts of Freedom in Kant;" Nelson Hall for "Philosophy as Literature;" and Oxford University Press for "Conscious and Unconscious Motives" and "How I Became Almost a Philosopher."

ix

Foreword by Robert L. Holmes:

Remembering Lewis White Beck

When I stepped from the plane into the cold Rochester winters night in 1961, I was met by a short, impeccably attired man who greeted me rather formally but with a cordial southern drawl; then, considering the lateness of the hour, delivered me directly to my motel, with a kind offer—which I declined—of the loan of some pajamas to offset the inconvenience of lost luggage. That was the beginning of 35 years of association with Lewis White Beck, who was to become both friend and esteemed colleague.

But not right away. Esteemed colleague he was from the start; but friendship took time to develop. I was for some time to him, "Mr. Holmes," he to me, "Professor Beck," and some of that formality first had to melt away. But there was always a thoughtfulness and unpretentiousness to Lewis that shone through the formality, and that quickly laid the groundwork for friendship. Knowing, for example, that he had to be out of town when I arrived the following summer, he—the distinguished Kant scholar and chair of the Department— offered this beginning assistant professor the use of his office until his return. This offer I accepted. So while I never slept in his pajamas— and never came close to stepping into his shoes—I began my years at Rochester sitting at his desk.

The department was small in those days, as it has remained, consisting of Colin Murray Turbayne, Jerome Stolnitz, and John Stewart, with Peter Winch visiting from Swansea ("Every philosophy department should have a British moral philosopher," Lewis once said, and a succession of British visitors followed). Keith Lehrer, James Cornman, Henry Kyburg, Jr., Rolf Eberle and Richard Taylor were among those soon to join the department, as the national reputation of its fledgling Ph.D. program soared. Colloquia with visiting speakers were typically followed by dinner at the Chalet, a small downtown restaurant whose proprietor hailed from Königsberg (a fact that probably had as much to do with our dining there as the beef stroganoff Lewis usually ordered) who would break out the accordion and regale us with song during dessert. We'd sometimes conclude with fireside brandy at Lewis and his wife Caroline's home where some of the richest free-flow of ideas would take place. Lewis never dominated discussion, but he was invariably centrally involved, setting the tone if not the direction. He would slouch comfortably into a chair, light his pipe, and then—as though those were the moments he lived for—venture into a cooperative, often serendipitous foray into the world of ideas.

It's been said that a man with a pipe has a decided advantage in an argument—and, one might add, in philosophical discussion. I've always thought of Lewis in this regard. An aura of reflectiveness would surround him, as he puffed deeply and looked off in thought, or jabbed the pipe into the air to reinforce a point, or simply lit and relit it endlessly while collecting his thoughts or just keeping his hands busy. Most fascinating of all, he had a way of holding the bowl of the pipe in his hand, crooking his thumb up over the top and tamping down the burning ashes—a practice that left his thumb looking like a piece of burnt cork. Though he later gave them up, he was a man for whom pipes were made. Clenched tightly in his jaw, his pipe was the finishing touch as he wore his (Sherlock) Holmesian hat and walked his beloved bloodhound, Snapdragon.

As relaxed and congenial as he was in informal settings, however, Lewis was a taskmaster in the classroom, and I learned early on to avoid scheduling my graduate seminars during the same semesters as his. His courses were so demanding, and he inspired such awe in students, that it was difficult to get them to devote time to other work when studying with him. He always said that Ph.D. oral examinations should be a "chastening" experience, and it was as though his courses were preparation for that experience. He would call on students without warning (as, to my chagrin, he did me years later when I sat in on a seminar of his after he'd retired), and the unprepared quickly learned humility.

At the same time, he would spare no effort to help committed students. Although best remembered by many for his concern for graduate students—particularly in his retired years through the vehicle of his *privatissimum* of invited students with whom he met regularly almost to the time of his death—his concern extended no less to undergraduates. Indeed, he was the first recipient of the University's Edward Peck Curtis Award for Excellence in Undergraduate Teaching (a fact which afforded him another opportunity for self-deprecating humor; his colleagues convulsed with laughter when he told them over lunch that he'd been assured by the IRS that the award wasn't taxable because it was "unearned"). He nurtured one outstanding student through her intellectual development, arranging special provision for her to take her Masters while still completing her undergraduate degree. "She's smarter than I am," he once chuckled, "she just doesn't know as much yet." But the most telling case to me was of a more personal nature, when the parents of one of our philosophy majors visited the university and arranged to talk with Lewis, who was then still chairman. He invited me to the meeting in my capacity as undergraduate advisor. Although they were unspecific about what troubled them, beyond reporting darkly that her roommate was seeing a thirty year-old man, the parents were distressed about the course of their daughter's life and were considering removing her from college. Lewis listened long and carefully. Then he spoke. Most of the details of what he said I've forgotten, but they weren't important. What was important was what he conveyed, and that I remember clearly. In the measured tones of his rich and well-modulated voice he counseled patience; but in a way that reflected a wisdom and understanding that carried far more weight than purely rational argument or platitudes about college being a time of growth ever could. The full extent of his concern for students—and not merely as students, but as persons as well—came through, and the parents left reassured that all would be well if they left their daughter in school, as, indeed, it was, when she graduated with flying colors. From that moment on I saw Lewis, not merely as the pre-eminent scholar, but as a man of humanity and compassion as well.

Our friendship fully blossomed during the summer of 1968. Lewis had been asked to do a second edition of his first book, *Philosophic Inquiry*, but it was a task for which he had little time, as he was hard at work on his *Early German Philosophy*. He asked if I'd be willing to co-author it with him—proposing revisions and doing whatever new writing was required. So we worked through that summer, Lewis on German philosophy, I on *Philosophic Inquiry*, dropping in one another's office frequently when there were points to discuss, talking through the positions to present on various issues, and lunching together at Earl's Tavern across the Genesee River. "It's my book, but you wrote it," he joked when we finished. Not true, of course; I merely added some embroidery to what he had done. But we bonded, as contemporary jargon would say, during that summer, and although we never again spent quite so much time together, the connection remained fast.

No one who knew Lewis well could forget his legendary, even cosmic, disdain for exercise. He was fond of quoting someone— maybe Chesterton, I've forgotten—to the effect that whenever he felt an urge to exercise, he'd lie down until it went away. So this made one particular encounter especially memorable during the last few years of his life. I was warming up before jogging on the University's indoor track, a portion of which runs through a tunnel underlying the gymnasium. It was an odd hour of the morning and I was sure I was the only one in the field house. Suddenly I looked up and there, to my astonishment, emerged Lewis from the tunnel, fully attired in street clothes, bow-tie, hat, and cane, walking laps in the center of the track. He looked at me and I looked at him. Then with characteristic aplomb, and without missing a stride, he said "Don't tell anyone," and continued on his way.

To many, Lewis was the consummate gentleman; and that he was. To others, he was the master scholar; and that he was also. To me, however, he was first and foremost a genuine man of learning— perhaps one of the last, certainly one of the very few I've known; and by this I mean not just a learned man, of whom there are many, who have extensive accumulations of knowledge (often as not accompanied by desiccated intellects that derive little pleasure from their learning), but a man who loved learning; whose natural habitat was the world of ideas, whether philosophical, scientific or literary, and who roamed far and wide in that world, delighting in new discoveries and taking relish in sharing them. He was respectful of those who accompanied him and supportive (particularly with students) when their visions led them on a different path from his. In this respect he was perhaps closer to the Taoist ideal than to any Kantian virtue in leading without trying to control.

Lewis White Beck was, as one former student put it, a magisterial presence in the department, but he was also a rare human being who exemplified some of the finest values to which the life of the mind can aspire. It was a privilege to have known him.

Introduction by Predrag Cicovacki:

Lewis White Beck as a Philosopher

How does a person become a philosopher? Does one always feel predisposed toward philosophizing, or does a call come suddenly? In one of his last writings, a short autobiographical piece: "How I Became Almost a Philosopher,"[1] Lewis White Beck (1913–1997) described how he "accidentally" found his way toward philosophy. The tale begins with young Lewis, a chemistry major at Emory University, aspiring to become a scientist. These hopes were blasted by the discovery that he was color-blind. Fortunately for him (and philosophy), in this moment of desperation Beck found "a real, living philosopher"—Leroy Loemker—who convinced him to devote his intellectual gifts to philosophy. For the rest of his life, lab experiments were replaced by thought experiments. After finishing a graduate program at Duke University and a "year of apprenticeship" with Nicolai Hartmann in then pre-war Berlin, Beck himself became "a real, living philosopher" for countless generations of students. Interacting with students, teaching them, and learning with them, was for Beck an indispensable aspect of his philosophical life.[2] His students (I had the special privilege of being one of them) could always count on his time, patience, and critical yet well-intended comments. Moreover, they could count on his honest and constructive advice about life issues, like that he once received from his teacher Loemker.

Beck spent most of his teaching career at the University of Rochester, from 1949 until 1979. Even after he officially retired and

---

[1] See Appendix 1 below.

[2] Several weeks after his bypass operation, at the age of seventy-nine, Beck wrote to me complaining about his doctor who demanded he stay at home and stop any activity at the university. In a Socratic manner, Beck replied to the doctor that, without discussing philosophy, life is not worth living and continued with his seminars.

for the next eighteen years, Beck continued to conduct informal seminars and meet regularly with graduate students to discuss their research and writing. The pride of Beck's later years was his private seminar—*privatissimum*, as he called it—held with a few select students, which he continued until two months before his death.

What kind of a philosopher was Beck? To prepare ourselves for answering this question, let us first briefly review each of the essays included in this collection.

I

In one of his first articles, "The Synoptic Method" (1937), Beck intends to establish what a synoptic method is and show that, besides analysis, this method is an important tool of empirical science and philosophy. As a method of perception and interpretation of reality, synopsis is (from the time of Plato) as common to philosophy as it is to biology and other scientific disciplines. Ordinarily, "synopsis" means something like a survey, or a process of seeing various things together. Beck argues that, although common, this definition is inadequate. In his view, the synoptic method is a way of seeing an object as a part in its relation to some objective (or real) whole. Unlike Hume, who believes that wholes are fictions, Beck argues that "The concept 'whole' is probably a primitive idea admitting of no definition. But it is possible to exhibit what we mean by the word" (7).[3] It is possible to do that because being a part of an objective whole makes an empirically determinable difference to the characteristics of some parts. A criterion of the objective wholeness is that an object may show characteristics when it is in a whole which it does not display when it is not a part. The philosophical significance of this view is that the application of the synoptic method may lead us to the discovery of some characteristics of objects that would not be discernible by means of a (causal or conceptual) analysis of the same objects. The contribution of Beck's article is in the following insight: "The concept of the whole is by means of the synoptic method brought into scientific categorization with as much legacy as that of cause" (12). With an unguarded

---

[3] This, and all subsequent references to the included essays by Beck, refers to the page number in this volume.

optimism, he concludes: "The concept of whole may well be the central category for philosophy, guiding us in a synthesis of our knowledge and showing the relevance of the determination of the parts by the whole to the general problems of metaphysics" (12).

The article on "The Formal Properties of Ethical Wholes" (1941) provides an illustration and application of the main points of the previous essay. Beck begins by criticizing Bentham, who (in Beck's language) attempted to provide an analysis of values and ethical wholes by means of a quantitative scale of values. This approach not only neglects many important complexities of our moral practice but, as G.E. Moore demonstrates, also suffers from the "naturalistic fallacy" of confusing value with one of its "natural accompaniments." With Moore, Beck argues that what the whole is cannot be predicted from a knowledge of the values of the parts which make it up. If there is to be any genuine criterion of wholeness, it must be found in the parts themselves, not in the whole as such. The problem is to find what this criterion could be without falling back into Bentham's quantitative scales. Moore tries to solve this problem by means of the idea of "intrinsic value," which he defines as the value a thing would have if there were nothing else in the universe besides it. Beck believes that Moore's attempt is unsatisfactory. Moore's proposal loses all empirical meaning because we could never determine empirically when the concept of "intrinsic value" is really applicable to a group of values. The value of parts of a certain whole cannot be fixed either in a quantitative way, as Bentham attempts, or in a metaphysical way, as Moore suggests. There simply is no regular proportion between the values of parts and the value of the whole. The relevant whole in this case is determined by our ethical practice, and a careful observation of that practice reveals that "the rank order of valuableness of any two things may vary according to the value of the wholeness of which they are parts." Moreover, "this variation in choiceworthiness is the sole criterion of the reality of an objective whole of values" (19). This kind of solution clearly leans toward "contextualism," a view highly unpopular at that time but more appreciated nowadays.

In the third essay, "The Principle of Parsimony in Empirical Science" (1943), Beck continues to emphasize the relevance of practice in this case scientific practice. Focusing on the principle of parsimony, which he understands as the demand for simplicity in explanations, Beck poses the following questions: 1. Is the principle of parsimony applicable in a definitive and unique way, permitting a decision as to the value of conflicting scientific theories? 2. Does the principle of parsimony have any realistic (i.e., objective or cosmological) implications for the material to which it is applied? After discussing four different ways (metaphysical, naturalistic, formalistic, and conventionalistic) in which philosophers attempt to make the principle of parsimony plausible, Beck's answer to both questions is negative. A closer look at scientific practice shows that in the normal course of the development of science, the principle of parsimony does not play a very significant role. In those cases, it is the principle of adequacy which is dominant. According to Beck, we cannot derive any specific rules for the application of the principle of parsimony. This principle "leaves entirely unanswered the question as to whether the metaphysical nature of the world is such as to make simple explanations 'true'" (43). The problem of the ultimate nature of reality is metaphysical, not methodological.

In one of his rare essays on aesthetics, "Judgments of Meaning in Art" (1944), Beck defends the traditionally disputed authenticity of art through the concept of meaning in art. This autonomous "form" of meaning in art cannot be accounted for either in terms of cognitive standards extraneous to art, or in terms of impressionistic and emotivistic conceptions of art. What, then, is characteristic for the uniquely artistic kind of meaning? In Beck's words, "Art which has a meaning is a sensuous presentation of connotations without denotations. If I may paraphrase Kant, art is 'meaning without the meant'" (52). If art is to have a meaning, its meaning cannot depend on a denotation to an external object or event. For that meaning we have to look at the content and the form of a work of art. Although Beck believes that both of these elements are important, he correctly emphasizes the relevance of form. The form of a work of art "serves as a sensuous receptacle for many specific connotations but is not limited to one, being a sensuous schema or essence but not a discursive universal" (53). This unique kind of "universality which transcends specificity of denotation also explains the paradox that we can both assert that a work of art has a meaning and yet deny in principle that we can enunciate its meaning" (53). The most we can do, according to Beck, is to say what a great work of art does *not* mean. Its positive meaning can never be fully determined and captured. If this provocative view is true, then we should think of a work of art as being essentially open-ended, rather than as a finished product. We should think of a work of art as inviting our participation, rather than a fully objective analysis.

In the next essay, "Psychology and the Norms of Knowledge" (1954), Beck is concerned with two distinct, yet related, projects of epistemology. One is to establish the internal epistemological norms by means of which we determine that something is an instance of knowledge. The other is to find out the causal connections of the occurrence of knowledge. Contemporary philosophers recognize an apparent incompatibility here, and try to resolve it by choosing between one or the other of these positions. Beck has a different approach. He first shows that the tension between these two projects is comparable to the one discussed in Kant's "Third Antinomy" of pure reason. In our case, the thesis would be that we cannot know anything unless we govern our thoughts by certain non-causal norms, and the antithesis would be that both the necessary and sufficient conditions of knowledge are causal. Like Kant, Beck wants to show that both the thesis and the antithesis could be true. Unlike Kant, Beck does not believe that the resolution is merely linguistic, i.e., that it is based on the equivocation of the word "condition." A genuine resolution needs to occur on a more profound level. Beck offers an original and insightful resolution of the tension in terms of the distinction between particulars and universals. The casual explanation regards the subject only in relation to particulars, which are not cognitive objects but stimuli or causes. "From this kind of behavior there can arise an awareness of universals when the subject can respond in some way to diverse causes. This awareness of universals is the necessary condition of awareness of or intention to objects, and behavior is under normative conditions when this intention or awareness exercises a discipline over the simple cause-effect sequences which would occur if the universal were not present in consciousness" (70-71). Beck's strategy has important implications for epistemology. If it works, his idea demonstrates what contemporary epistemologists stubbornly refuse to admit, namely that both the causal aspect and the normative aspect may be indispensable for the possibility of knowledge.

The seventh essay, "Conscious and Unconscious Motives" (1966), gives further consideration to these issues. The accent is now on human behavior, not knowledge, but the anti-reductivist and anti-determinist way of thinking is present as well. To the same question about an agent's behavior we can give different answers. There is first a generic difference between what Beck calls "agent answers" and "spectator answers," each of which can be further subdivided. We can have, for instance, a "motive answer," an answer that reports a disposition and has a predictive value for other behavior of the same agent. Or we can have an "intention answer," which is not dispositional, but refers strictly to the episode in question. Beck also discusses what he calls an "obstacle" answer and a "compulsory" answer. The former informs us about an external obstacle that prevented an intention from being fulfilled, and the latter indicates a reduced degree of deliberate control in comparison to a normally motivated action. There are, furthermore, causal answers, which in turn could be mental causal answers or physical causal answers. One of Beck's central aims in the article is to show that there is no continuum of intentions and motives, through compulsions and responses to obstacles, along the range of mental causes. There is also no reduction from the former to the latter, which means that there is no ground for mechanicistic determinism of intentional actions, which is so popular in empirical psychology.

Beck's other aim is to show that there can be genuine unconscious intentions and motives for action, and that they should not be confused with causes, as is frequently the case in psychoanalysis. This confusion arises, according to Beck, because of our dogmatic commitment to causal determinism, "as if there could be no other kind of determinism or predictability in intentional actions" (89). Beck argues that Freud obviously confuses motives and causes. One interesting question that Beck does not raise is: What about Kant?

One of the most interesting articles in this collection is certainly "Extraterrestrial Intelligent Life" (1973). Many philosophers have believed that there is extraterrestrial life: Aristotle, Nicolas of Cusa, Giordano Bruno, Gassendi, Locke, Lambert, Kant, and William Whewell, among others. After reviewing numerous ancient and modern arguments in support of our belief in extraterrestrial life, Beck expresses his doubts that an adequate argument can be found. The main problem is that it seems impossible to avoid one or another form of anthropomorphism. Nevertheless, Beck does not reject these speculations about extraterrestrial intelligent life as irrational or irrelevant. Together with Carl Gustav Jung, Beck believes that the insistence on keeping alive the archetypal idea that we are not alone reveals something important about the human condition: "We are now suffering from technological shock, destroying by radiological and chemical, if not moral, pollution the only abode of life we know. Are we not enough like our ancestors to respond with the same desperate hope they did? ...The eschatological hope of help from heaven revives when the heavens of modern astronomy replace the Heaven of religion" (116). Beck is not opposed to our search for extraterrestrial intelligent life. "But somewhat like people who object to spending money needed in the ghettoes on exploring the moon, I think the best hope for our survival is to be based on understanding human predicaments here on earth, not on expecting a saving message from super-human beings in the skies" (117).

"World Enough, and Time" (1979) is yet another article that reveals Beck's deep humanistic orientation. He deals with one of the perennial problems of philosophy, that of relation of appearance to reality. The extreme views are well known: one takes eternity as ontologically real and basic, and the other focuses the attention on time as empirically experienced and quantified appearance. The first view reveals the other-worldly orientation, and the second finds this world "quite enough." The second view is characteristic of the Enlightenment philosophers, and Beck discusses in detail its four great figures: Newton, Locke, Leibniz, and Kant. He summarizes the attitudes of these philosophers by quoting from one of his favorite books, *Finnagan's Wake*: "Shake eternity, and lick creation." How does Beck understand this sentence? "It suggests to me that man can master the world ('lick creation') if he breaks up the solid, static, Eleatic world ('shake eternity') of which the world of his knowledge and action was thought to be only a moving image—perhaps not exactly an illusory image, but at least one lacking the ontological dignity and perfection of true reality" (142). For the philosophers of the Enlightenment there is world enough and time to rationally explain all the past, present, and future states of the universe, without appealing to miracles, the act of creation, or God. As Beck summarizes the predicaments of the Enlightenment, "We were left with the time without any pretensions to eternity; time was quite enough" (144).

In "Philosophy as Literature" (1980), Beck continues to philosophize in an inspired, almost poetic, way and baldly asserts at the beginning of this essay: "For me, philosophy is, among other things, a genre of literature" (145). To answer the question: What is literature about?, Beck distinguishes between two meanings of "about": "reportorial about," i.e., truth about, which is relevant for science, and "fictive about," i.e., truth to, which is relevant for literature. The "fictive about" cannot be entirely fictitious. "High literature" is true to life: it "contains ideas and beliefs and doubts which have traditionally been the subject matter of philosophy: fate and freedom, nature and convention, truth and illusion, man and God, the one and the many, what is and what ought to be, vice and virtue, happiness and misery" (151-152). Does that make literature a genre of philosophy, we may ask? Not quite. "A philosopher has to prove, and each of the twenty-one steps in his proof is equally important, no matter how tedious it may be" (153). By contrast, the poet does not prove; he exhibits. The poet will make us see philosophical models; his logic is the logic of images, not of abstract concepts. Does this mean that the "philosophical about" is the "reportorial about"? Not entirely, replies Beck. For philosophy is also concerned with the human world, with the world of human creations, human values, and human suffering. That is what philosophy and literature have in common. Moreover, argues Beck, the relation between the content of philosophy and its literary expression will depend on our understanding of philosophy. Plato did not accidentally write dialogues, nor did Nietzsche whimsically use the aphoristic style. A dialogue, that perennial form of philosophical discourse, "is the outward dramatic form of dialectic, which Socrates defined as the discourse of the soul with itself" (160). Beck's message seems to be that to answer the questions of what philosophy is and what form of expression it should take, everyone's soul must enter into dialogue with itself.

In the essay "Kant on the Uniformity of Nature" (1981), Beck deals with a frequently discussed issue concerning the nature of causal inference. He first reconstructs three principles that underlie Hume's understanding of causal inference: 1) the principle of universal validity, which says that everything that begins to exist necessarily has a cause; 2) the principle of necessity, which argues that between a case of A and a case of B there stands a necessary relation such that the case of A could not (*ceteris paribus*) have been followed by a case of non-B; 3) the principle of the generalizability of the causal connection, which asserts that like causes necessarily have like effects. Although these principles are logically independent, Hume believed that there is a deep psychological connection between them. Believing that the origin of the last principle is due to the psychological mechanism of association, Hume tried to enquire into the validity of the other two principles. He concluded that the regularity of nature, based on the causal principles, was not grounded in nature itself but in our mechanism of association. Hume's failure to demonstrate the objective validity of the causal principles woke Kant from his "dogmatic slumber." Kant reacted to Hume, and Beck tries to show in this article how complex, ambiguous, and changing Kant's position was toward Hume's causal concerns. On the one hand, Kant agreed with Hume that every specific causal connection must be discovered empirically. On the other hand, Kant tried to show in the "Second Analogy" of the *Critique of Pure Reason* that the generalizability principle is not the result of an induction of naïve and raw experience. Against Hume, Kant argued that Hume's third principle epistemologically presupposes the other two. Beck's principal concern in this essay is that, even if Kant was correct on this issue, the question of whether Kant himself was able to establish the validity of the principles of universality and necessity still remains open. In the "Second Analogy" Kant tried to establish that the principle of universality is the constitutive principle of our knowledge of objects of experience. As is well known from the enormous secondary literature, there are problems with Kant's argument. Beck believes that perhaps Kant's best overall reply to Hume was the one from the *Critique of Judgment*; there Kant suggested that the causal principle(s) should be regarded as the regulative, not the constitutive, principle(s) of cognitive experience. Yet if that was Kant's best try, then—with the exception of the "Second Analogy"—"the differences between the Humean and the Kantian conceptions of the regularity of nature [are not] as great and as sharp as has generally been believed" (179).

As its title indicates, Beck's essay "Five Concepts of Freedom in Kant" (1986) reconstructs various ways in which Kant understands the concept of freedom. The first of them is an empirical concept of freedom, in the sense of something done voluntarily, without coercion. This concept is relevant for an empirical determination with respect to whether a specific act is done freely. The second concept is that of moral freedom. For Kant, this concept is analytically connected with the concept of pure moral law. In its negative sense this concept points toward an intuition about freedom that cannot be merely understood as an effect of natural causes. In its positive sense, this freedom is called autonomy, i.e., an ability to undertake actions in accordance with, and out of respect for, the moral law. The third concept of freedom refers to a broader, non-moral conception of freedom, relevant for any decision making. Both the second and third sense of freedom presuppose, according to Kant, that one's decision, moral or otherwise, is not causally determined in advance. They presuppose what Beck marks as the fourth concept of freedom, i.e., transcendental freedom. This concept of freedom emerges from Kant's attempt to resolve the "Third Antinomy" of the *Critique of Pure Reason*. There Kant confronts the possibility of a non-temporal causality (of the first cause, for instance) in the thesis, and a complete natural causality in the antithesis. Kant's solution is to locate the natural causality in the phenomenal world (which can be known), and the non-temporal causality in the noumenal world (which cannot be known). Beck does not find this solution satisfactory, and believes that Kant himself changed his mind about it as well, at the time when he was writing the *Critique of Judgment*. Kant's initial solution proves both too much and too little, according to Beck. It proves too much because it implies that, if every phenomenon has its transcendental ground or noumenal causation, then any human action must be free, which is not the case. Kant's solution also proves too little because, according to Beck, the ubiquity of noumenal causality trivializes the concept of freedom. Beck argues that Kant needs a fifth concept of freedom, which would be more flexible than the fourth conception. This new concept is based on the "two-aspects view," instead of the unacceptable "two-worlds view." The phenomenal man and the noumenal man are nothing but different aspects of the same personality, of the same reality. Accordingly, the natural causality and the non-temporal causality are two aspects of the same reality. The difference between them is not ontological but perspectival; it is the difference of regulative principles chosen with regard to the divergent purposes and contexts of two kinds of inquiry. In Beck's words, these principles are "on equal footing and, in different spheres of experience, equally inescapable. Their truth is not absolute, for they limit each other; their truth is in the context of their respective employment definite and justified; outside the respective contexts there are no criteria for their correct application" (194). In this, as well as in the previous essay, Beck's message amounts to saying that the first two *Critiques*, the *Critique of Pure*

Reason and the *Critique of Practical Reason*, should be read from the point of view of the *Critique of Judgment*! The final essay in this volume, "What Have We Learned from Kant?" (1981), has a very important place in Beck's opus. The first version of this essay was written already in 1946 ("What Can We Learn from Kant?"), and Beck kept revising and expanding it for the next four decades. Beck does not hide why Kant was so important to him: "Great philosophers such as Kant speak not just to the professoriate, but to all who agree with Socrates that the unexamined life is not worth living" (199). Kant makes it clear that the interests of the school are subordinated to the interests of humanity. Beck takes it that the central question of Kant's—and apparently Beck's own—philosophy is: What is man? This is a single common theme running through Kant's three *Critiques*, although Kant nowhere offers a simple answer to it. A closer look at Kant's critical philosophy reveals that Kant is always preoccupied with discovering the ways in which the mind's own activities are projected into and reflected back by nature. The creative activity of the mind is, then, the leading motif of Kant's philosophy, and Beck takes it that Kant's answer to the question of the nature of man is: Man is creator. In Beck's words: "Man is no god, but in his creativity he may be godlike, and many of the tasks previously assigned to god in creation and governance of the world are reassigned by Kant to man" (209-210). Beck speaks here in Kant's voice, but it is hardly possible to resist the impression that he is revealing his own deepest convictions. This is particularly true of one of the concluding passages of this essay: "For Kant, only reasonable human beings, in spite of all their errors, can create a world in which there is some chance for well-being and happiness, and only the criticism and discipline of reason can lead toward the requisite wisdom" (210). This statement may well be the best expression of Beck's own philosophical orientation.

II

Walter Kaufmann once remarked that there are two inspirational sources of philosophy: science and religion. As we have already indicated, for Lewis White Beck, that source was initially science. The first five essays (which belong to the first two decades of his publishing

activity) show that Beck's early philosophical approach was "analytic."
He was mostly preoccupied with the use of the scientific method in our
attempts to explain various aspects of reality. Beck took for granted
our reliance on science and its method. Yet he questioned what the
proper scientific method really is, and, even more frequently, he asked
whether this method was the only tool that we could, and should, use in
our efforts to understand reality. As much as he was opposed to
irrationality and superstitions, Beck argued against the one-sidedness
and narrowness of the prevailing positivistic orientation in science and
analytic philosophy with equal animosity. Whether he wrote about
metaphysical, epistemological, ethical, or aesthetical questions, Beck
tried to show the complexity of the issues involved, and to demonstrate
the need for a variety of complementary approaches and
methodological devices. The guiding idea of his early philosophy was
that philosophical questions are synoptic, which Beck explained as
follows:

> By synoptic vision we mean 'seeing things whole', seeing
> everything in its bearing upon everything else, seeing things in
> their internal togetherness. This characteristic of philosophy really
> sums up all the others. Whereas science and many of the special
> branches of philosophy deal with only particular aspects of things
> or narrow 'universe of discourse,' philosophy itself is an attempt to
> remain keenly aware that we live in *one* world.[4]

While Beck entered philosophy through the royal gates of science, in
the late 1950s his interests shifted more and more toward ethical and
religious questions. Characteristic of that shift is the following
example. While his first book, *Philosophical Inquiry* (published in
1952) concluded with two chapters on naturalism, the second edition of
the same book, published in 1968 and co-authored with Robert
Holmes, ended with an extensive discussion of "faith, inquiry, and
conduct." This shift of focus is already visible in 1960, when Beck
published two books: *A Commentary on Kant's Critique of Practical
Reason*, and *Six Secular Philosophers*. Beck's interest turned from
naturalistic towards humanistic concerns, from what could be roughly

---

[4] *Philosophical Inquiry*, p. 21; Beck's emphasis. For a full reference of
Beck's works, see Appendix 2.

called "philosophy of nature" towards what he called "philosophy of man." In Beck's words:

> [T]he synoptic function of the philosopher, who is supposed to see things steadily and see them whole, is lost if the philosopher does not remain sensitive to those concerns which have given religion its central place in life. Without this sensitivity, philosophers only take in each other's technical washing in logic and epistemology and metaphysics, and do not keep alive that wonder in which, Aristotle said, all philosophy begins.[5]

The shift from philosophy of nature to philosophy of man coincides with Beck's growing and deepening interest in Kant's philosophy.[6] This development is not accidental. Kant himself initially found motivation for philosophical thinking in science, only to later base his critical philosophy on the primacy of "practical" over "theoretical" reason. Kant intended to show that what reason cannot accomplish in its theoretical, speculative use, it could achieve in its practical use, i.e., in its efforts to guide our behavior and give a rational foundation to our hopes. Over the course of his philosophical career, Kant moved from the question of the nature and limits of knowledge to questions like: What ought I to do?, What may I hope?, and ultimately to the question that also became Beck's preoccupation: What is man?

With good reason, then, in philosophical and wider intellectual circles Beck was considered a Kant scholar. Beck was undoubtedly a philosopher who found much inspiration in Kant, and who agreed with Kant on many issues. I hope, however, that this collection of essays will help us rethink the impression that he was mainly a "Kant-scholar." The essays included here also show that Beck was a philosopher who stood on his own ground, and had a philosophical approach of his own. To clarify this, it may be useful to compare Beck with Ernst Cassirer, who was also deeply indebted to Kant, and whose

---

[5] *Six Secular Philosophers*, p. 17.

[6] Beck's books *A Commentary on Kant's Critique of Practical Reason*, *Studies in the Philosophy of Kant*, *Early German Philosophy*, and *Essays in Kant and Hume* mark important milestones in Kant scholarship. For a renewed interest for Kant's philosophy in the English-speaking world, Beck's translations of the *Critique of Practical Reason*, *The Foundations of the Metaphysics of Morals*, and Kant's numerous essays in political philosophy were no less important.

book *Kant's Life and Thought* still is, I believe, the best introduction to Kant's philosophy.

Both Cassirer and Beck start their philosophizing with a deep and fundamentally sound understanding of Kant's philosophy. For both of them, an informed and comprehensive scholarship is a starting point and a necessary component of any serious philosophical thinking. Their writing is clear and engaging, their thinking sympathetic and yet not apologetic. What both Cassirer and Beck are interested in is finding out what is still valid and significant in Kant's philosophy. For many more decades to come, all of those seriously interested in the lasting legacy of Kant's philosophy will be well advised to turn to the texts of Cassirer and Beck.

This comparison between Cassirer and Beck is neither accidental nor arbitrary. Beck frequently mentioned that Cassirer's *Substance and Function* was one of the first philosophical books that he seriously studied, and he advised his students to do the same. Beck was also always willing to admit that "the influence of Cassirer on my thought is visible in almost all my writings."[7]

There are, however, some important differences in the way Cassirer and Beck understood philosophy. Cassirer was interested in the perennial questions of philosophy, but he was also preoccupied with finding definite answers to these questions. His monumental work, *The Philosophy of Symbolic Forms*, is a clear testimony of his desire to offer, if not exactly a philosophical system, then certainly a synoptic vision of the history of Western civilization.

As can be seen from his early essays published in this volume, Beck started his career by insisting on the synoptic function of philosophy. In the late essays, however, we do not find that synoptic vision. What is missing is not the insistence on such a vision, but the presence of any definitely shaped vision. Viewed wrongly, this lacuna is deceptive since it is largely responsible for our perception of Beck as nothing but a Kant scholar. A closer look at his essays will show that this picture is one-sided and inaccurate. There should be no doubt that Beck was a Kant scholar. Yet the message that emerges from his work is that, while scholarship is important, it is not so in itself, on its own ground. We see there that the value of scholarship for Beck consists not in resolving problems and providing definite answers, but in intensifying

---

[7] *The Actor and the Spectator*, x.

those perennial questions concerning our humanity. As Beck himself explains,

> Philosophy has been defined as a 'persistent attempt to think things through.' The characteristic attitude of the philosopher is, or ought to be, patient and open-minded inquiry in a serious, disciplined, and ambitious effort to find the general traits of reality, the significance of human experience, and the place of man in the universe as a whole. Philosophy is a vigorous attempt to think about the ultimate questions that are usually 'answered' by our emotions and vague hopes and fears. It is a reasoned effort to see facts and ideals, emotions and truths, man and the universe, in such a way that they will, when taken together, make more 'sense' than when taken piecemeal.[8]

This passage, which epitomizes Beck's way of thinking, contains several noteworthy insights. First, Beck does not think of philosophy in terms of definite answers or the resolution of fundamental questions. As the last sentence indicates, philosophy is an attempt to *make sense* of the world. Philosophy is a deliberate, rational effort to understand our role and place in reality as much as it is possible. Second, the questions that philosophy considers are not unique to philosophy. Beck would presumably argue that, strictly speaking, there are no uniquely philosophical questions. Philosophy deals with questions that are of general interest, the questions that concern us as human beings. As the following essays convincingly show, Beck does not believe that there is one prescribed way of dealing with these questions. Philosophy is, above all, an attitude that we have toward the questions that concern the world around us and our humanity, and everyone has to find a way of dealing with them through a dialogue with one's own soul. Third, in the quoted passage or elsewhere, Beck does not speak in the first person. He does not use his own voice not because he is only concerned with what Kant had to say, or because he himself docs not have anything original to say. Beck thinks of philosophy as a joined effort. Philosophy is not a competition of this philosopher against that philosopher, of this ego against that ego. Philosophy is a cooperative human effort, an effort in which we are trying together to understand and improve our reality as much as possible. In this effort

---

[8] *Philosophical Inquiry*, p. 4.

we will not find ultimate and definite answers to the problems which preoccupy us, but we can correct some errors and gain deeper insights. That is why his interactions with his colleagues and students were so important for Beck. That is why Beck was a tireless teacher and an ever-learning student.

The picture that the following essays paint of Beck as a philosopher is something along the following lines. Beck was not a philosopher of bold claims or theories, nor was he a philosopher of memorable refutations of his opponents' arguments. He was a philosopher of balance and modesty. He was a genuine seeker and lover of wisdom, always aware of our human (and especially his own) limitations and finitude. Why else would he refer to himself as "almost a philosopher" at the end of his illustrious career? Who else would be able to write with such honesty and self-criticism in one of his last writings: "Nietzsche draws a distinction between philosophers and philosophic workmen. I am among the latter."[9]

Let me summarize this portrait of Beck as a philosopher by quoting one of his contemporaries, Hans-Georg Gadamer:

> However much he may be called to draw radical inferences from everything, the role of a prophet, of Cassandra, of preacher, or of know-it-all does not suit him. What man needs is not just the persistent posing of ultimate questions but the sense of what is feasible, what is possible, what is correct, here and now. The philosopher, of all people, must, I think, be aware of the tension between what he claims to achieve and the reality in which he finds himself.[10]

I have never known anyone to whom these words apply more fully and adequately than Lewis White Beck.

---

[9] See Appendix 1 below.

[10] *Truth and Method*, second revised edition; translated by J. Weinsheimer and D.G. Marshal, xxxviii. New York: Continuum, 1993.

Essays by Lewis White Beck

1. The Synoptic Method*

Since Plato, in the *Republic,* said that "the dialectical mind is the synoptical," it has been customary for philosophers of various schools to say that it is their task to interpret reality synoptically. The dialectical ideal for philosophical conceptions is that they should form an organic whole, and English philosophers since Martineau[1] have spoken of this demand for unity as the synoptic aspect of their thought. In contrast to this dialectical ideal, the special sciences have generally been said not to be synoptic, but abstract. And in so far as synopsis is the method of ordering all the categories of being in one system, philosophy alone deserves to be called synoptical.

But the word has of late taken on new meanings, and it is commonplace today to say that the sciences are synoptical, in that they investigate their objects as wholes, supplement the analytical inquiries with a regard to the unique properties of their objects which are said to be lost or at least neglected in many forms of analysis. In biology, organismic theories are replacing narrow mechanistic and vitalistic conceptions which seek to explain the unity of the organism as a result of certain conditions of its parts; psychology has largely abandoned atomism; even in physics the procedure which would assert the sole adequate account of molar phenomena to be in terms of microscopic products of analysis has apparently shown difficulties.

That these new approaches in science may legitimately be called synoptic, even though they are not comprehensive like philosophy, may be seen from a comparison of the types of objects which are investigated in metaphysics and in the special sciences. The philosopher demands systematic unity in his conceptions simply

---

* Reprinted with permission from *Journal of Philosophy* XXXVI (1939), pp. 337-345.

[1] James Martineau, "The Unity of Mind in Nature" (1853). In *Essays, Reviews and Addresses,* London, 1891, Vol. III, p. 105.

because he believes the world, at least in so far as it is rational at all, to be a unity, a whole. It may have complexities and irreducible differences, conflicts, and contradictions in it, but after all he supposes it to be one world even though in some senses it may be a plurality: since Plato wrote his *Parmenides,* there has been no difficulty in supposing it to be both one and many. Likewise, the scientist who is earning the name "synoptist" deals with his object as a whole: it would be only a monistic prejudice which would deny that some things, though parts of the world to be sure, may be wholes without being *the* whole. And the psychologist or biologist in supposing the personality or the organism to be a whole requires a consistency of assertions concerning it which is quite analogous to that which the metaphysician requires when he makes assertions about the whole world.

It is the nature of the method of dealing with such wholes which I wish to investigate. To do this requires a consideration of our experience of wholes and of the criteria to which we appeal when we say a thing is a whole. The former inquiry will lead us to the striking conclusion that those who have offered definitions of synopsis have not by any means meant what they said.

Obviously, a definition of synopsis must involve some reference to a whole. Etymologically, the word means "seeing together," and a "togetherness" of a set of objects is at least one condition for their being parts of a whole. But "seeing together" applies to two different procedures: a process of seeing things in their togetherness or a process of seeing together various things. As an example of the first, the word "synopsis" has been used to refer to the experience of the continuum of immediacy, for it is a complex unity of experience of a variety of content which is not synthesized from parts, but which can be analyzed and broken up into "elements." Kant uses the word "synopsis" in this way; he says, "As sense contains a manifold in its intuition, I ascribe to it a synopsis."[2] But since the primary reference here is to the wholeness of an awareness rather than to the knowing of a whole, we obviously have a situation which is altogether universal and necessary for knowledge in general. Synopsis, as a word used by the layman, means an extension of this comprehension, a syllabus or survey. But this is not what we are here investigating, a controversial method in science. I do not deny, of course, that an extension and clarification of this

---

[2] *Critique of Pure Reason, A 97.*

comprehension is an essential part of all fruitful thinking, and the importance of the original synopsis for methodology should not be neglected. It appears as the first extended apprehension, the *prius* of the analysis which is to follow. Subsequent analysis has it as material and as the guide to the synthesis of the analytical results in a clearer, more articulated, presentation of the original subject-matter.

The first serious attempt to describe the seeing of things together was made by J. Theodore Merz, who used "synopsis" as a translation of *vue d'ensemble*. His description of synopsis as the view to which "every object of contemplation ... is a whole, a totality,"[3] has been repeated and accepted without question by those who urge the synoptic methods in philosophy and the sciences. But fundamentally, this definition and the others like it are not descriptive of the procedures which do go under the name of synopsis. For it is elementarism—the theory that the properties of wholes are inherent in the parts—which in effect regards every object as a whole. To take an example, the one-sided development of biology following Schwann resulted from the exclusive interest in accounting for the whole organism as a resultant of the parts, i.e., its cells. But this had as its corollary the centering of interest in the cell itself as in no essential sense a part, i.e., as a whole. True, it occurred in a whole, but it was not significantly different from what it would be in a culture dish where it would be an independent whole. Schwann, but not his followers, recognized that the *organism* as a whole was the seat of some functions (i.e., growth), but it was not until the cell was seen to be not an autonomous whole, but rather a dependent part of a more complex but fundamental whole, the organism, that biology could be said and is said to have become "synoptical." It is then clear that synopsis is not the method which sees all things merely or primarily as wholes.[4]

In dealing with objects in a "togetherness," that togetherness may be merely subjective, as it is when I see a butterfly and a locomotive in one experience-moment; but it may be real and objective, as it is when I know the center and the circumference of a locomotive wheel to be there together, regardless of the fragmentary state of my momentary

---

[3] J.T. Merz, *A History of European Thought in the Nineteenth Century* (4th. ed., London and Edinburgh, 1928), Vol. III, p. 612.

[4] It is interesting to observe that Merz, in accordance with his definition, praised the theory of Gemmules as a "synoptic" theory.

experience. In the latter case, each object I contemplate is not essentially a whole, but a part. Against Merz's definition, it may be urged that synopsis is a knowledge of an object as a part in its relation to some objective whole.

An important consideration will then be, of course, what the conditions are under which I can assert the object I contemplate to be a part of a whole other than the whole of my experience, of which, of course, every object experienced is a part. This question of the criterion of wholeness and partiality was not clearly put by Merz, but at least the beginning of an attempt to answer it is to be found in another part of his description of synopsis. He believed that synopsis affords more than analysis could ever discover or deal with.[5] But if we inquire into the nature of the alleged inadequacy of analysis it appears that he did not distinguish between an acquaintance and a synopsis. In other words, he failed to see the formal identity of the concept of emergent and that of a Gestalt quality. In making synopsis a knowledge of wholes, he erroneously supposed that its distinctive contribution was an acknowledgment of an oversummative property. Merz's attack on the adequacy of analysis presupposed that the wholes had oversummative properties, and the reference to them was apparently for him a guarantee that he was dealing with a whole and that his method was synoptic, for in analysis he held that "something is lost."

But it is only an accident (of size) that we call some properties "emergents" (e.g., the wetness of water) and others "Gestalt qualities" (e.g., the beauty of a picture). In the former case we do not see the parts of the whole which has the oversummative property, and we call the knowledge of it an acquaintance, a relatively unstructured intuition. In the second, we do see the whole which has the oversummative property; we see its internal structure, and we see that the new property is not a sum of the others. But it does not follow that our experience of *it* is synoptic. Our knowledge of *it*, in its ineffable novelty, is still an acquaintance. The Gestalt property does not have as *its* parts the parts of the Gestalt to which it appertains; synopsis can apprehend this property only because "opsis" or acquaintance in this case is a part of synopsis.

---

[5] J.T. Merz, "On the Synoptic Aspect of Reality," *Proc. Durham Philos. Soc.*, 1913, Vol. V, p. 54.

From this we may learn two lessons about synoptic method. The limitation of synopsis to the experience of some "poetic" or incommunicable quality or value of a whole is unfruitful. We have such experiences in cases we do not call synoptic (e.g., any sensuous awareness); and in the cases which we do call synoptic experiences, we do not find the presence of an intuition to be essential to its being a knowledge of structural relationships of parts and wholes. The second lesson is a corollary to this: the presence of an oversummative property, while perhaps a necessary condition of there being a whole, is not a sufficient condition for asserting knowledge of a complex possessing such a quality to be synoptic.

If we consider the structure of wholes, though, it will be possible to discover the desired criterion. The concept "whole" is probably a primitive idea admitting of no definition. But it is possible to exhibit what we mean by the word. When we call an object a whole, we mean at least that it is both singular and plural. It is a single thing, but it is not simple. It is several things considered as one, or one thing considered as several because several things may be found "in it." Since Hume, wholes have been thought of as fictions: cabbages and kings, the Counties in England, and myself are three wholes when taken separately, or one whole when taken together, because my assertions have united them in one complex reference. Needless to say, this theory has as disturbing consequences for a theory of wholes as Hume's other opinions had for other parts of metaphysics. Is there no ground for supposing that the head and heart of George III belong in one whole in a sense in which his head and a cabbage do not constitute a significant whole?

The most widespread answer to this question would be one which, if true, would limit synopsis to the uses Merz described and which I rejected on the basis of the preceding clarification of his confusion between acquaintance with the property of a whole and synopsis of the objects having the property. This answer asserts that some objects constitute wholes because they give rise to unique qualities which attach to them together but not separately. These properties are oversummative properties, and their presence is a necessary condition of wholeness. Now to show in a more rigorous fashion that synopsis can not be concerned only with wholes, if such a property is the necessary and sufficient condition of the existence of the whole, as it is asserted to be in this answer, we may adopt an argument of Peirce's.[6] Peirce showed that any two objects taken at random possessed a property in common when taken together which neither possessed alone, and which no other object had in common with them. Consider two objects, *A* and *B*. *A* has the property of *a*-ness, and *B* that of *b*-ness. All objects other than *A* have the property of *a*-lessness and all except *B* have that of *b*-lessness. These two properties constitute a complex property of *a*-*b*-lessness which all objects except *A* and *B* have. Therefore only *A* and *B* possess the property of un-*a*-*b*-lessness when taken together.

This is not by any means trivial. The complex quality of random objects together has the same logical status as the Gestalt quality of a particular type of foolishness attaching to a whole consisting of George III's head and my cabbages, or that unique being of George III enjoyed by all of his organs, or the beauty attaching to a set of esthetically indifferent lines when they are put together.

The criterion of individuality which is used in many branches of science is a mere adaptation of this principle of unique qualities. Their discovery seems to be sufficient indication of a real whole, whose parts and structure must be studied in synopsis. The principle of individuality is not narrowly qualitative, of course, but involves unique properties of groups. This can be seen through the extension of Peirce's argument concerning unique quality. The criterion of individuality which is derived from this may be called the Principle of Inhomogeneity. If there are three objects, *a, b,* and *c*, such that the relation of *a* to *b* is of a different *kind* from that of *a* to *c* and of *b* to *c*, then *a* and *b* together are inhomogeneous with their context or environment *c* and constitute a whole. For example, the "mechanical individual" is determined by a "balance of motion and rest" among its parts, as Spinoza held; but Spinoza also saw that the relations of motion and rest were so ubiquitous that, strictly speaking, only the whole universe was a mechanical individual. We distinguish some relations, though, between some parts of the mechanical world and other things, e.g., our own purposes. An automobile, though not a mechanical individual since relations among its parts and between it and its context are homogeneously mechanical, is an individual in that a group of objects (its "parts") has a definite and unique relation to our purposes

---

[6] C.S. Peirce, *Chance, Love, and Logic* (London, 1923), pp. 112-113.

which other objects, such as the roadbed, do not have. These objects, then, are "parts" of a whole, which in this case is determined by a relation to our purposes which, in effect, give some objects (its "parts") when taken together a property which some other things, connected to them by mechanical relations, do not have.

When a procedure of analyzing a manifold of objects reaches certain points, the methods of analysis and the categories on which it is based may have to be changed. I may analyze a body of water, but at one stage I come to an object which can not be treated under categories of hydrodynamics. A fish requires new categories—it is inhomogeneous with its surroundings, and so it is a whole. Not every case is as simple as this; many controversies in biology rest on the diverse answers to the question, When does the investigation require us to introduce specifically biological concepts into the analysis of a situation? This is, in other words, the question, When do we reach a biological whole? What are the limits of the organism?

That this criterion is used there can be no doubt. But it can not be considered faultless. First, inhomogeneity is a relative term, ranging in meaning from Peirce's un-*a*-*b*-lessness on one extreme, which in itself we do not consider empirically significant, to an organism in an unfavorable environment on the other. There is no adequate means of distinguishing *kinds* of relations from each other; in fact, *kind* itself presupposes significant inhomogeneity. And in the second place, an inhomogeneity might be resolved into a complex homogeneity with more refined methods; this has been the fate of many chemical "elements." The monism of science is a healthy ideal, for this criterion of individuality is a statement of ignorance; that is an individual whole which we have not *yet* reduced to the status of a homogeneous part. We can not attribute individuality at any level merely on this criterion without breaking into the continuity of investigation. Thirdly, when the determination of significant inhomogeneities is intentionally instrumental, as in the case of the automobile, it is *a fortiori* subject to change. For these reasons, this criterion can not be said to give us a dependable guide to the attribution of real wholeness in the object: in every case the admission of inhomogeneities may rest only on our limited experience of the object.

The more dependable criterion of the reality of the whole is to be found in the synoptic consideration of an object which we may suppose for the time being to be a part. If it is a part of an object which is a real whole, it can be exhaustively explained only if in addition to its own intrinsic nature we study also its histrionic nature as playing a rôle in a determinable whole. The synopsis of the object begins with it and examines its relations to its parts and then its relations to other objects, together with which, it is now supposed, it constitutes a whole. The necessity of the use of this synoptic procedure in order to give an account of the part is a criterion of the partiality of the objects it investigates, and this implicates the objective existence of a real whole independent of my chance predications.

The supposition on which the synoptic method is based is that being a part of a real whole makes an empirically determinable difference to the characteristics of some parts. We may give a symbolic characterization of a whole as follows:

We may consider b and b' to be distinct wholes consisting of parts and exhibiting the inhomogeneities necessary for our asserting their integral existence. c and c' are parts of b, and b is a part of a. Now it is the ideal of scientific methodology to carry on analysis until a limit of supposed simplicity is reached; this is the atomistic aim of science. It is just as true, though, that in any specific investigation we are interested in analyzing only to the next lower level of complexity. The complete analysis of a chemical compound would be into electrons and protons, but we are generally content to stop analyzing when we reach recognizable ions whose analysis has already been performed. If a is a real whole and b is a real whole, our knowledge of b is sufficient for most purposes if our synopsis leads us to a and our analysis to c and c'.

Now it is my contention that the only legitimate test of the reality of a as an objective and empirically determinable whole is to be found in certain characteristics of the b-level which are discovered in a synoptic consideration. Why this is so can best be seen in Mr. Spaulding's "A Defense of Analysis."[7] He insists that the products of analysis must be independent of the process of their discovery if the allegation that

---

    [7] E.G. Spaulding, "A Defense of Analysis," *The New Realism*, New York, 1912.

analysis "falsifies" is not to be justified. But Mr. Spaulding admits that an object may show properties when it is in a whole which it does not have when it is not a part. It is just this fact which is our criterion of real wholeness, but it is a fact which is available only to a method which is synoptic. Mr. Spaulding, while admitting the difference to exist, can not claim that it is a discovery of analysis, for analysis is not to affect the things it discovers. With a strictly analytic procedure, we can not make a comparison between independent elements and parts to see that an object has a property when a part which it does not have when it is not a part, else at least one analysis would "falsify." If we know, as Mr. Spaulding knows, that the properties are not always the same in the two cases, we are prevented, if we make a subsequent analysis of the part, from attributing its entire nature when a part to *its* parts and their intrinsic relations. But if we can not suppose this subsequent analysis to begin with this same part and treat it as a whole by investigating its parts, obviously analysis is not an exhaustive investigation of the part. To return to our diagram: if we analyze *a* into *b* and *b'*, and then begin an analysis of *b* which will then be regarded as a whole instead of as a part, and find that *b* in the two cases is not empirically the same, then we can know that *a* is an objective whole since it makes an empirical difference to *b* when it contains it as a part. But this discovery of difference results from our use of a method which forces us to regard the object *b* as essentially a part. And this is just what is meant by synopsis. This dual direction of interpretation of an object, by reference to both the next higher and the next lower level of complexity, gives us occasion to determine to what extent its properties are intrinsic to it as oversummative to its parts, and whether or not there is some more inclusive whole which has an effect on it. A categorial framework for interpretations of experimental results (e.g., of regeneration) may be worked out with reference to these structural relations.

So considered, synopsis seems to me to be an unavoidable aspect of scientific method, though many who have held to the narrow elementaristic presuppositions of analysis have not appreciated the great significance of the statement that an empirical analysis may change the properties of the parts. In fact, by so considering synoptic method many of the ambiguities in appeals to the whole as ground of explanation are avoided in that the concept is given an empirical, even an operational, meaning. No doubt the careless appeal to the "whole" as the explanatory ground for all mysteries might at times provide an obstacle to investigation: it need not do so, however, if one recognizes that an appeal to the whole means no more a surrender of empirical method than an appeal to the parts does. For this reason, I can not think Dr. Needham's terms such as "obstructive organicism" need frighten us all into accepting his organicism which admits of no discontinuities.[8]

The concept of whole can thus be brought into scientific categorization with as much legitimacy as that of cause, and canons for its application can be formulated. And philosophy will have to learn the same lesson with regard to it as it learned with reference to causality: what is a real whole and what is a cause are matters for empirical investigation, and no amount of ratiocination alone will answer these questions. This is not to deny, of course, that both cause and whole have *a priori* aspects which must be investigated, in one case leading to the concept of ground and in the other to that of system. These two concepts in their *a priori* aspects have an important rôle to play in the synthesis of scientific knowledge, but their application extends far beyond the natural sciences. The concept of whole may well be the central category for philosophy, guiding us in a synthesis of our knowledge and showing the relevance of the determination of the parts by the whole to the general problems of metaphysics.

---

[8] Joseph Needham, *Order and Life,* New Haven, 1936.

2. The Formal Properties Of Ethical Wholes[*][1]

At the present time the descriptive sciences are moving away from their former elementaristic positions. This shift in interest and emphasis from the end-products of analysis to its original starting point is having an effect outside the limits of scientific study. It is shown in a new conceptual orientation to social and ethical problems. In what sense is this orientation "new"? It is new for a scientific community and for all those beyond its pales who have enthusiastically and uncritically followed the scientific belief in the ultimacy and adequacy of analytic procedures. It is not a new emphasis for the common man or for the phenomenologist who has never surrendered to the forces of analysis alone. The scientific analysis of mental content into sensations or other elements is opposed to "common sense," and the movement towards organismic or personalistic conceptions in psychology is accurately characterized as a "return." Similarly, social and ethical investigations which quantified values and broke up their unities to facilitate an examination of their components seemed "far from life," and consequently the relatively recent theoretical emphasis on the unanalyzed contexts of value is likewise a return to a healthy "naïveté."

---

[*] Reprinted with permission from *Journal of Philosophy* XXXVIII (1941), pp. 5-15.

[1] In its original form this paper was read at a meeting of the Southern Society for Philosophy and Psychology at Durham, N.C., April 7, 1939. It has been somewhat expanded here to take account of suggestions and criticisms made in the discussion at that time, and for these I am indebted to Professor Helmut Kuhn of the University of North Carolina and Dr. Henry S. Leonard of Duke University. In its present form it is a continuation of, and presupposes, my article, "The Synoptic Method," *Journal of Philosophy* XXXVI (1939), pp. 337-345. [Reprinted in this volume, pp. 1-12.]

The purpose of this essay is to examine the position of thinking about wholes of value within the general context of ethical study. I wish not to discover what specific wholes we should reëmphasize, but rather to investigate the logic of the new interest in ethical wholes as such. My task, therefore, is entirely formal. Does the emphasis on the "whole situation"[2] as the locus of value in ethics mean a renunciation of the methods of analysis, definition, and construction which really distinguish science from common sense, ethics from actual moral contemplation of specific given problems? In my previous article I have denied that this is the case in the natural sciences; here I think a more "holistic" ethics can be defended from like charges of unscientific satisfaction with the mere given.

Many of the great ethical systems have taken sciences as their model; this is as true of Aristotle's as it is of Bentham's. The difference between them lay in what science was fundamental. In modern times the science which underlay all others was mathematics, and much of modern ethics is dominated by the desire to make mathematics support it. Arithmetic with its serial orders and cardinal quantities has been taken as the model for making ethics "scientific"—a wholly different purpose from that which Plato had when he used mathematics in ethics. In patterning their inquiries after the most abstract field of knowledge, it was to be expected that many concrete qualitative aspects and many important complexities of the subject-matter of ethics would have to be neglected by moralists. This we can see actually occurred in the over-simplifications of Bentham and the Utilitarians: in reducing value-relations to relations merely of more or less of something, those characteristics of moral issues which make morality so problematical were simply left out.

All attempts to establish a quantitative scale of value suffer from what Mr. G. E. Moore has called the "naturalistic fallacy" of confusing value with one of its "natural accompaniments," a psychological or a social actuality.[3] The "natural accompaniments" are made to provide the material for the arithmetization of the value they accompany. The procedure is: first, an abstraction is made from a group of *prima facie* valuable things and a genus is thereby established for the good.

---

[2] For example, see C.W. Morris, "The 'Total Situation' Theory in Ethics," *International Journal of Ethics* XXXVII (1927), pp. 258-268.

[3] *Principia Ethica*, p. 13.

Second, this abstraction is chosen in such a way that an intensity gradient can be found within it. Third, a scale of degrees of intensity of the abstracted accompaniment of value is established for the original group of objects from which the abstraction was made. Finally, this scale is stated to be equivalent to the order in which the objects *should* have been placed at first in their unanalyzed valuableness.

In this procedure, besides the "fallacy" knowingly and intentionally committed by most of those Moore criticizes, there are methodological difficulties which can not be avoided. If the order in the abstracted series is the same as that in the originally and naïvely evaluated group, the scale of value is useless since all we need to know is the rank order in the original scale of naïve approvals and preferences. Sometimes, however, the established scale has a more ambitious use; it usurps the place of the original order, and the paradoxes it introduces into the original moral preferences (e.g., "Pushpin is as good as poetry") are accepted as corrections of naïve errors. But when this usurpation occurs, we have something analogous to that which Whitehead describes as the "fallacy of misplaced concreteness." For the scale on an absolute gradient is an artifact, and as such it would be meaningless were it not derived from a series of actual preferences and appreciations which can be legitimized only by indicating in advance that abstraction by which they should be compared. Thus such a paradox as that of Bentham is worse than an ordinary paradox: it is simply the failure of an hypothesis to fit the only facts by which it could possibly be tested, i.e., the preferences which underlay the construction of the system from the beginning.

More than that, though, the abstractions underlying any scalar relation of values can not be self-justifying in the same way as an immediate intuition that one thing is to be preferred to another. The order of items presented by the quantification of the abstraction is dependent upon the standpoint chosen as the principle of evaluation. Now abstraction always involves a certain arbitrariness in the choice of a perspective. Due to the arbitrariness, there is no reason to suppose that the rank-order of an item on one scale will correspond to its position on another. The result is that every possible scale of value is beyond criticism from the standpoint of another abstraction, which must have been made just as arbitrarily. Conflicts inevitably result from taking an abstraction to be the value-equivalent of the original object, and the consequence of the linear quantifications of the abstracted qualities or accompaniments is not an ethic at all; the quantifications and the skew relations between them are merely descriptive. They could become normative only if we knew on other grounds which scale was "right." These other grounds, of course, can be only a comparison with the naïvely accepted choiceworthiness in the naïve order of preferences we feel to a group of objects or actions, for it is to this that we always go back in deciding whether an ethical theory is adequate. But such a comparison as this means a return to the authority of the original and naïve preferences which, as we have seen, entirely vitiates the usefulness of any theoretically established abstract scale.

But one ground on which an arithmetical scale of values is thought sometimes to be preferable to the original and uncritical appreciations is its supposed greater exactness. But here as elsewhere exactness is purchased at the cost of neglecting the complexities of actual conditions which must be introduced again at least as "probable errors" when the mathematical calculations are used in practice. These complicating factors render the predictions of evaluations made from an abstract scale utterly unreliable. For in the medium of ethical values there is a kind of non-linear determination which is different from the arithmetical one of mere position in a gradient between two other values.

In my previous article (p. 9) I formulated the criterion of real wholes as being the difference accruing to an object upon its entering a complex originally defined by the criterion of inhomogeneity, as stated on the page before. This criterion is applicable to values. If an object has no unique value, it is because the value it has at any moment is dependent upon relations which are variable. The variable relations which affect values and which keep them from having a definite and unique position in a series of preferences are relations of means to end, symbol to value symbolized, and part to whole.

The first two of these require no discussion. It is obvious that one can not decide whether a hammer or a saw is "better" until he knows what the goal or the value is which lends each one whatever significance it has. Also it is obvious that a cross has a variable value independent of its intrinsic properties and dependent solely upon its relationship of symbolizing something else of value. Its value is determined not by the mere fact that it is made of iron or wood, but by the fact that it symbolizes military valor or religious redemption. The specific ways in which these complexes of value differ from wholes has been exhaustively treated by Moore and Stern, respectively.[4] Only the third type of variability requires discussion here. It is, since Moore's epoch-making work, obvious that the value of a whole can not be predicted from a knowledge, however exhaustive, of the values of the parts which make it up. Moore's vigorous assertion of this as the principle of "organic unities" was not, however, necessitated by its being a new discovery of his, but rather because this truth which is available to common sense and unbiased inspection had been neglected or explicitly denied by those who wished to display mathematical relations between measured values. Still, Moore's statement of this principle leaves much to be desired. Specifically, one might object to two points in his presentation: (1) He considers organic unities defined by the absence of regular proportion between the value of the whole and the "sum of the values of the parts"; (2) The part of such an organic unity, he says, though it may be more desirable in these circumstances (this unity) than in others, has no more intrinsic value than it would have if the whole did not have more than the sum of its value and the values of the other parts.[5]

First, the concept of "sum of values" is meaningless. Moore is here falling back into the position he is attacking—namely, the view that values are related to each other as more to less of some quantity. Pleasures perhaps can be added to each other, but values[6] like degrees of temperature, can not. The reason for this is that degrees of temperature are ordinal numbers with no corresponding cardinal significance, and the same is true of values. Moore does not attempt to establish a unit or a standard by which values could be quantified; all his descriptions enable us merely to see that in a choice between two

---

[4] Moore, *op. cit.*, pp. 31-33; William Stern, *Wertphilosophie, Person und Sache*, Vol. iii, pp. 126 ff. However, Moore differs from many writers in so sharply distinguishing between part-whole and means-end relationship; for example, Kant *(Grundlegung zur Metaphysik der Sitten*, A 417) and H.H. Joachim *(The Nature of Truth*, p. 66) argue that the latter arises only in the former. And Stern's entire system is "holistic," so that he regards symbolic values as *Strahlwerte* from *Personen*.

[5] Moore, *op. cit.*, p. 29.

[6] Cf. A.P. Brogan, "The Fundamental Value Universal," *Journal of Philosophy* XVI (1919), pp. 96-104.

things, one will be seen to be the greater in value. By carrying out indefinitely this process of choosing, it will be seen that values can be, at least at a given moment, arranged in a linear series of worthiness, but their relative position in this scale does not tell us anything about the *quantities* of value involved. For this reason, the notion that two values could have a definite and conceptually determinable sum is meaningless. Thus we can never tell, according to this, when an organic unity appears, for if we can not predict the "sum" we can not tell when the process of actual addition leads to a *de facto* error which is the criterion of organic unity or wholeness.

Second, if there is to be any criterion of wholeness it must be found, as would be expected from the criteria developed in my previous article, in the parts themselves, not in the whole as such. We discover cosmologically real wholes and distinguish them from mere conceptual or imaginative unities by shifting something into their context to see if it is changed in a significant way, significance being defined by the principle of inhomogeneity. We must do the same for values if we wish to discover specific actual wholes. This does not mean that the intrinsic choiceworthiness of an object or an action is to vary with the other things of which it is not a part, for this is an effect only upon its extrinsic value as a means. What is important here is that the choiceworthiness of a part-action or of a part-object is not the value it would have under the condition that it was on an equal footing with all other things in an all-comprehending whole or medium; the effective choiceworthiness of such a part under actual complex conditions is the value we discover in it in the whole of which it actually is a part, and we must recognize that this value may vary from time to time as the whole of which it is a part alters. If this is not allowed on the basis of some metaphysical theory of the permanence and internality of all intrinsic value—as when Moore falls into extreme elementarism in saying that the intrinsic value is the value a thing would have if there were nothing else in the universe besides it[7]—Moore's valuable concept of organic unity loses all empirical meaning simply because we could

---

[7] *Ethics*, pp. 162, 163. In his *Philosophical Studies*, p. 260, intrinsic value is defined as that which "depends solely on the intrinsic nature of the thing in question." Thus "better" is not an intrinsic character of the two things between which this relation obtains. This by itself indicates to me the ethical poverty of the concept of intrinsic value.

never determine empirically when the concept was applicable to a group of values.

With these points in mind we can, however, refine Moore's principle so as to make empirical use of it: *The rank order of valuableness of any two things may vary according to the value of the wholes of which they are parts, and this variation in choiceworthiness is the sole criterion of the reality of an objective whole of values.* To show the methodological fruitfulness of this principle, we must investigate three questions: How can we determine the "value-minimum" of an object or an act so as to be able to discover the variations in its choiceworthiness? How can we discover the value of the whole which induces these variations? How is the value of the whole related to the values of its parts?

(1) It is not absolutely essential that we know the "elementary" value of an entity or action even though this is equivalent to its intrinsic value in Moore's system. But if we could discover its elementary value, i.e., the value it has when we suppose it not to be determined by a supervening whole, we should then in all cases be able to determine its positive and negative "histrionic" values in separate cases, i.e., the values it has by virtue of its rôle as a part. Strictly speaking, of course, nothing is really isolated; and if Professor Brogan's thesis, which I am here following, is correct in saying that value does not appear except in a hypothetical comparison of two things, *a fortiori* valuable things can not be isolated so that we might study their "atomic" value. But we can attempt to exclude a value-object from any wholes we can empirically discover within the realm of ethical discourse. To be sure, we can not insulate values from the sphere of awareness, affective state, some kind of society, etc., each of which may be a whole; yet these wholes are pervasive and whatever effect they have on one value can be neglected because they will have the same effect on all others, thus leaving the relative orders undisturbed. Such a whole which does not have visible effects and whose extent is so great that its effects on its parts can not be discovered by studies and comparisons of the parts themselves we may call a *medium*. A medium is the upper limit of an empirical whole. Then we can define an "elementary" value as the value an object or an action has when its superordinate whole is a medium. We can not require analysis to break these wholes down; we are satisfied when we have conceptually excluded the intermediate wholes between

the given thing and this medium. For practical purposes it may be neglected.[8]

Any variation in the value of a thing from this elementary norm-value gives evidence that the medium has been replaced or distorted or transformed into an equally real but specific value-whole. For example, a pain, without any reference to or knowledge of its conditions, occurs in a state of consciousness; in this medium it has a certain (negative) value. Its value, i.e., the order in which we should choose or reject it when it is a question of this pain or any other equally unexamined sensation we compare it with, is its most nearly elementary or intrinsic value; a comparison with an "unfelt pain" does not enter into consideration. But sometimes the pain has *another* value or position: we find a martyr exulting in it, another person seeing it as a due consequence of justice, etc. When this change in value occurs it means that the context of the specific thing has changed; it has either become a part of a whole which is different from the original or, more accurately, it has passed from membership in a medium to the status of part in an intermediate whole.

(2) How can we discover the value of the whole which induces these changes in values of partial objects or actions? Though we have seen that Moore's statement that the value of the whole is not in any regular proportion to the sum of values of the parts is misleading, it is nevertheless true that the value of the whole bears no regular relation to the values of the parts considered severally. Therefore we can not infer anything about the value of the whole from the value of any one of its parts or of each of its parts. All we can do is this: we can compare the hypothetical elementary value with the actual value of the part, that is, its elementary position in a scale of preferabilities with its position affected by its histrionic rôle as a part; and if the resulting position on the gradient of choiceworthiness is higher than the position of the partially identical elementary value, we can say that there is a valuable whole influencing the values of the parts. For example, in evaluating pleasures we say "other things being equal" the more pleasure the better. If, therefore, we find in a certain case that we approve of some

---

[8] But we should be very sure that it is truly a medium. We are required at every stage to seek further and further for the medium, and to distrust all finality. This is Plato's warning that in the dialectic we should not make great jumps.

pleasure less than the maximum, we conclude that "other things" were not equal, that the less intense pleasure (the lower "elementary value") was a part of some more valuable whole, which gives it a higher histrionic value.

As to the values of the wholes themselves, nothing can be said in an essay on the formal properties of values. For the value of a whole is in precisely the same ontological status as any other value, whatever we may think that to be. We have no formal ground whatsoever for differentiating between the values pertaining to wholes and those pertaining to parts, and *a fortiori* no grounds for arguing, as a monist tends to do, that the whole is the ultimate locus of all value. Moreover, there is no significant epistemological difference in our acknowledgment of the two values. It is conceivable that all values are "oversummative" properties, that value itself is an emergent from some kinds of wholes. Just as "emergent quality" and "gestalt quality" have the same status (as I argued in my previous essay, p. 6) so also the same kind of intuition or insight or conviction is required to discover what things are valuable, and that indifferently whether they are wholes consisting of other values or not. The only difference between them arises in the case where we wish to discover the valuable whole *as such* (and not its specific value); for there we have to have *two* intuitions or moral sensings or appreciations of the parts, one to determine their elementary and one their histrionic value. Whether the significant wholes of value are persons, families, races, nations, or something else is, compared to the formal problem, an empirical or material problem to be solved—come the day!—only by exhibiting the actual evidence. For the present, unfortunately, the relation of this great practical problem, which separates men, to the formal system here under discussion is analogous to that between the way women choose their hats and the laws of the science of optics.

(3) How is the value of the whole related to that of the parts? In answering this question, we must remember that between the elementary values and the value of the whole there is no regular proportion. This is the same thing as saying that between the elementary and histrionic value of a single thing there is no regular relation. But it is *not* equivalent to saying that there is no regular relation between the value of the whole and the *histrionic* values of its parts. So far from meaning that, the case is rather that here a very definite relation can be found. By a study of these relations we may

clarify the subsumption of a part under the diverse wholes which may contain it. It is this diversity of possible wholes which may contain a part or an action which makes these considerations important for practice. Every value-object or value-act can be a member of various wholes, and it is only through a study of the nature of these wholes that we can determine the proportionate relevance of the various "allegiances" a part may have.[9] There are five factors which determine the relation of value-parts to value-wholes and thereby the relevance of the various possible integrations in the different possible wholes.

(a) The discrepancy between the elementary value and histrionic value, as shown by the displacement on a scale of preferabilities (of the values themselves, not of their accompaniments), varies directly with the intrinsic real value of the whole itself. I may approve of a good intention; I approve of it still more highly (that is, I *displace* it in the scale of elementary preferences) if it is carried into effect, if it is changed by being a part of a more valuable social or public whole and not simply in the mere medium of a state of mind.

(b) The discrepancy varies directly with the degree of structuredness of the whole. Thus I am a member of a relatively unstructured whole which I call my "circle." I am also a member of a highly structured whole which is my family. Because of the more elaborate and intense organization of the latter, it affects more sharply my value than the circle or group does. Therefore, if the values of the whole were equal, the more structured the whole the greater displacement, positive or negative, there would be in my histrionic values. An example of this effect where condition *(a)* does not obtain, where we have two wholes of different values and different degrees of structuredness, arises in so-called "professional ethics" which may shift histrionic values far from the more nearly "elementary positions" in the medium of society itself.

(c) The higher the degree of substitutability of parts in a whole the less is the discrepancy between elementary and histrionic choiceworthiness. This is a corollary to *(b)*, since the more highly structured the whole the greater the determinateness of the parts and

---

[9] For example, the contrast between cosmopolitanism and nationalism is relevant, and Marcus Aurelius states it in terms of membership in and allegiance to different wholes. See *Meditations* VI, 39.

thus the less probability of substitution.[10] If I were twenty years older than I am I might still be surrounded by the same friends, but I could hardly occupy the same position in my present family. Similarly, my friends could more easily find substitutes for me than my family can, with the result that the greater discrepancies between elementary and histrionic values seem [more] justified in the latter case than in the former. The law recognizes this in allowing wider legal immunities to members of a family than to members of other social groups; that is, the law allows a greater discrepancy from abstract social norms in one case than in another.

(d) The comprehension of a whole, measured by the variety and number of the value-parts, affects the histrionic value of each part. Other things such as structuredness and intrinsic value of the whole being the same, the greater the whole the greater degree of displacement may occur in the elementary values, since displacement in the value of any one implies a like displacement of more different parts. Thus while the rank-order within the whole may remain the same with the growth in comprehension, each of the parts may deviate further and further from its own original and elementary value. For example, other things being equal the duties to a nation can be seen to call sometimes for a greater shift from elementary values (e.g., the sanctity of life as such) than the duties to a political party could justify; the reason for this, put formally, is that the nation enjoins a shift in more evaluations of more persons.

(e) Finally, the "distance" from the part to the whole has an effect on the displacement of value in a series of choices. This relation is, in a general sort of way, roughly inverse. Thus it appears at first sight to be in conflict with *(d)*, and in actual fact it does limit its application. Nevertheless, in order to be faithful to the naïve preferences which ethics seeks to rationalize, this principle is necessary; some wholes just appear to be more *urgent* to us than others do, even though the others might be preferable by all the preceding canons. For example, cosmopolitan ideals are commendable on score *(d)*, but we should not let them obscure our personal duties to wholes which are close to us; we feel imperious duties to aid this particular man even when it seems that mankind as a whole might suffer. The conflict between Christian

---

[10] Cf. A. Angyal, "The Structure of Wholes," *Philosophy of Science* VI (1939), pp. 25-37, especially p. 35.

"nearest love" and Nietzschean "furthest love" is the same as that between *(e)* and *(d)*. We are here at the extreme limit of formal considerations in ethics, and there is no methodological principle whereby we can weigh the relevance of these two principles.

Practical ethical reflection is well acquainted with these facts. Because ethical theory for the sake of generality over-simplified the actual complexities of ethical choice into a "this or that, now and forever, world without end," ethical theory has failed to rationalize a large part of practice. The purpose of this essay has been to show that without loss of theoretical rigor our values do not have to remain fixed to a quantitative rack by which attempts have been made to hold them in place.

3. The Principle Of Parsimony In Empirical Science*

Seldom in the history of thought has one man's name become so universally attached to a principle which he did not formulate as has that of William of Occam. Hamilton called the demand for simplicity in explanations "Occam's Razor" and this name has remained as a testimonial to Hamilton's felicitous phrase-making rather than to his otherwise great acumen as an historian of thought. His designation has survived in spite of the fact that the principle to which he attached it was not formulated until about three centuries after that philosopher died.[1] Nevertheless, though Occam probably did not say *Entia non sunt multiplicanda praeter necessitatem,* he *might* have said it, and there is some justification for giving him some credit for it. Though many a philosopher before him had objected to an opponent's ideas on the ground that they were not sufficiently simple (for example, Aristotle's criticism of the classical theory of ideas), few philosophers have been in greater need of such a principle than some of Occam's opponents, and few philosophers as ruthless as he in cutting away what he thought were metaphysical extravagances.

The attribution of this principle to Occam, even though not vindicated by historical fact, is symbolical also of two characteristics which have attended its later use. First, it has almost always been explicitly associated with nominalism, due to the *prima facie* simplicity of the latter in metaphysics; and, by contagion, one may say, it has characterized most antimetaphysical systems because of their relation to sensationism which historically grew from nominalism. Secondly, the use of the principle has been largely polemical. It is most apparent

---

* Reprinted with permission from *Journal of Philosophy* XL (1943), pp. 617-633.
[1] For a more accurate account than that of Hamilton see W.M. Thorburn, "The Myth of Occam's Razor," *Mind* XXVII (1918), pp. 345-353.

in polemics and dialectic, not in orderly systematic thinking from established premises. Naturally it appears often in controversies over relative degrees of simplicity, and many a thinker has accused his opponent of extravagance when perhaps his own work might not have served as a perfect exemplification of the rule. One reason for these controversies lies in the fact that the principle is so abstract that it warrants divergent applications,[2] and other reasons will become apparent as we proceed.

These two controversial aspects of the application of the rule constitute the subject of this essay. We shall attempt to answer two questions:

(1) Is the principle of parsimony applicable in a definitive and unique way, permitting a decision as to the value of conflicting scientific theories ?

(2) Does the principle of parsimony have any realistic, i.e. objective or cosmological, implications for the material to which it is applied ?

These questions can not be handled separately. The answers to them will come out in an examination of the diverse formulations and justifications of the principle itself. There are various ways in which the principle may be made plausible, and the implications of each must be examined. These modes of conception we shall call the *metaphysical,* the *naturalistic,* the *formalistic,* and the *conventionalistic.*

I. The Metaphysics of Parsimony

The demand for simplicity in scientific formulations is, at least in modern times, an historical outgrowth of a particular metaphysical theory, in which the Christian doctrine of the unity of the world and the Greek belief in its intelligibility formed the stage on which new mathematical and empirical interests produced a renaissance of science. Originally the demand for simplicity was not antimetaphysical; it was a principle within speculative philosophy, and Occam was particularly attacking a theory of reality which he considered to be extravagant metaphysics.

---

[2] Cf. J.W. Nogge, "Regarding the Law of Parsimony," *Journal of General Psychology* XLI (1932), pp. 492-494.

The methodological aspects of simplicity were only corollaries of this, for if nature were simple, concepts of it should likewise be simple. It is in line with this tradition that Newton both renounces metaphysical hypotheses and yet appeals to a realistic cosmological, and even a metaphysical, basis for his attempts to simplify the scientific picture of reality. In a famous passage he says,

> We are to admit no more causes of things than such as are both true and sufficient to explain their appearances. To this purpose the Philosophers say that Nature does nothing in vain, and more is in vain when less will serve; for Nature is pleased with simplicity, and affects not the pomp of superfluous causes.

Specifically, this search for simplicity involves a reconstruction of both science and metaphysics; instead of a "vertical relation" between hidden causes (occult qualities in the Aristotelian System) and visible effects, science should seek to establish "horizontal relations" between various observations; this is the meaning present in his famous *Hypotheses non fingo.* Obviously, however, Newton could not be a positivist, so his principle of exclusion of causes is not a limitation of scientific concepts to direct observation, but lies in the answer to the question, "Does the assumption of such and such a cause permit mathematical prediction of observation?" This question changes the direction of metaphysical interest from speculation beyond experience to a justification of experience by its own resources critically examined and extended where necessary. Cooley has shown that in modern times, when metaphysics has thus become largely a handmaiden to science, metaphysical simplicity has not been so much a logical basis of the methodological rule as an attempt "to make simple explanations possible [in a realistic sense] by conceiving of the subject matter in such a way that simple explanations will fit it."[3]

Consequently, it is difficult to speak of a metaphysical derivation of the rule of parsimony. Rationalism, the leading example of the development Cooley mentions, is not so much a metaphysical justification of the new science as it is its metaphysical consequence, though both the metaphysics and the science strengthen each other by

---

[3] W.F. Cooley, "The Lure of Metaphysical Simplicity," *Studies in the History of Ideas,* Columbia University Press, New York (1925), Vol. II, pp. 161-182.

their inner harmony in dealing with one world. In the long run, as it ends in positivism, this relationship leads not only to a simplification and impoverishment of metaphysics, but eventually to its renunciation, when to speak of justification is an offense to the positivistic thinker. And after Hume and Kant had shown the independence of method from any particular presuppositions in cosmology, the need for a metaphysical justification of methodology from the side of the object disappeared.

But the contribution of Hume and Kant opened the way for a new kind of metaphysics and a new route of justification. From them comes the modern preoccupation with the rôle of the scientist rather than with that of his object; from the former's psychology come attempts to justify method on psychological grounds, and from the latter's logic there arises at least the incentive for, if not the guide to, a formalistic defense of methodology.

II. Naturalistic Theories of Parsimony

The term "naturalistic" is used here in a broad sense to cover all theories of methodology which regard economy as a consequence of the natural functioning of the mind in scientific thinking. Such interpretations were suggested by Hobbes, Hume, and Mill; they become almost inevitable after Darwin, and they reach their classical formulation in the work of Mach.

Mach was led to his theory by three chief considerations. The first was that the history of science (as traced in his great history of mechanics) was a continuous development in the direction of more and more simple representation of observations; great discoveries in science are not so much new observations, but new simplifications in the interpretation of old facts. His account of the development of the concept of mass is a perfect illustration of this tendency in science. Second, "minimal principles," for example, those in optics and mechanics, impressed him as being one of the highest kinds of scientific generalizations, and he regarded science itself as a "minimal problem." Finally, his debt to the thinkers mentioned previously was his conviction of the dominant rôle of control in science and of the importance of the fact that science is to be evaluated as a tool.

These three factors led him to his view that the construction of a scientific theory was a process of finding abstractions to cover the widest variety of observations "with the least mental effort." "Science itself . . . may be regarded as a minimal problem consisting of the completest possible presentment of facts with the least possible expenditure of thought."[4] When we comprehend a thing without effort, "it is *explained* for us," and this comprehension is equivalent to "discovering everywhere the same facts." [5]

Two objections to Mach's theory have rendered it untenable at least in the relatively simple form in which he presented it; and though it perhaps stands as a description of the parsimonious tendency and attitude of the scientist it is in no sense a justification of them.

The first is that the kind of simplicity Mach was seeking was inconsistent with another kind which might be equally desirable, and the incompatibility between them makes any absolute reckoning of simplicity on his basis impossible. Mach was seeking to simplify scientific description, to "find the same facts everywhere," but in order to achieve this, he had to go against an economy which would not permit multiplication of entities. (The opinion that these entities have only a fictional status and that the only real things are sensa is important as a metaphysical proposition; but the scientist has to use atoms and the like, and to call them fictions does not simplify his thinking.) Such entities or fictions as atoms immensely complicate a simple system based on sensationism. Thus Mach had to complicate one aspect of his work in order to show how the mind attains to its natural destination in simplifying its *prima facie* objects. If Mach's system is justified, then, it must be on pragmatic grounds of control through simplicity of formulation rather than on the basis of representing a maximum simplicity in general.

The second objection to the naturalistic theory has been stated in its classical form by Husserl. This well-known argument need not be repeated. Suffice it to say that he exposes the psychologistic basis of the theory, and then refutes all psychologism in science by showing

---

[4] E. Mach, *The Science of Mechanics,* English translation, Open Court Publishing Company, Chicago (4th ed., 1919), p. 490.

[5] E. Mach, "The Economical Nature of Physics," English translation, *Popular Scientific Lectures,* Open Court Publishing Company, Chicago (1919), p. 194.

how it eventuates in scepticism. Economy of thought, he admits, may be a fact of nature; this, however, does not justify the logical consequences seemingly derived from it, and its regulative and normative use is inconsistent with its own descriptive basis.

> A psychological or epistemological law which speaks of a *striving* to accomplish *as much as possible* is an absurdity. In the pure sphere of facts there is no "as much as possible," in the sphere of law no striving. And from a psychological standpoint there is in every case something definite, just this much and no more.
> To identify the tendency to the highest possible degree of rationality with a biological tendency to adaptation or to derive the former from the latter, and yet to impute to it the function of a basic psychological force—that is a mass of confusions which finds its parallel only in the psychologistic misinterpretations of logical laws and in their conception as natural laws.[6]

Nevertheless, Mach was insisting upon an important fact, that science does reduce things to their lowest common denominators and substitute the latter for the former, obtaining greater generality than would be possible with unreduced observations, and saving thought by substituting a few rules for many unique observations. The extent to which this is important as guiding methodology will be determined later.

III. Formalistic Derivations of the Principle of Parsimony

The formal justification of the principle of economy did not arise historically as a result of Husserl's attack on Mach, but it can nevertheless be best understood as a substitute for the discredited liaison of naturalism with positivism (as this was assailed almost simultaneously by Husserl, James Ward, and others). By the formalistic theory I mean the view that the principle can be regarded as a logical formula, derivable like other principles such as that of identity from a

---

[6] E. Husserl, *Logische Untersuchungen*, Niemeyer, Halle (1913), Vol. I, pp. 204, 207.

few basic axioms which are not themselves normative but which have conclusions which may be applied regulatively. Such derivations must be regarded as valid; their usefulness in directing or judging scientific work, especially in empirical fields, is, however, more doubtful.

Whitehead has remarked, "As hypothesis increases, necessity diminishes."[7] Erich Becher, attacking the fictionalists, was perhaps the first to derive the principle from considerations of probability, for he held that it was applicable without qualification only to fictions, where probability (usefulness in prediction and nothing else) was at stake.[8] Hailperin[9] showed that

$$P(p \bullet q) \leq P(p)$$

which he called "essentially the basis for Occam's Razor," though actually it is, of course, only a necessary condition, and he does not prove the sufficient condition.

Nelson[10] went further and showed that, if we assume (a) explanation consists of one or more independent hypotheses, (b) hypotheses consist of groups of propositions in mutual implicative relations (i.e., hypotheses are independent of each other), and (c) the independent hypotheses have equal *a priori* probability, then

$$P(E) = P(H_1 \bullet H_2 \ldots H_n)$$

and

$$P(H_1) > P(H_2 \bullet H_3).$$

---

[7] A.N. Whitehead, *The Organisation of Thought, Educational and Scientific*, Williams and Norgate, London (1917), pp. 175-176.

[8] E. Becher, *Die Voraussetzungen der Naturwissenschaften*, Barth, Leipzig (1907), pp. 19-20.

[9] T. Hailperin, "Foundations of Probability in the Mathematical Logic," *Philosophy of Science*, Supplement, IV (1937), pp. 125-150.

[10] E.J. Nelson, "A Note on Parsimony," *Ibid.*, III (1936), pp. 62-66. (I have simplified the symbolism in this brief account.) It should also be noted that the deduction outlined above is by no means the whole of Nelson's contribution to the problem. He states that this is not the only or the most important type of simplicity, and among the others he lists: number of entities assumed; type, degree, and number of relations or functions; simplicity of numerical coefficients, and a number of terms in polynomials.

This proof depends only on the multiplicative axiom in probability theory.[11]

We have said that this connection between probability and simplicity has been formally established. As thus proved, it is of immediate application in mathematics, though probability itself can not be taken in any sense other than "likelihood of involving inconsistency (error)." In mathematics, simplicity is absolutely required. Since independent assumptions are made and their consequences must be self-consistent, and since we can not be sure of meeting these requirements in any absolute sense (but only through eventual demonstration of an isomorphism between a subset of the postulate system with a part of an *assumed* paradigm of simplicity such as the real number system or the Euclidean geometry), the danger of inconsistency is reduced by assuming as few independent starting points as possible, for it is within them that latent conflicts may be hidden.

But in empirical science, the conditions which would render Nelson's deductions applicable do not ordinarily, and perhaps never, obtain. We can see this in three ways: (a) The condition of complete independence of hypotheses is not fulfilled and is not desirable. (b) The condition of equal probability does not obtain in an empirical science. (c) The field of application to which hypotheses are applied is not a limited one as in a deductive science wherein the field of application (the scope of the theory) is generated by implications of the postulates; where this basic difference between a deductive and an empirical science is overlooked for the sake of simplicity of construction, science becomes dogmatic.

(a) The hypotheses making up a scientific theory are not completely independent so that their probabilities could be separately determined. Take, for example, the basic assumptions of Newton's system. It would be erroneous to suppose that one could be deduced from the other

---

[11] Another formalistic deduction of the rule is independent of considerations of probability, and is capable of being extended to a realistic objective basis, but it is not derivable simply from the principle of sufficient reason. It depends upon two premises: (i) Every event has a sufficient reason; (ii) Every event is the sufficient reason for another event. Then A has a sufficient reason a, and a is alone sufficient to explain or cause A. If, however, $a + b$ is assumed, then the effect by (ii) will be $A + B$; but if the effect is A, then to assume $a + b$ as the cause is inconsistent with (ii). Therefore, every increase in the complexity of a cause increases the complexity of the effect.

(within Newton's system). Yet it would be equally erroneous to call them independent in the sense that their plausibilities (or probabilities) are irrelevant to the conjoint assumption of the entire set. The definition of time, for example, is not derivable from that of space, yet it would be materially improbable that one would be of use without the other; the second law of motion, furthermore, is improbable without the first, yet it is not deduced from it. To break them down into their truly independent parts and then to judge the system on the basis of its simplicity would certainly be foreign to the grounds on which Newton's system recommended itself for two centuries as the simplest cosmology. It was certainly not this sort of simplicity which was sought by Newton; his desire for simplicity was largely directed against the loose ends of Kepler's work and Descartes' extravagance in physical models.

Another example of this same interdependence in the "axioms" of empirical science is obvious from an analysis of Darwin's system. From the existence of life and variations and the concepts of overpopulation and heredity, Darwin derives the principle of struggle for survival, natural selection, survival of the fittest, and the consequent establishment of new kinds. This is not to say that the theory is not less simple than the one it replaced, but merely to point out that its simplicity is not discovered by *counting* postulates or independent hypotheses; it is simplest because its starting points are not only few in number but also because they are of "one kind," with none of the discontinuity and arbitrariness of the various subhypotheses of the theory of special creation.[12]

(b) What has been said about the interdependence of the hypotheses or concepts implies the second objection, namely, that the requirement of equal probability can not be met with in practice. Yet it is necessary for the establishment of the formal minimal principle, because three hypotheses each with a probability of .99 have a total probability higher than two with probabilities of .50, even though the total explanation is numerically more complex.

---

[12] Popper's concept (*Logik der Forschung*, Springer, Vienna, 1935, p. 94) that simplicity is equivalent to "falsifiability" and thus a positive function of empirical content is a better reason for preferring Darwinism than any counting of hypotheses.

(c) The scope of a scientific theory is not limited by what is implicit in its postulates, but is also determined by the kind of facts to which the theory is later exposed and to which it ought to apply. (Since the postulates serve as criteria of relevance, however, it often happens that they do limit the scope of the theory in a way not empirically warranted.) For these reasons, scientific simplicity is always tentative and is not something that can be judged once and for all. What is rightly judged to be a simple theory one day may have to be acknowledged complex the next by the enforced addition of an *ad hoc* hypothesis occasioned by an "interference" from the outside where none was expected. One may say formally, of course, that theory A plus *ad hoc* B is not the same theory any longer, and in a purely deductive system where all hypotheses are logically independent it would not be. But in an empirical science where this independence does not obtain, the *ad hoc* in effect belongs to the system, since its very suitability to the tone of the whole has made it acceptable in place of the infinite variety of *ad hoc* hypotheses theoretically available if the requirement of complete independence is fulfilled.

A scientific theory is to be judged not only on grounds of its internal simplicity, but also from the standpoint of its relevance to other similarly simple systems. Here, as indicated previously with regard to Newton's laws, we do not have either complete independence or complete inferability. Naturally, the entire set should be as simple as possible, and the synoptic function of great theories in science is to tie lesser theories together. But often we are not using the entire set; and in such a case we do often prefer a more complex hypothesis than is required by the particular problem in order to achieve relevancy to a larger field of scientific experience. Peirce,[13] for example, limited considerations of simplicity not to the probability of the separate components of a theory but to its "total probability." Thus, he says, it may be more parsimonious to explain any specific human action in terms of pure egoism, but it is more probable that, remembering the wide variety in behavior, there are other causes, and an admixture of other motives into the explanation of a single action should not be ruled out by too narrow an application of the rule of simplicity.

---

[13] C.S. Peirce in Baldwin's *Dictionary of Philosophy and Psychology*, article on "Parsimony."

Wertheimer[14] goes so far as to distinguish between the truth-values of partial and systematic propositions.

Still another danger in the use of the minimal principle is apparent from the work of Hugo Dingler. A short introduction to one aspect of his thought will serve to clarify the following criticisms. Dingler is an "operationist" and is often called a "conventionalist," though he renounces this appellation with good reason. He holds that the apriority of scientific propositions lies in the fact that they are all defined by a finite number of repeatable operations. For them to be uniquely defined, some formal principle must be agreed to which will uniquely determine the operational series by which they are defined. The formal principle is that of simplicity, which is thus derived from the requirement of uniqueness. "The solution which is suitable," he says, "is the only one which can be uniquely defined by the methodological means then available. Such solutions have then naturally the characteristic of also being the logically simplest, that is, they require the fewest determinations."[15] Now, Dingler continues, the simplicity which such a solution has is purely systematic or internal (*innenbestimmte Einfachstheit*), because it is a simplicity resulting from a concatenation of the only possible operations with the fewest possible *Grundfähigkeiten*. It does not coincide, however, with what is frequently desired, a simplicity in application to a particular case, or *aussenbestimmte Einfachstheit*.[16] For example, the unique determination of a plane is a necessary condition for the reproducibility of a measuring instrument, and it is uniquely determined only in Euclidean geometry, which, in turn, is based on a minimum of *Grundfähigkeiten*, namely, the acknowledgement only of distance and the plane. Therefore, he holds the "methodological means" at our disposal at any time to be Euclidean, and measurements, to be systematically simple, must then be interpreted in a Euclidean manner. This may, however, complicate actual calculations and predictions (or render them impossible). But such criticism, made from the standpoint of external simplicity, he regards as invalid, or at most as only temporarily justified by the exigencies of "front-line science," since, if taken systematically (as he objects that Einstein does), it destroys the

---

[14] M. Wertheimer, "On Truth," *Social Research* I (1934), pp. 135-146.

[15] H. Dingler, *Die Methode der Physik*, Munich, Reinhardt (1938), p. 86.

[16] *Ibid.*, pp. 284-285.

foundation of the instruments by which both systematic and external simplicity are reckoned. He is especially critical of those who regard "measurement as an external absolute."

The effect of this sharp distinction between internal and external simplicity is to make a breach in the unity of a scientific theory, since Dingler admits that "front-line science" can not be restricted always to the systematically simplest procedure. The new discoveries must often be taken care of *ad hoc,* meaning that the total complexity of the theory is increased. When this is decreased by a systematic integration of the *ad hoc* there is a consequent loss in external simplicity. There is no other alternative.

An increase in the number of presuppositions or basic operational possibilities is needed to avoid the conflict between generality and simplicity which is engendered by Dingler's *a priori* decision as to what is to be permitted. If his original presuppositions, which need not, of course, be self-evident or psychologically prior, were those of a more general geometry, subsets of the hypotheses would be applicable within different ranges and the molar instruments would not have to be calibrated for microscopic and macroscopic deviations from Euclid. This would necessarily lead away from his numerically minimal simplicity, but the effective simplicity (a function of the presuppositions, the total number of determinations necessary, and the shortness of the deductive route from presupposition to observation) could be reduced to far less than it is when Dingler attempts in terms of his neo-classical physics to treat the phenomena on which relativity is based.

There is another systematic danger in Dingler's use of simplicity which would be avoided were he less of an absolutist and more the conventionalist which he is often considered to be. This is the threat of dogmatism (which he does not escape) resulting from an *a priori* determination of the structure which a scientific theory must have. That is, he allows his rule of exclusion of operations to become the general rule of the incorrigibility of postulates, which is characteristic only of a deductive science in which everything may be presumed to be known *ab initio.* This transition, which is made in the name of uniqueness or simplicity, actually reduces the data to an entirely secondary position, making physics a formal science. Fruitfulness is replaced by elegance; the physicist need not go to the laboratory. To appeal to simplicity becomes itself merely an assumed maxim, and the absoluteness which he seeks proves itself to be merely arbitrary convention.

IV. A Conventionalistic View of Parsimony

Simplicity may be regarded merely as a desideratum, an ideal which should be sought but whose locus is not fixed *a priori*. Naturally, each of the other accounts of the principle which we have surveyed has its normative aspects too, yet in each case the principle has been derived from something which does not purport to be normative—from some theory of the nature of the object or the nature of man or from a mistaken identification of the conditions of formal with those of empirical thinking. In each case, due to the formalism and abstractness of the derivation, either the demand for simplicity was carried so far as to nullify some of the other desirable features of a scientific system, or the conditions required for the application of the principle could not actually obtain. If we do not derive the law of parsimony from extra-scientific considerations, but regard it exclusively as a rule of the game, refusing to acknowledge the legitimacy of an explanation which assumes more than is necessary for resolving the particular *type* of problem before us, we have what may be considered the conventionalistic theory of parsimony.

It is obvious that simplicity is not the only convention of this character. Formally distinct from it, but equally difficult to justify in any of the ways mentioned previously, is the principle of sufficient reason.[17] A third requirement would be that of generality; due to the systematic nature of science, an explanation of a single observation

---

[17] The conventionalistic relation between parsimony and sufficient reason has been stated by Kaufmann with what I consider to be parsimony basic. He says, "The rules of scientific procedure contain the *conditions for an exemption from the general prohibition to change the corpus of a science.*"— Felix Kaufmann, "The Logical Rules of Scientific Procedure," *Philosophy and Phenomenological Research* II (1942), pp. 457-471, esp. p. 459. It would seem to me that the name for the "general prohibition" would be not "the methodological principle of sufficient reason" as he suggests, but the principle of parsimony (or exclusion); the rules determining exemptions express sufficient reasons. In another essay I hope to examine critically various theories of the status of the law of sufficient reason.

must be adequate to it and also contain any complications necessary to render it applicable to a reasonable maximum variety of other observations; an "explanation" of one fact alone is a misnomer. It is clear that the principle of simplicity is now very restricted and can be applied effectively only after the adequacy of a set of hypotheses has been established.[18] An overly conscientious use of the principle of parsimony may be expected to lead to theories which are too narrow, since every scientific convention becomes in time a principle of exclusion or a criterion of relevance and appears to the careless thinker as a natural law.

Simplicity in a closed field of deductive science may be regarded as a final attribute; in empirical science, of which we may say not only a minimum of assumptions but also a maximum of observations are needed, it is always relative to generality and adequacy. Adequacy we may regard, in its turn, as like an Hegelian synthesis of the principles of sufficient reason and parsimony; it is a demand we make on science because the two principles are, in isolation, incompatible in their effects on scientific thinking. There is a conventional dialectic resulting from this antithetical relationship and the constant leaven of new observations which should not be inhibited by either.

The historical transition to the heliocentric astronomy may serve as an example of this.

Copernicus is quite explicit in his attempt to introduce a greater simplicity into the Ptolemaic theory.[19] Kepler found, however, that the systematically justified parts of the Copernican system (i.e., those parts not treated analogously to the Ptolemaic system, which in fact are the forty of the original eighty odd cycles which Copernicus could replace) were *too simple*, and that this was the cause of the necessity of assuming the remaining *ad hoc* epicycles. Through a fundamental

---

[18] Lloyd Morgan says, "We do not know enough about the causes of variation to be rigidly bound by the law of parsimony." *Animal Life and Intelligence* (1891), p. 174.

[19] I refer here not to the passage in the preface in which it is stated that the hypothesis is put forward only to facilitate calculations, since this is now regarded as spurious. Cf. H.S. Jones, "Copernicus and the Heliocentric Theory," *Nature* CLI (1943), p. 573. The reference is rather to the argument that it is simpler to suppose one globe to move and many to be stationary rather than the reverse.

change in the postulate of circular orbits, by which this concept was replaced with a more complex elliptical concept,[20] he increased the field of the systematic concepts without the use of *ad hoc* hypotheses. The systematic part of his work, however, is less parsimonious than the systematic parts of Copernicus' work.

It is thus quite apparent that the formal principle with its minimal numerical concept can not be very relevant to empirical work. Even within some parts of mathematics, where certain results are intentionally sought, simplicity of the axiom system must also be tempered by the desire for adequacy. In this case, the locus of simplicity is shifted from the axiom set (which is logically independent of the particular consequence we wish it to justify) to the total solution of the problem, since, if the axiom set is inadequate, hypotheses *ad hoc* would be necessary for the particular solution. If these latter are to be systematically justified, the total complexity is increased or the entire system regarded as a subset of some more general axioms.

But the problem of how high a price (in *ad hoc* hypotheses) we are willing to pay for axiomatic simplicity is a central one in empirical science. To show this, let us take two cases, one decided and one still under debate.

In physics, the Newtonian system predicted a positive result for the Michelson-Morley experiment. None was found. Three ways were open to the physicist. (i) He could give a nonphysicalistic hypothesis *ad hoc* which would save the simplicity of the system. He could say there was an experimental error and forget the experiment. To follow this path means, however, ultimately to regard the laws of physics as "legislative" for nature and to render science dogmatic. (ii) He could formulate a physicalistic hypothesis *ad hoc,* which would leave his basic system simple but adapt it to this particular contingency. Thus he could suggest the Fitzgerald-Lorenz contraction hypothesis. This, however, when looked at critically is, of course, an increase in systematic complexity, since to the extent that it is logically

---

[20] Popper (*loc. cit.*) mentions a similar case as one of his examples to show what he means by simplicity. Since it takes fewer determinations to decide whether a given set of points lie in a plane than for determining whether they are on a quadratic surface, the "linear connection is simpler than the quadratic." That is, a linear connection is more easily "falsified" than a higher curve surface.

independent it ought to be put at the beginning with the laws of motion instead of *ad hoc* at the end. (iii) He could try to show that the *ad hoc* hypothesis and the axioms are not logically independent but rather special consequences of another hitherto unformulated axiom set which may have either fewer logical independents or more basic suppositions whose interconnections give them a plausibility which the Newtonian axioms together with the *ad hoc* contraction hypotheses do not have. This was the course of Einstein, who says that the inadequacies of the Newtonian system "are not logical objections to the theory. They form, as it were, merely unsatisfied needs of the scientific spirit in its effort to penetrate the processes of nature by a complete and unified set of ideas."[21]

The other example is taken from so-called "psychic research." The existence of para-psychological phenomena is still under debate, and what is said here is not intended as suggesting a positive or negative decision on this question; it, like the one in physics just described, is a technical matter for experts alone. But the behavior of psychologists in this field is relevant to our considerations. There have been systematic objections to Rhine's work, but in addition to these (which do not concern us here) there have been purely defensive reactions from the side of many psychologists who reject the results because of their apparent inconsistency with deductions from accepted principles or presuppositions. One psychologist has said that he will never be convinced of the existence of a psychical phenomenon by any experiment whatsoever, because he knows *a priori* that it is impossible. To support this exclusion, which he defends on the basis of simplicity, since to take Rhine's results seriously would require either a new postulate or a restructuring of the whole, he may be forced more and more to bridge the gap between theory and the experimental observations by *ad hoc* hypotheses. These may include some legitimate psychological concepts; in this case they add to the total complexity of his theory. Or they may be nonscientific, as the accusation that marked cards were used, etc. What makes such a standpoint as this relevant to our purpose is that it will either replace science with dogmatism or else

---

[21] A. Einstein, "Isaac Newton," *Annual Report of the Smithsonian Institution*, 1927, pp. 201-207. Cf. also J.H. Jeans, "Newton and the Science of Today," *Proceedings of the Royal Society*, Series A, CLXXXI (1943), pp. 251-262, especially pp. 252, 258-259.

eventually force the question which we have seen the formalist to be unable to answer: How complicated can a theory become at the conclusion level without forcing a restructuring at the premise level? Obviously, no mathematical answer such as "One premise is worth five hypotheses *ad hoc*" can be expected; but unless a fairly definite answer can be given in a particular case, simplicity in the sense of the formalistic minimal or numerical concept is no guide to scientific construction.

Simplicity, it seems to me, is more a matter of "scientific strategy" or "tact" in judging the value of a shift in the base of operations. If it is so, we can not derive hard and fast rules for its application, nor can we regard it as determined finally for each theory, thus permitting a choice among them on this ground alone.

There are several inferences which are justified by this concept of simplicity.

(1) We have not discussed the recent psychological accounts of the principle of simplicity in which the pattern-character of perception is taken as the natural ground for simplicity in science. I did not mention them because, in principle, they resemble Mach's work too closely. But in conjunction with the conventionalistic theory, they become very relevant, since they are an acknowledgment that suitable conventions do have a psychological basis. What appears suitable at a given time will depend in part upon the "intellectual climate," the scientific environment, and the character of the scientific thinker. This gives a basis, even if a variable one, for estimating the relative simplicity of two theories. R.B. Lindsay, having also concluded that formalistic criteria of simplicity arc inadequate, states that the simpler of two theories is the one with which a normally intelligent person can, in the shorter time, become sufficiently familiar to obtain correct and useful results.[22] While this may not be the kind of interpretation we expect from one of the most honored and ancient traditions of methodology, as a "rule of thumb" it is probably as good a way as any for determining the "effective simplicity" in an empirical science. It must be borne in mind, of course, that this kind of simplicity may not coincide with logical or formal simplicity, and that for the latter type

---

[22] R.D. Lindsay, "Simplicity in Physics," *Philosophy of Science* IV (1937), pp. 151-167. See especially p. 166.

there is no substitute in a deductive science, no matter bow much the difficulties in understanding may be multiplied by the maxim.

(2) The type of simplicity within a scientific system will depend upon the purpose of the explanation. If sciences are distinguished not so much by the answers they give as by the questions they ask, it is obviously unimportant to arrange them in order of simplicity, as attempted by Comte and Spencer. It is also obvious that some sciences use the concepts of others, that this borrowing is not always mutual, and that where it is not, the science which borrows is to this extent dependent on the other and formally less simple. For example, the conceptual field of biology is less simple than that of physics to the degree to which physical laws are presupposed within the scope of the biological questions. We naturally prefer, when possible, a physical explanation for most purposes, but often we are content with sciences which are "autonomous" only to the extent that they are simple in Lindsay's sense. Still, to prefer physics as a matter of principle because of its minimal simplicity is erroneous. It is even more groundless to equate its conceptual simplicity with its truthfulness outside of the context of a specific type of problem and to admit into cosmology only what is physicalistically defined.

(3) Simplicity has appeared to some writers to be primarily an esthetic category. As long as scientific simplicity was read in terms of the formalistic minimal principle, such suggestions could only be tolerated perhaps among popularizers of science. When simplicity, however, is regarded as an attribute of a system (rather than of a series), its resemblance to the simplicity of a work of art, which is not a simplicity of blank identity or sparsity of ideas, is more striking. If the suggestion made above that the simplicity of science is not so much a matter of counting postulates as an expression of what for lack of a better term we called "tact," the resemblance between great scientific theorizing and artistic creation is manifest.

(4) The metaphysical implications of the principle of sufficient reason are somewhat different if the approach is conventionalistic rather than otherwise. It strengthens the case against a metaphysics based merely on the positive results of science, because the principle of exclusion, which is the form in which the law of parsimony is used, is now regarded as itself a variable, dependent upon many factors besides the cosmological nature of the objects of science. And when the conventionalistic interpretation is substituted for the naturalistic and

formalistic, it shows that the history of science can not be construed as a straight-line development in the direction of an absolute minimum of complexity.

It leaves entirely unanswered the question as to whether the metaphysical nature of the world is such as to make simple explanations "true." It does not tell us whether simple ideas work because they are true or they are true because they work; it does not indicate whether the simple laws we have discovered have been disclosed merely because they are simple, or whether the entire natural organization is simple and homogeneous with that which we have brought to light. It introduces into science itself a variability and relativity (which has been suspected more and more in recent years), and this is a warning against absolutizing the results of science into a final metaphysic. In a word, it puts the problem of the ultimate nature of reality back where it belongs, in the hands of the metaphysician.

Human beings have seldom been at a loss to imagine sufficient reasons for things. The great trouble, if we may judge from the conflicts which occur in times of scientific crisis such as the sixteenth century and the end of the nineteenth, has been in getting rid of unneeded explanations. It is for this reason that, in critical turning points in the history of science, parsimony rather than adequacy has been the battle cry of the revolutionary forces. In the normal course of a science's growth, however, when to a stable axiomatic basis more and newer facts are assimilated, it is the requirement of adequacy which is dominant. And when a critical juncture comes, their applications modify and check each other so that nothing useful is lost in the process of simplification.

4. Judgments Of Meaning In Art*[1]

May works of art have a meaning as one of their esthetic properties? Answers to this question whether affirmative or negative have driven many critics and estheticians into untenable positions, yet it is a question which requires an answer doing justice to the esthetic experience and harmonious with an acceptable philosophy of art.

The following study of meaning as an esthetic property begins with two explicit assumptions. The first concerns the definition of an esthetic judgment and the second concerns the methodology of esthetics. First, it is obvious that many kinds of judgments and many different predicates can be employed in estimating those objects generally considered to make up the field of the fine arts. It is equally clear, however, that many of these judgments and their predicates are irrelevant to that by virtue of which certain artifacts do so constitute the field of the arts. Those which are irrelevant relate the work of art to non-artistic material, i.e., to material not esthetically refined and presented in the same integral creation. A judgment that a picture costs a thousand dollars is such a judgment, which is about art but not an esthetic judgment. We may decide in general whether a particular judgment is genuinely esthetic by seeing if an affirmative answer can be given to the question, "Does tracing out the relation indicated by the judgment in question contribute to the direct and immediate sensory experience?" If it does not, if it dissipates the esthetic impact and corrodes its wholeness by diverting attention from the immediate givenness, it is not an esthetic judgment. This criterion is applicable within all esthetic theories which do not surrender the value of the

* Reprinted with permission from *Journal of Philosophy* XLI (1944), pp. 169-178.
[1] This paper is based on one with the same title read to the Fullerton Club at Bryn Mawr College, December 11, 1943.

esthetic experience to that of some other kind of experience, such as moral edification, for example.

Second, we have to presuppose the *prima facie* validity of judgments which claim to be esthetic and which meet the first requirement outlined above. In some fields of philosophy, and perhaps in all of them, it seems to me that the thinker should have a very high respect for relatively naïve judgments. I do not propose that we always admire complete naïveté or accept the doctrine of the incorrigibility of common sense. I merely mean that before theoretical construction begins, the "facts" on which it is to be based must be accepted as such, even if only tentatively. In the appreciation of art, basic judgments of preference have to be accepted as evident even though they are only provisory, since dialectical and phenomenological elaborations may sharpen some distinctions and obliterate others; but if the expectation that they will stand analysis is not at least held—for it is obvious it will not always be fulfilled—no theory of esthetics can get started and even less can it be tested, for these judgments, though occurring in a value context, have the office and authority of fact. To be sure, even in the construction of a scientific experience facts are to some extent variable, and consequently to look upon values as facts does not of itself guarantee their permanence. Yet certain empirical judgments will retain their credentials in science regardless of what interpretations are put on them and no matter if they are translated into a conceptual language different from that of the pre-scientific judgment. At least the same primacy must be conceded to the basic deliverances of the esthetic attitude.

These two presuppositions provide a starting point and give direction to the following discussion. The "basic fact" of the esthetic experience with which we here begin can be expressed in such a judgment as, "The hundredth symphony of Haydn is very beautiful, but it lacks the meaning (or meaning-fulness) that one of Beethoven's later quartets has." Both inexperienced listeners and connoisseurs can be heard making such judgments as this. It is conceivable that their approval of the latter is misstated in this terminology, but we should not decide dogmatically in advance that this is the case. If an esthetic theory can not find a place for the predicate "meaningful" in its categories, or can not find a more acceptable way of expressing this preference, it is simply inadequate to the fact which it should explain. The place of meaning need not be the same after an analysis has been carried out as before, nor does it matter to our present purposes that artists and critics can not agree as to what has meaning and what lacks it. All that is asserted here is simply that some esthetic situations seem to demand the judgment that they have meaning, and this is a fact which should not be forgotten or simply explained away in the light of some *a priori* construction based on more convenient predicates.

The validity of the concept of meaning in art is most radically denied by those who follow the present enthusiastic developments in semantics. With a positivistic definition of meaning, it is quite obvious that most art can not have any meaning. In sharply distinguishing between the emotive and the symbolical use of language or any communicative medium, and in restricting art to the former, they make it a gesture which is a symptom of emotions in the creator and a stimulus to emotion in the observer. The statements art makes are to them merely "pseudo-statements," and the difference between a yawn and a concerto is not that one has "meaning" or "beauty" but that it has a structure which is supposed peculiarly to adapt it to stimulation of certain desirable emotional states. But the "Ohs!" and "Ahs!" to which they reduce the lyrical gesture can not compete with the simple yawn as a stimulus in arousing (and even sometimes in calming and satisfying). Though the theory is in part correct in pointing to the fact that most art does not leave our feelings "cold," this fact is hardly sufficient to support the entire edifice of a philosophy of art which attempts to deal justly with the manifold complexity of phenomena in esthetics. It will suffice to indicate only three disadvantages which are closely related to the present problem. (1) It does not explain why a certain pattern of lines or tones (though the case is easier with words) is adequate to represent and to cause feelings; empathy can accomplish much, but how "meaning" supervenes upon the physiological empathic reaction is not revealed. (2) It does not adequately explain why two gestures which we may consider equally expressive and exciting may have such obvious differences in their *prima facie* esthetic value. If it attempts to do so, it must be in terms of kinds or real objects of the aroused emotion, and art is surrendered to all kinds of extraneous standards. (3) It directs attention away from the esthetic immediacy since there is no requirement that our emotional excursion entered upon because of the esthetic stimulus should bring us back to our point of origin with a richer experience of it.

Nevertheless, the attempt to escape these difficulties by a completely objective reading of the immediate experience does not lead us much further towards an understanding of meaning in art. The Kantian esthetic is typical of this, and though it preserved art from all sorts of Philistinism and subjective sentimentalism, it did so only by denying that art was a communicative medium. Its autonomy was preserved, but its content was dissipated in order to preserve its universality.

A third theory remains, and that is one which holds art to be communicative because it consists of signs of particulars. To prove this constituted the program of impressionism, but the instability of the impressionistic attitude can be discovered equally well by reviewing its actual history or by examining its presupposition. The latter was the assumption that the artist pictures things as he sees them, that he sees them as they are and not as they have come to appear as a result of habit and practical interest, and that he then immediately represents them. Immediate representation, however, is self-contradictory, since representation implies mediation by perspective, selection, and accent. The fact that the artist has an arbitrary choice in each, not dictated by the material, is the fatal element in the program, because he can not humanly choose all of the possibilities in each and therefore has to make use of non-imitative canons. That is, he has to import into imitation an element foreign to his object and thus forbidden by his own theory. (Positivism had to do the same, and if a comparison between positivism and impressionism is appropriate, then their respective issuance later in voluntarisms and expressionisms of various sorts is no less revealing of their instability.)

But it is nevertheless true that much art has its imitative components, selected and modified by artistic demands. To trace out these indications, however, is like discerning that of which art is a symptom, in that both require us to leave the field of the esthetically given without any assurance of being brought back to it. On the other hand, to remain within it to the exclusion of all else seems to be, from the example of Kant, to deny the validity of the concept of meaning. Meaning by its very structure seems to entail a reference from the given here-and-now to the not-given. If this is all there is to it, we must suppose that our first presupposition is inconsistent with our second when applied to judgments of meaning.

But can we find meaning within the medium, not in a bridge between it and something else? We can not save meaning with a theory that the esthetically formed content both means and is meant in the same esthetic experience. Various forms of this theory of inherent meaning have indeed been valuable as defenses of esthetic immediacy against the theories we have examined which hunt for a meaning outside. But this theory involves an equivocation which lies in allowing the word "meaning" to denote both the act of reference and that which is referred to, and while acknowledging that it denotes both, it allows them to coalesce in one object or one moving process. How absurd it is can best be seen by analogy: if one claimed that a word had meaning, but when asked what was its meaning replied that it meant itself, we would quite rightly conclude that it meant nothing.

This analogy is not merely destructive, however, for if we observe the ways a word seems to have meaning and yet turns out either not to have any or to have a different meaning from that which it seemed to have, I think we shall get some information which will help us to see how art can have a meaning without justifying the inadequate theories which we have already examined and rejected. The following account of the genesis of some communicative forms is not, of course, a genetic one; it does not purport to be a history of language so much as a gross anatomy of one or two of its parts.

In an ideally simple case, we would have a sound or a mark universally agreed upon for every discriminable entity. Such a "perfect language" would be absolutely transparent in both the objective and the intersubjective dimension. It would, however, be so complex that it would be unusable; its structure would be as complicated as the world itself, and for practical purposes we might be able to find no structure in it at all. Actual language has little or nothing in common with this ideal schema by which the semanticists wish to make the "verbal maps" fit the "geography of objects." One of the greatest differences lies in the fact that our language consists largely of class names, not proper names; a distinctive feature of class names is that they themselves form classes, and the whole apparatus of the calculus of classes gives the schematism of connotational structures. These patterns and the structural relationships among the things outside the medium are probably never isomorphous, and this has led many philosophers from Heraclitus to Bergson to regard language as deceptive. Certainly language can deceive us, but the knowledge that it can do so is useful for keeping it from actually doing so, and the deceptions which we fall into are occasions for restructuring either the connotational or the denotational patterns. Of the two, the former is the easier to change.

The ease of restructuring the connotational pattern in comparison with the difficulty of changing the objects to which the former is supposed to correspond is the source of two divergent modes of symbolistic change. The first begins with what we call "correcting" ideas in the light of experience. In this change, however, it is observed that the most valuable relationship for practice between the connotational and the denotational structures is not that of 1:1 congruence, but that it is rather a direct relationship between only a few terms of the one and a few observations of the other, with the terms themselves being connected into complex systems of relations which need not be supposed to hold in exact congruence in nature. The only requirement we make of a connotational structure is that it keep its feet on the ground, so that whenever a term which has a denotation occurs in the connotational system, its factual counterpart can be found objectively in the denoted system under the conditions defined by the total connotational context. This status of meaning, which is the normal one in science, indicates that meaning can be preserved even when its elaboration goes on entirely within the symbolic medium and under the domination of its own logical, semantic, or mathematical laws. Its freedom from the vain ideal of perfect picturing of denotations can be called, for obvious reasons, "semantic dissociation," and its ultimate stage would be reached in a system of mathematics which would fit Mr. Russell's definition.

The other symbolistic change brought about by this greater plasticity of the connotational structure is what Friedrich Engels called "the innate casuistry of man, to change things by changing their names." This change may be called "semantic arrest." Here the footing of the connotational structure may be lost by inadvertence or intention so that the referential contact with the object is broken off. This occurs because, if we are careless, words and other symbols come to be regarded primarily as things and not as the meanings of things,[2] and

---

[2] Though this account is not meant to be genetic, it is nevertheless well to point out that primitive language is at this stage and its development goes in the direction of a more stable denotative vocabulary and a connotational structure which is to a considerable degree semantically dissociated. This fact

sometimes because it is useful to us to talk without saying anything, as in phatic communication and delusory propaganda. Many of our words, names of values which Nietzsche said are merely "banners marking the spot where men have experienced new blessednesses," gain intersubjective currency but lose meaning in the dimension of denotation because they are names of ill-defined objects of desire which lie in a region all too far from that of practical enjoyment, thus building up substitute satisfactions in pseudo-environments of words and rituals and illusions. These symbols are freed from the corrective intercourse with their objects, and they become super-charged with meanings derived from their manifold uses as ideals and substitutes— that is, they become "overdetermined," as the psychoanalyst says— because they serve too great a variety of the intentions to do full justice to any; thus they lose their denotations and become useless or even dangerous when denotation is needed. But the visible structure of meaning is preserved, since the incongruence between the two realms is not visible in the single experience when we are looking at only one; its strength lies in its feigning a meaning.

Semantic dissociation is more likely to occur when the elementary material which may have denotations is largely irrelevant to our emotional interests; semantic arrest occurs most readily when the material which may relate to an object or the object itself is strongly colored with emotions and interest. In the former case, the meaning may get through at selected points so long as a vocabulary of denotation is preserved; in the latter it may be peremptorily arrested because the denotations become completely indefinite, appearing only as incomplete acts of reference having direction (intention) but not specific termination. But in both, the appearance of meaning is preserved.

Now let us apply these distinctions to meaning as we find it claimed in some esthetic judgments. We have seen that though art may indicate an object and may let us discern the artist, this reference is not esthetic meaning. It has also been shown that we can not completely cut art off from all relationship to things outside it and still preserve the concept of meaning without equivocation. We have seen ways, however, in which the phenomenon of meaning can be preserved without there

is relevant to the genesis of art if artistic communication depends upon the kind of arrest of the "normal" reference which is described here.

being any necessity other than a practical one (which is arbitrary for esthetics) for checking the precision of the reference, and the phenomenon is all that is needed in art. In a word, the question of the meaning of art is altogether different from (though perhaps basic to) that of its "truth."

It is my thesis that art has a meaning because its esthetically formed content is isomorphous with connotational structures which might be specified by contents which could have mediate meanings by virtue of the vocabulary-relations of the content to objects or non-esthetic ideas. Art which has a meaning is a sensuous presentation of connotations without denotations. If I may paraphrase Kant, art is "meaning without the meant."

Semantic dissociation will account for the significance of formal structure; semantic arrest comes into play when the contents of art are not just sounds and colors having sensuous relationships to each other, but when they are chosen from things we know in non-esthetic experience with which we normally associate them when we do not take up the esthetically detached attitude.

Absolute music and abstract painting have a meaning-structure but lack a vocabulary and thus have meaning but no denotation; representative and narrative art has a connotational structure and, through its use of situations which are not restricted to the artistic medium, it often has an apparently specific and, in many cases, a real denotation.   But due to the centrality of quality in the esthetic experience, or to our psychic distance in neglecting non-esthetic implications, the content is allowed to become relatively opaque in the denotative dimension.   Thus it can be overdetermined for the spectator and can thereby gain in connotational richness (and intersubjective clarity) what it loses in having its denotation out of focus.   I say it is "allowed" to become opaque, for it is obvious that it sometimes is prevented from this by our attempts to see through it to a denotation; my attitude to a novel, for example, can be that of a historian seeking information, and when it is I may both lose the esthetic immediacy and therewith any purely esthetic meaning it may have, and find that the non-esthetic or denotative meaning is in error and does not really lead me to things at all. But in the esthetic experience it has a meaning, and the fact that greater circumspection may show it to be denotatively delusory is irrelevant to the appreciation itself.

The meaning of a work of art, then, may lie in the contents which might in other circumstances be meaningful to us because of the denotations they have; but these salient meanings are arrested by the quality which will not let us go through it lightly. Ambiguity in it may be looked upon as a positive quality dependent upon overdetermination instead of being merely a name for lack of determinateness. Or meaning can lie in its form, which serves as a sensuous receptacle for many specific connotations but is not limited to one, being a sensuous schema or essence but not a discursive universal. The work of art can thus be the locus of the phenomenon of meaning without committing the artist to anything specific about the real world, moral or physical, subjective or objective; but the work of art is not isolationist for this reason, for it has the potentialities of an almost infinite number of references, no one of which it need specify because to specify means to deny other meanings. It is in this sense that even the non-verbal arts are more "philosophical" than history. This universality which transcends specificity of denotation also explains the paradox that we can both assert that a work of art has a meaning and yet deny in principle that we can enunciate its meaning. For any narration in a language makes specific denotative commitments which the artist has transcended; if it does not do so it is clear that it will necessarily remain the unclear and confusing outpourings which are accepted as "art appreciation" and which have no more specific meaning and considerably less interest than the art itself. It is not the fault of the interpreter, however; it lies in the nature of the task he has rashly assumed. We can at most tell what a great work of art does *not* mean; to express its full meaning would be to recreate the work (and critics are not too competent here). To attempt to express a phase of its meaning may be in part successful, for the form of the work will often fit many particulars; not one program but an indefinite number can be found for a piece of music if one sets about the task with imagination; but to hold that the form is preeminently congruent with one particular narrative pattern which is specified by having a denotative vocabulary is to miss the esthetic meaning which is potentially a great variety of specific meanings which never should be allowed to become actual by denying the equal appropriateness of the others. Thus Beethoven's third symphony can not be exclusively interpreted as an elegy to a great man without our losing some of the richness of meaning its phenomenon suggests as possible; but at the same time it is obvious that it does not mean, even in this tenuous way, the situation suggested by his "Fury over a Lost Penny." When a definite program is provided, or when the structure is organized in such a way as to make it conform obviously to one particular denoted circumstance, we get program music with a denotative meaning, the interpretation of which leads us away from the medium and thus reduces the pure esthesis.

Although we can not say what a work of art does mean, we can nevertheless point out some of the conditions in a work of art which seem to call for the particular response of a judgment of meaningfulness. Both the form and the content must be considered. First, the form must exhibit a pattern which a directly communicative system could have. Regardless of the differences in content, the analogy between music and mathematics has long been obvious; they both have an abstract semiotic structure. They are characterized by a variety which almost breaks through the limits of the allowable heterogeneity (of ideas or contents), but are saved from disintegration by subtle harmonies and a synoptic integrating unity in complexity; they are marked by a simultaneous progressive development of both the apparent variety and actual and (at least eventually) obvious wholeness; they are marked by assertion if not denotation;[3] their contents are unambiguous (fitting) in their own contexts no matter how far they are from uniqueness of denotation; and finally they go through various phases of development in which there is both a progressive and retrogressive effect upon the connotations of all other parts.

If we turn to the contents of those arts which seem to have a denotative meaning, it is even clearer how they can have a genuinely esthetic meaning. They have such a meaning to the extent that their vocabulary is overdetermined without semantic arrest causing the phenomenon of meaning to fade. Thus a photograph does not have the meaning that a painting of the same person can have, because its

---

[3] This distinction is made clear in Wheelwright's "Principle of Paradox: that two quasi-contradictory statements which lack full propositional assertibility may both be accepted as true, or both as false, within the same context." Cf. Philip Wheelwright, "A Preface to Phenosemantics," *Philosophy and Phenomenological Research* II (1942), pp. 511-519, especially page 517. This entire essay, explaining the modifications in ordinary semantic canons required by their application to "transformal" or "meta-logical" contexts (of which art is one) can not be too highly recommended.

vocabulary of indicators of something outside it is too transparent to hold attention to itself. Or when photography reaches the status of art it no longer lets the attention go through it to the object so directly that it can not enrich itself with a variety of connotations (and thus ceases to be "photographic" in the ordinary pejorative sense of the word). Something between the extremes of complete objective opacity and transparency is required; *Finnegan's Wake* does not have as much meaning (at least to many people) as *Portrait of the Artist as a Young Man*, because in the former semantic arrest is so complete that the phenomenon of meaning is itself weakened and can be found, if at all, only in the form.

If we use "beauty" as the name of a specific esthetic category and not as a term of general esthetic approbation referring to perfection in all relevant values, it is clear that meaning can be a category of quality which may be distinguished, and though it is not independent of other esthetic qualities, it is nevertheless acceptable as a predicate in genuinely esthetic judgments. Not all esthetic objects have it; nor can it be said that the phenomenon of dissociated or arrested meaning is restricted to works of art. But works of art are preëminently receptive to it, for in creating the mood of immediate acceptance of the given and satisfaction with the phenomenon we do not feel uneasy in view of the intrinsic ambiguity of the meanings adumbrated.

5. Psychology and the Norms Of Knowledge[*]

1. The Two Problems of the Theory of Knowledge

The theory of knowledge deals with two distinct kinds of problems. There is, first, the question of characteristics of knowing, by which we can decide what mental events qualify for the generic title of "cognitions." I shall call this problem the *epistemic*. In solving it, we do not need to go outside the phenomena of the mental life; in Farber's words, it is of no more importance in this inquiry that we think with our brains than that we breathe with our lungs.[1]

We wish also to know what are the causal conditions of the occurrence of knowledge. These conditions are studied piecemeal in various special sciences, but each of the piecemeal approaches has something in common with the others, the investigation of which is a philosophical problem. They all explain the occurrence of cognitions as specific events in terms of existing entities and their causal interrelations; they do not describe knowing in terms of its immanent but non-causal structure and essence. All their inquiries, therefore, may be referred to under one name; I shall call them *causal*. Causal inquiry into knowledge assumes that knowing has existential conditions and that techniques can be applied in discovering them that are like those used, for instance, in discovering the conditions of a headache.

[*] Reprinted with persmission from *Philosophy and Phenomenological Research* XIV (1954), pp. 494-506.
[1] *The Foundation of Phenomenology*, p. 568.

Each of these divisions of the theory of knowledge makes an assumption. That of the first is: "Some truths are known and it is known that they are known." And of the second: "There are causal conditions for the occurrence of knowing."

2. An Antinomy in the Theory of Knowledge

Through these assumptions, the theory of knowledge is related to the sciences in a two-fold manner. First, the validity of some specific cognitive claims, examined by epistemology independently of any knowledge of causes or other results in psychology, is presupposed in all scientific work. Second, the fact that knowing occurs is accounted for in terms of the facts which are discovered in psychology and other sciences. Knowledge is epistemologically prior to the sciences, but the facts discovered by the sciences are causally prior to knowing and to the theory of knowledge. Epistemology examines the criteria of knowledge which are used in the sciences; the sciences examine the facts which are responsible for there being cognitive events. The theory of knowledge thus stands at two extremes. In one sense it seems basic to the sciences; in another, the sciences seem basic to it.

What is assumed at one extreme cannot, in a coherent philosophy, be incompatible with what is assumed or concluded at the other. But if the psychologist says we think as we do because of certain causal conditions—he cannot fail to say this and remain a psychologist—then there is an antimony between the extremes. For the practicing logician or methodologist must say that certain thoughts *ought* to follow from certain others by laws of inference, and unless we say this and unless we can actually discipline our thinking by this "ought," there is no discovering even the *alleged* psychological conditions.

Prima facie the laws of logic or methodology are entirely consistent with the psychological laws of, say, the association of ideas or conditioned reflexes. But they are consistent because they are irrelevant. They are formally consistent since they explicitly deal with different things. The question is, however, whether it is possible to say both that the necessary and sufficient conditions of cognitive acts are causal and that we cannot know unless we can govern our thoughts by certain non-causal norms. The question is comparable to Kant's third antinomy. He there demonstrated that all events have phenomenal (causal) conditions, yet that at least some events have intelligible (in our terminology epistemic) conditions; and he tried to show that both these propositions can be true. But the solution he finally reached, in the third *Critique*, is far from merely pointing out the equivocation involved in establishing the antinomy in the first; rather, it involves a thorough revision of the theory of the relation between the phenomenal and the intelligible worlds.

I mention this historical fact merely to suggest that it does not suffice to resolve such an antinomy by means of formal logic, through exposing the equivocality of the word "condition." We are dealing not with the consistency of two sentences but with the possibility of a discipline of mental events by norms and of a causal account of behavior which is not interfered with or limited by any non-causal conditions.

Let me give an illustration to show why I do not think the problem is a mere equivocation. A psychologist describes the cognitive behavior of a subject and attempts to explain it in terms of psychology. But if these causal conditions are taken to be adequate to an explanation of cognizing, they will apply to his own knowledge of what the subject does, and his own report on the subject's behavior will be reduced simply to another item of behavior to be explained in terms of its own causal conditions. If he is to meet the requirements of a universal theory of knowledge establishing conditions for cognitive acts generally, he would have to say that he himself judges that the subject did so and so not for the epistemically relevant reason that the subject did in fact do so and so, but because of another set of causal conditions such as the momentary state of his own brain. If he denies this, he seems to deny the generality of any causal conclusions which he may put forth; if he asserts it, he gives a causal discount to his own knowledge-claims since the conditions he cites as sufficient for his own cognition do not involve any norm by which it could be judged.

Suppose that, in order to avoid such self-destructive psychologism, he generously allows that his subject as well as himself may have genuine knowledge disciplined by norms of validity and not conditioned merely by neural processes. Then he credits his subject with the possibility of behaving with respect to norms that have no causal status. Though in doing this he conforms to common sense, in principle he has asserted that there is at least one event in the world for which adequate causal conditions cannot be found.

3A. First Attempt at Solution: Division of Labor

To save the validity of his own knowledge, he ought, in honesty, to give up the ideal of a completely causal explanation. That is an uncomfortable position, so what does the psychologist do? He makes a division of labor, putting the psychology of cognition at the complex end of knowledge where it can presuppose all the results of the sciences, and epistemology at the other, where it can support the method by which these results have been obtained. He leaves the occurrence of cognitions unexplained in one place and their validity unnoticed in the other. He does so by a convention that the causal conditions of knowledge are studied in sciences which exclude epistemological concepts from their categories of explanation.

3B. Second Attempt: Rules and Norms as Causes

It has sometimes been argued that such a convention is not needed because the psychologist can deal with "rule-governed behavior." In this way it is thought that even the epistemological rules can be adduced in causally explaining behavior, and that we can thus have a "psychology of the psychologist" without destructive psychologism. But the word "rule-governed" is ambiguous. The subject in a psychological experiment is rule-governed in the sense that his behavior conforms to or illustrates certain laws or rules empirically discovered; the person solving a mathematical problem in a psychological test-situation is rule-governed in exactly the same sense that a falling body is rule-governed. But if the observer makes any valid knowledge-claims, he, the observer, must be rule-governed in quite another sense. That is, he must govern himself by rules which are not *causes* but *norms* of behavior. In this case the rules governing behavior are prescriptive, not descriptive; they are not laws stating efficient causes of behavior but norms of a process of explanation of behavior; they are not discovered by psychology, but prescribed to it. In the case of the observer, therefore, we must distinguish two aspects of rule-governed behavior. First there is the law stating the cause of the observer's obedience to rules, and this law can be discovered in the same way that he has discovered laws of the causes of his subject's behavior. Second, there is the rule that the observer intentionally obeys or tries to obey, and this rule is not adequately described as a cause at all. Only the first of these two aspects of rule-governed behavior is the subject of psychology, but without the second set of rules there would be no psychology.

It is an important gain in psychology that rule-governed behavior is now dealt with scientifically without fear that recognition of this mode of behavior would lead to unscientific teleology. The psychologist in dealing with such behavior, however, has sometimes supposed that his science has therefore become normative since it deals with behavior in which knowledge of or belief in norms is among the causal conditions of behavior. (For instance, he could hardly explain a subject's constructing a syllogism without citing the attitude or set he has towards the rules or norms of inference). The fact that psychology can deal with behavior for which attitude to a norm is a causal condition should not, however, obscure the fact that the explanations are formally identical whether or not the subject's attitude is directed to a valid or a spurious norm, while the *explainer's* attitude must be deference to a *valid* norm if the explanation is acceptable. In distinguishing between the normative behavior as it is explained and the normative behavior of the explainer, it suffices to say of the former that it is normative, but of the latter it is necessary to go further and say, "It is normative, and rightly so." Obviously the expression "normative, and rightly so" cannot occur in a purely causal account of knowledge, but must occur in an epistemological evaluation.

3c. Conclusion

Hence, even when psychology deals with rules and norms there remains a division of labor between the investigations of the psychologist and the epistemologist. A division of labor is useful and legitimate if the labor can eventually be reintegrated. In this case, however, we are not really dividing a big problem into little ones with the plan eventually to put them together again; we are rather agreeing henceforth to ignore one problem and its results whenever the other problem and its results are mentioned. This is because we are using incompatible categories in the two phases of our work, and our overall results would be inconsistent if we did try to pool them.

The epistemologist's account will conflict with the psychologist's because the epistemologist says that one of the conditions of knowledge is non-causal, while the latter has committed himself to giving a causal account of knowledge in which he can never be forced to say, "Here is a case in which causal conditions are insufficient determinants of behavior." The psychologist will avoid such an *ignava ratio* with the same vehemence that he would reject the analogous admission of a free will.

Having now made as explicit as I can what I believe to be an antinomy in the theory of knowledge, I shall propose two steps which may allay the conflict. The first is a hierarchical conception of the diverse categories involved, and the second is a suggestion concerning the way in which a subject can make a transition from one level to another within the hierarchy.

4. Hierarchy of Contexts in Explanation

For the first step, let us remember our illustration of the psychologist and his subject. There are two contexts or realms of discourse here, which I shall now call respectively the "context of explanation" and the "explained context." The subject is in the explained context, and the explanation of his behavior includes only causal concepts such as stimulus-response theory provides. The context of explanation is that of the observer, who ignores his own causal conditions and formulates judgments concerning the causes of the subject's behavior, using concepts and rules which are not causal but epistemic, such as logic and methodology prescribe. There is no reference within the explained context to rules that are "normative and rightly so," and in the context of explanation there is no reference to the causal conditions of this specific explanation, though there is reference to the causal conditions within the explained context.

In this way no actual conflict arises between the uses of the two sets of conditions in a psychological experiment. Though in both cases the observer and his subject may perform cognitive acts, they are different acts. The explained context is imbedded in a context of explanation in which the psychologist avails himself of some categories he denies to the subject in the context explained. Psychological explanations always refer to the explained context, and the explained context is always a complex state of affairs functioning as object in a context of explanation. We have a causal object-language and an epistemic meta-language.

I have argued, however, that the problem is not solved by this linguistic distinction or the division of labor it signalizes. But inasmuch as it gives rise to a clear conception of a hierarchy of contexts, it is a help in making our first step, which is to show how the two contexts are related. With this distinction in mind, then, let us turn to a slightly different illustration, the case of students in a class in experimental psychology.

Student *A* does an experiment on student *B*, dealing with visual size-perception, and explains *B's* response to a stimulus in causal terms. Then *B* does a similar experiment on *A* and gives a comparable explanation. If these explanations are accepted simultaneously, we have seen that they cancel each other out. So we accept first one and then the other. We must consider the reasons which lead us once to accept *A's* report and on another occasion *B's*.

B looks at an unfamiliar object through a reduction-screen and adjusts a diaphragm until it appears to him to be the same size. *A* observes *B's* behavior, but *A* knows how large the object and the diaphragm are, while *B* knows neither. We commonly say that *A* knows how large the object is, while *B* knows only how large it appears. (In earlier times it would have been said that *A* sees the object, while *B* sees only his sensation of it.) In current terminology, the statement that the object *looks* such and such a size is relegated to the language of the explained context, while "actual size" which is "normative and rightly so" with respect to the apparent size is in the meta-language of the context of explanation. But the fact that whatever is said about *B* can also be said, *mutatis mutandis*, about *A* when *B* is the observer shows that there is nothing unique about *A's* epistemic abilities to get at the real object.

There is no radical discontinuity between what *A* does and what *B* does. Very nearly the same psychological processes are described in the explained context and performed in the context of explanation, though the categories of the two contexts, i.e., causal and "normative and rightly so," are different. The absence of radical discontinuity between the behaviors is even more clearly brought out if we add another stage to our example. Let us make such an addition. *A* may object to the mark that his instructor gives him on his report on the behavior of *B*, and he takes his objection to the head of the department of psychology. Two things may happen each of which is very instructive.

4A. Causally Discounting the Explained Context

The first possibility is this. The teacher, let us say, has *criticized* the student for drawing an inference erroneous in the light of the norm he appeals to and to which the student failed to conform, and at the same time he *explains* the student's behavior in some causal terms such as nervousness or the aura-effect. Note what has happened: *A* explained *B's* behavior in causal terms of peripheral neural processes; the teacher explains *A's* behavior in terms of a larger context of causes including central nervous processes. The causal context in which *A* behaved is thus more comprehensive than that in which *B's* behavior occurred. The head of the department examines the paper, decides that the teacher's mark was incorrect, and—showing bad academic taste—tells the student that the teacher is prejudiced against him and that that is the *cause* of his low mark. The head of the department in this way causally analyzes the teacher's context of explanation, and, admitting that the teacher used normative principles, denies that they are "normative and rightly so." (He can do so regardless of whether he finds the teacher's behavior correct by his own norms or not, though he is, of course, more likely to do so if he finds there is some error calling for explanation). All that he needs to do is to find some more comprehensive causal context—in this case a social one—in which the teacher's behavior is causally explicable. The teacher may not like the *ad hominem* of the head of the department and take the matter to the dean; the dean may say the head of the department is senile; the president may intervene with an *ad hominem* against the dean, and so on.

This hierarchy of contexts can be carried upward indefinitely, with the higher context causally discounting the included ones. There is in principle no way to terminate a series of contexts each of which causally discounts and denies the relevance of considerations of validity in explaining the behavior in its included series. At least we find no break in such a series, after which there appears some existentially immaculate conceiver, though some philosophers have supposed that the series does end in some omniscient mind, or *actus purus*, or absolute consciousness.[2]

4B. Dialectic Reconciliation of Contexts

The second thing which may happen in the dispute about the student's mark is quite different but equally instructive. The head of the department may go over the student's report and the teacher's correction, and then tell the teacher, "I believe you made a mistake in giving *A* such a low mark. The class is really too small to justify the curve you used in distributing your grades." In this case, the teacher, the student, and the head of the department are all as it were in a single context of explanation, and there is no explicit reference to a causally explained context. Ideally there is a single set of proper norms that apply to the student's work, the teacher's mark, and the evaluation by the head of the department. All the argument will be on one level; each argument will have the form: "You ought to have done so and so in the light of the evidence and under the sound rules of method." The only disagreement will be on the meaning of the "so and so" that ought to have been done; the ideal of the argument is to discover the principles which will uniquely determine this "so and so" that ought to be done. In this case we are not emphasizing a hierarchy of explained and explanatory contexts, as in the explanation *A* gives of *B's* response to a stimulus, but a dialectic for bringing out the full implications of limited points of view.

The principles which are sought, when thus explicated, have two characteristics which show the universality of norms. (1) They are held to be applicable to all three of the men. But these men, under our hypothesis, form a series from less to more comprehensive explained contexts, since the student's context is, at least ideally, more restricted than that of the teachers. Generalizing this, we find that a logical or epistemological principle is "normative and rightly so" for all behavior which might be included in the contexts. (2) The principles enunciated as a basis for agreement are—if they are logical and not merely preferential rules—those principles which hold their own in the dialectic dispute of the three men and which are posited as able to hold

---

[2] Cf. *Space Time and Deity*, I, pp. 19, 20.

their own in a still further dialectic. The principles formulated by our group of three men will not satisfy them and conclude the argument unless they feel sure that the principles will be acknowledged when carried to a still higher court, say a dean. Of course this acknowledgement may not be obtained, but the argument does not stop until there is a conviction that it will be forthcoming. Generalizing this, we find that a logical or epistemological principle is expected to, and if valid will, retain its imputed validity when submitted to examination in a larger context of explanation with a more comprehensive base. Taking our two generalizations together, they save the ideal of the universal applicability of norms to both lower and higher levels of a dialectical development.

5. Causal Conditions for Application of Epistemological Norms

My illustration and its ramifications are in accord with the theory of types; but linguistic considerations do not in the least illuminate the circumstances wherein the same event under causal conditions can come to be also under the epistemological. Such linguistic considerations tell us merely what rules we must obey if we are to act as if such a transition were or could be made. Hence the time has come to take a second step which will, I hope, bring the presence of these two determinations out of the realm of a dualistic mystery yet not relegate it to a purely linguistic realm. In taking this step, I shall again use our illustration of the two students.

In our experiment, A, the observer, has more potential modes of reaction than B has, not because he possesses some transcending soul or the like, but because A, in order to explain $B's$ behavior, reduced the number of variables by operationally isolating some of $B's$ afferent processes and behavior-potentials from others. Unless he does so, he cannot control the experiment. In a well-conducted experiment, in estimating the size of the object B has no cue to act upon except retinal size. He reacts to a terminal member of a single causal series, the optical chain ending at his retina. In such an experiment, it is found as a matter of fact that two objects of the same size but at different distances will be judged by B to differ in size in almost exact proportion to the difference in size of their corresponding retinal images. *A*, on the other hand, has many cues at his disposal. They constitute what Brunswik has well but almost untranslatably called *Entwederreihen*, and which I shall call "alternative cue-series." For instance, *A* sees the size not as proportional to the retinal image and hence inversely proportional to the distance, but as relatively constant, because he simultaneously sees the distance of the object, feels its size with his hand, infers its size from a reading on a scale, and remembers its size from having constructed it. Each of the data he receives among these alternative cue-series is causally and phenomenally diverse, because the neural conditions of one are quite different from the neural conditions of the others. But—and this is the crucial consideration— these diverse data are normatively equivalent in the context of his behavior. They are for the most part interchangeable in serving the behavioral purposes of the organism. Different pairs of them have the same pragmatic meaning; a retinal image in conjunction with the visual cues of distance is functionally the condition for the same adaptive behavior as that initiated by tactual data resulting from feeling the object with the hand, and so on.

Out of the Heracleitean flux of consciousness, or from a shifting mosaic of momentary data, these behavioral equivalences appear as regulative, normative, and object-controlled. If they will hold their own in a larger context of causes, they are "normative and rightly so." Our data are not constant, but from their behavioral equivalences we construct one of the first of all universals, that of a persisting object with constant size. In the behavioral identification of various experiences as evidence of a single constant object, we have the beginnings of consciousness of universals and the process of substitution, for substitution requires identity of meaning. The laws of logic can function as norms of conscious behavior only where the actual contents of consciousness lose some of their existential *hic et nunc* saliency and are seen as instances of meanings which might be transmitted by other causally diverse experiences. The great experiments of Helmholtz, Katz, Koehler, Thouless, and Brunswik on object-constancy contain the essentials for the solution of the transition from mere causal stimulus reactivity to normative object-response or intention. Whatever be the ultimate metaphysical status of universals, awareness of a constant object is awareness of a universal and a norm over against the blooming buzzing confusion of isolated data; only when the organism has developed and integrated alternative cue-routes can such consciousness of a universal arise. But when it arises, all the formal rules of combination and substitution of symbolized meanings become relevant and available to the organism in the intelligent control of its behavior.

The size of the *object*, which is available to *A*, in contrast to the size of the retinal image which is available to *B*, is a constant and a universal, and mathematical manipulations with this size will give *A* more knowledge about the external world. The size of the object is a factor regulating *A's* goal-seeking behavior, but the size of the retinal image, if it alone regulates *B's* behavior, will only mislead him in his dealings with the constant aspects of his environment. The disadvantage suffered by *B* arises because *B* cannot respond to functional equivalences among various data from diverse cue-series, for the data which would be equivalent simply are not available to him, having been eliminated by the experimental conditions. *A's* response to these functional equivalences frees *A* from the mosaic of isolated reaction-mechanisms so that he can respond to their common meanings or functional equivalences.

This is the reason why we accept *A's* report of the experiment as being true, but take *B's* report as simply a case of behavior. Reduced to its simplest terms, it is simply that *A* knows more about the object than *B* does. The more comprehensive causal or explained contexts to which I previously referred are behavioral contexts in which there is a greater number of behavioral equivalences (or better established equivalences), and recognition of them is equivalent to more knowledge.

We can summarize and generalize the results of our example by saying, first, that as the causal conditions are made more explicit or pronounced, as in an explained context, there is a regression from consciousness intending the real object to consciousness of causally determined data with little or no epistemological or pragmatic significance for knowledge of the external world; second, that in the context of explanation the relevant conditions are not the brute given data but their behavioral equivalences signifying properties of a common object; third, that this equivalent significance (and not the data themselves) is content of rules of an experience which is seen as "normative and rightly so" as well as stimulus-caused.

6. Conclusion

I must point out what I have tried to do, and carefully distinguish it from another task, which I have not attempted to solve but which is closely related to my own. What I have not tried to do is to give or defend a metaphysical theory of universals. Any theory of universals will work equally well or poorly within or without the framework of my analysis. For instance, if similarity is an unanalyzed relation and is the fundament of universals, then similarity—but among responses—must be admitted in my analysis as the foundation of universals, and we have no more insight into the grounds of similarity of responses than we have into the grounds of similarity of data. Analogous use could be made of any other theory of the metaphysical status of universals. All that is accomplished by the argument with respect to universals, if anything, is that the attention has shifted from the immediate data of experience to the behavioral and conscious structures which supervene upon them. Not memory or inspection, but goal-seeking is the first stand of the universal in experience.

The problem I *have* dealt with is how behavior, including consciousness, can be causally explained yet normatively disciplined. My answer to this question is that in causal explanation we regard the subject only in relation to particulars, which are not cognitive objects but stimuli or causes; while from this kind of behavior there can arise an awareness of universals when the subject can respond in the same way to diverse causes. This awareness of universals is the necessary condition of awareness of or intention to objects, and behavior is under normative conditions when this intention or awareness exercises a discipline over the simple cause-effect sequences which would occur if the universal were not present in consciousness. The behavior is "normative and rightly so" only when these equivalences are left intact by a dialectic in which other diverse experiences are found to be behaviorally equivalent to the members of the pairs already linked together. When the subject does come in this way to guide his consciousness and behavior by reference to universals, all the rules of substitution and inference can be normatively applied to the judging and guidance of his behavior.

My conclusions, if tenable, permit a somewhat different approach to the problem of knowledge from that usually followed by philosophers who emphasize the genetic or causal side of knowledge. Their approach is usually to determine how it comes about that a mind can be conversant with anything more than its own momentary contents. It seems to me, on the contrary, that it is more profitable to ask how the mind becomes cognizant of sense-data instead of being naturally aware of objects. In other words, given an organism with what Driesch called equi-finality (i.e., identical terminal states resulting from diverse initial states), how can the organism come to know the initial states as such and give them such salience that it then seems to be a problem of how to "get outside the mind"?—a problem never yet settled when put into the center of the philosophical stage.

This question could be discussed, if time permitted, by reference to the quest for certainty which runs through the history of epistemology from Locke to Price. Since this would be a familiar story, however, I propose to give three instances of the way in which there is, in actual experience, a regression from knowledge of objects to concern with the contents of consciousness. These examples are: a psychological experiment, ordinary ignorance, and some types of nervous disease.

First, *psychological experiment.* Titchener's warning that the stimulus-error must be avoided can be made into a general principle: in all causal explanation the data and the functional equivalences known to the subject must be fewer than those available to the observer. Otherwise the experiment cannot be controlled. The restriction may be effected by reduction screens, use of naive observers, and, in the case of animals, surgery.

Second, *ignorance.* When we explain a man's mistakes as being caused by ignorance, we give a causal explanation of his behavior in the light of the more we know about him and his situation. In the more adequate knowledge we believe ourselves to possess, there are functionally equivalent data and the expectation, based upon past experience, that certain equivalences will be confirmed in further experience. These expectations cannot arise without the previous establishment of alternative cue-series, and they are the conditions of that "acting to the absent as though it were present" which is one of the marks of an intelligent and learned person.

Finally, *disease*, especially lesions in the central nervous system. Goldstein distinguishes between concrete and abstract (or categorial) behavior in a way almost parallel to my own distinction between the causal and epistemological, though his distinction had clinical origin.

Concrete behavior is a trigger-like response to a sign instead of a more adequately adaptive response to the same stimulus as a meaningful symbol. He explains concrete behavior as due to a radical simplification and isolation of more or less automatic stimulus-response arcs from the homeostatic organic whole, this isolation being a result of lesions in the central nervous system which impair its integrative function. Unlike abstract behavior, concrete behavior is uncontrolled by recognition of functional equivalences because of the ineffectiveness or absence of alternative cue-series. Under such circumstances the unfortunate individual cannot make abstractions or give an explanation of his behavior, which must be supplied in a context of explanation by the physician who can recognize the functional equivalences hidden from the suffering patient.

My purpose has been to show that the problem we face cannot be solved linguistically, but failure to show that it is only an equivocation does not imply that we must therefore fly to a metaphysical dualism. I have seen no need to assume a vitalistic or Cartesian dualism, such that we could say that only the organism plus something non-causal is able to know. Rather, the behavior of an organism is explained only in a context from which another person as it were "looks down upon" the simpler context of the behavior to be explained in terms of its causes, while the explanation appeals not to causes but to norms for its own validity. The causal account of knowing seems to be the limiting case of the epistemological when the effectiveness of its normative principles is reduced in any of the various ways we have discussed.[3]

---

[3] I am indebted to Professor David C. Yalden-Thomson for advice on the terminology used here.

6. Conscious And Unconscious Motives[*]

I

An educated man walking down a street notices a bookstore on the other side, which he has not visited for many years. He suddenly starts to dart across the street when an automobile, with screeching brakes, almost runs over him. He succeeds in jumping back to the sidewalk and avoids injury or death. But he becomes extremely nervous and agitated.—This is the first chapter of a little story that we shall examine in order to bring out some types of questions and answers that are involved in the understanding of human behaviour.

We ask the man: "Why did you try to cross the street?" We may expect him to give one of two answers: (1) "I love books and like to browse in bookstores" or (2) "I wanted to browse in this bookstore." We shall call the first a *motive* answer and the second an *intention* answer.

Normally they are so nearly alike and understood in so nearly the same way that they are interchangeable. We would be equally content with either. A person is not likely to give both, but it does not ordinarily matter which he gives; if either is given, we can supply the other. They are, nonetheless, not equivalent answers. The former reports a disposition and is an answer that has predictive value for other behaviour of the man. It classifies him as being one of those who do often or habitually visit bookstores and libraries and who might be expected to give answer (2) if asked why he crossed a street towards a bookstore, a bar, and a movie. The second answer is not dispositional; it makes no general statement, but applies to the episode before us. It refers to a specific situation and has, by itself, no predictive value for the future actions of the man. It classifies the action of crossing the street as a case of going to a bookstore; it does not classify the man as

[*] Reprinted with permission from *Mind* LXXV (1966), pp. 155-179.

one who could be expected to cross a street when there is a bookstore or library on the other side.

Only when combined with (1) in our own minds do we find answer (2) satisfactorily explanatory. If the man were thought to be indifferent to books, answer (2) would be puzzling, not explanatory. (If I explained to my friends that I crossed a street because I wanted to breathe the air on the other side, they would have to make fantastic guesses about me or about the street before my "explanation" would mean anything to them.) In normal circumstances, answers of type (2) will not be given unless it is assumed that the hearer himself can supply the appropriate answer of type (1). If the man in our story were known not to be a booklover, and he gave answer (2), we should not be satisfied with it until we had found (or he had given us) some answer of type (1) to terminate the series of questions: "Why did you cross the street?," "Why did you want to go to the bookstore?," each of which might be given an answer of type (2). In general, answers of type (2) are intelligible and adequate as explanations of behaviour only when they seem to suggest or imply some appropriate answer of type (1), but to ask for an answer of type (1) when an answer of type (2) is given suggests that the normal connection of motive and intention is not present or at least not discerned.

The man in our story might, however, give a different type of answer to the question, "Why did you want to go to the bookstore?." He might reply, for example, by giving what I shall call a situational answer, *e.g.* "I promised to pay a bill there today." If he had said, "I wanted to pay a bill" we might ask again, "Why?" But reference to the rules and proprieties of a society ordinarily stops the questioning before this, because they make the previous answers adequately intelligible. Such references are not to the wishes or desires of the individual but to the proprieties of a situation which make a demand upon every person in it. They are anonymous and impersonal in a way in which motive and intention answers are not.

The question we have been considering was asked of the man who tried to cross the street, and his answers begin with the word "I." But we might address the same question to an acquaintance of his and get the same answers introduced by the word "He." We shall call the answers given by the man himself *agent answers* and those given by his acquaintance *spectator answers*. They must be consistent with each other, or at least one of them is wrong. The agent is invariably in the better position to give an answer of type (2). He knows why he is crossing the street, in the sense of knowing his intention, directly and not by inference. If one were silly enough to ask him, "How do you know you want to go into the bookstore?" he would be at a loss to give any evidence that he does so, but he need not begin to wonder if he did indeed want to go to the bookstore. If he cannot in this way say what his intention was, both he and the spectator might well say that the action was unintentional and that the proper answer to the question "Why did you try to cross the street?" could be answered only by saying "For no reason at all; I just did it." A man always knows what he is doing (or trying to do) if he is trying to do anything at all.

On the other hand, the spectator can never be sure in this way that his own answer of type (2) is correct. He must be told, or he must infer it from the agent's past behaviour through his guess at the agent's motive: if a booklover goes across a busy street towards a bookstore, it is reasonable to suppose that he intends to go to the bookstore. But the spectator is in a somewhat more favourable position to give an answer of type (1) than of type (2). Indeed, he may be better qualified to give a type (1) answer than the agent himself is. A man does not infallibly discover his motives by introspection, and even when he thinks he does we may think he has made an honest error. For motives are not items in consciousness given, as it were, all at once in self-knowledge, as an intention may be; motives are dispositions. As Aristotle says, one swallow does not make a summer, or one good act a virtuous man; similarly one desire or intention to look at a bookstore does not make a man a booklover, and a desire to see a book is not the same as the love of books. It may come as a real surprise to a man to discover that he has become a booklover or an alcoholic or a vengeful man or a man in love, even though his attentive acquaintances have known it all along.

Let us come now to the second event in our story. When darting across the street, our hero was nearly run down by an automobile, but he quickly jumped out of the way. We now ask him, "Why did you jump?" and he gives a simple causal answer: the onrushing automobile, which he saw, was the cause of his jumping; or, more accurately, his seeing the automobile was the cause of his jumping. This is the answer we expect, and it would be silly to ask him, "Yes, but why did *that* make you jump?" No doubt if we asked this jejune question he would realize that his questioner was a philosopher, so he might give a motive answer such as "I love life," an intention answer such as "I did not want to be injured," or a situation answer such as "It was the only thing to do." We would no doubt think that there was something factitious about such an answer; we know that he jumped and only later thought of a reason for it. A thought of the reason did not precede a decision to jump, as the thought of the bookstore may have preceded his decision to cross the street. The correct answer to our question is the one he gave first: he refers to his perception of the automobile as the cause of his jumping. Let us call this an answer of type (4), a *mental cause answer*. Presumably we would get the same answer whether we asked him or some sensible person who saw the near-accident; a spectator could give the same mental-cause answer that the agent would give.

Such an answer is like any other causal sentence. It asserts a connection between two events, each independently definable and (except sometimes for technical reasons) each independently observable, such that we can say that one is a member of one class of events and the other a member of another class of events, that one member of the former class always precedes and is close to one member of the latter class, and that the classes are defined independently of temporal sequence of their members, etc. That one of the events is a mental event (the perception of the car) experienced only by the agent while the other (the jump) is observable by both agent and spectator is a minor technical complication, but it does not affect the causal schema of the answer that both agent and spectator give.

Some spectators, however, will not give this answer; in C.D. Broad's words, such spectators are either fools or physiologists. We will have nothing to do with the fools; let us consider the physiologists. They will say something like this: "The stimulation of the retina in such and such a way caused (or was followed by, according to the schema in the previous paragraph)...and this caused the contraction of such and such muscles." Let us call an answer of this type (5) a *physical cause answer*. The agent can give only a sketch of such an answer, since he is engaged in jumping out of the way, not in observing his nervous system; he is observing the automobile, not himself. He may subsequently (with the help of the physiologist) discover the physical causes but in so doing he has become a spectator of himself. The spectator proper, however, might, at least in principle, discover this causal connection without any help from the agent.

We now have ten answers to questions about the man's behaviour:

(1) Motive answers by agent
(1a) Motive answers by spectator.
(2) Intention answers by agent
(2a) Intention answers by spectator.
(3) Situational answers by agent
(3a) Situational answers by spectator.
(4) Mental cause answers by agent
(4a) Mental cause answers by spectator.
(5) Physical cause answers by agent
(5a) Physical cause answers by spectator.

For the moment we can ignore the generic differences between agent and spectator answers, and concentrate on the agent's answers. What we say about them will apply, for the present, to the spectator's answers, *mutatis mutandis*.

Answers (1) and (2) form a natural pair, and (4) and (5) another. Some answer of type (1) is required by an answer of type (2), while neither requires an answer of type (4) or (5) nor is required by them; we shall see later that answers of types (1) and (2) *exclude* answers of type (4) and (5). Answers of type (4) and (5) do not seem, *prima facie*, either to require or exclude each other, though on some metaphysical theories only one of them can be true and on others both may be true. Answers of type (3) and (3a) obviously belong with the first pair.

It is one thesis of determinism that the first pair of answers is reducible to the second pair or to one of the second pair. This is the thesis that motives and intentions are causes,[1] so that all questions about human behaviour must ultimately be answered in sentences of type (4) or (5). Answers of types (1) and (2) and (1a) and (2a) are regarded as only *façons de parler*. This is equivalent to saying that for the determinist the proper question is not: "For what reason did you cross the street?" but "What caused you to (or made you) cross the street?"

The question, "What caused you to ... ?" is an appropriate question to ask about an action like jumping out of the way of the car or

---

[1] The other theses, which we shall not discuss, are that motives and intentions are effects, and that answers of type (3) are reducible to those of type (1) and thus to (4) or (5).

breaking one's arm. It does not seem to be appropriate, in normal cases, with respect to an action like crossing the street. If he knew we were asking for a cause, the man in our story might respond, "Nothing caused me to do it; I did it because I wanted to." (It would be even clearer if the question were phrased in the more colloquial way, "What made you do it?" Then the reply would be, "Nothing made me do it; I did it because I wanted to" or "decided to do it" or the like.)

Still there are occasions unlike the jumping from the path of the car when the question of cause is appropriate. "What made you do it?" may be an appropriate question when the act is so unusual that the spectator cannot imagine what the motive or the situation was. "What made you (a book-hater) go into the bookstore?" is a perfectly normal question, even though the answer may be of form (1), (2), or (3), *i.e.* reasons, and not (4) or (5), *i.e.* causes. In such a case, it is as if no motive we concede to the agent would be sufficient. Actions which are done "for no reason at all" seem also to be appropriately questioned in this way. And there are occasions in which the agent's freedom to do what he intended to do is restricted, so that an intention answer to explain why he did what he did in fact do would not fit. Suppose, in our story, a sudden rain had come up, and the man sought shelter in another store. We or he could say that the rain caused him to seek shelter, or even that the rain made him do it and kept him from going to the bookstore. Or suppose he had gone not to the bookstore but into the bar, and when asked he might say that he was driven to do this—"I tried not to go in, but I couldn't help it."

Such answers we shall call respectively (6) *obstacle answers* and (7) *compulsion answers.* We get answers of this kind with respect to any agent's failure to fulfill some situational propriety or intention he has or might be expected to have. We ask "What caused you to make that mistake in arithmetic?" it being assumed that one who works a problem tries to get the right answer; we do not ask, "What caused you to get the right answer?" Similarly, we might ask, "What causes him to drink so much?" but hardly, "What causes him to visit bookstores?" As we have seen, the latter question can be sensibly asked, if going to a bookstore is sufficiently unusual to require as explanation. "What makes him drink?" suggests that there is some motive which is not under normal rational control, so that a man is thought to drink because he *has* to, not for any *reason.*

Obstacle answers and compulsion answers are hybrids between the two pairs of kinds of answers we have previously distinguished. They apply to actions which seem to have traits which require to be dealt with by answers of kinds (1), (2), and (4) or (5).

They are related and similar to kinds (1), (2), and (3) in that they can be given only in relation to behaviour about which motive and intention answers are *appropriate* but inadequate or incorrect. Without motives, intentions, or situational requirements, nothing can be an obstacle; an obstacle is something that prevents an intention from being fulfilled. And compulsions are said to exist only for actions which are structurally like intentional actions, *i.e.* a compulsion can stand in the same relation to an intention that a motive ordinarily does. One can have a compulsion to pick up a glass and drink, but one does not have a compulsion to jump from the path of the onrushing car—he just jumps. If he has a compulsion to go to a bar and drink, then he may answer the question, "Why did you cross the street?" either in terms of his intention, *viz.* "I wanted to go to the bar" or in terms of the compulsion, "I cannot stay away from a bar." Compulsive actions differ from normally motivated actions primarily in the degree of deliberate control to which they are subjected. In compulsive action, the man seems to be driven to an act and the act to follow the compulsion with an almost mechanical regularity as from a cause.

On the other hand, precisely this last point shows the relation of compulsion answers and obstacle answers to the pair of causal answers which would be appropriate to the act of jumping from the path of the car. For in the case of compulsions and obstacles, like those of caused reflex behaviour, the agent's apparent freedom of choice is restricted. Something *makes* him take shelter, *viz.* the rain over which he has no control; something *makes* him go to the bar, *viz.* his alcoholism over which he has no control. Thus a compulsion answer and many obstacle answers have the effect of excusing the person for his action, just as many mental cause answers and any complete physical cause answer would. On the other hand, no motive answer or intention answer of the kind we are discussing has this effect upon our imputation of responsibility.

II

We have spoken mostly of the appropriateness of different kinds of answers to various situations. We have seen that, ordinarily, we do not ask for reasons for the actions for which we ask for causes, nor for causes when we ask for reasons even though the language of the questions ("What made you …?") may sometimes be the same. But we have found two cases in which we do not quite know which question to ask, since actions in the face of obstacles and actions issuing from compulsions seem to resemble both actions with reasons and actions with causes.

Might we not, then, establish a kind of gradient, without sharp lines of demarcation, with causality of varying degrees of salience spread over the whole instead of being located only at one pole? That we can do so, as I have said, is one thesis of determinism. When it is done, philosophers at least since the time of Spinoza have distinguished free actions (like going to the bookstore) from unfree actions (like going to the bar or jumping from the path of a car) in terms of the *kinds* and *locus* of causes involved. If the cause of the action is something lying in the agent's personality, and not something outside it (like an obstacle); and if the cause is modifiable by deliberation and hence rational, and not something irrational and uncontrollable (like a compulsion), then it is said that the action is free even though it has a cause and could be predicted from knowledge of the cause. Such a theory teaches that intentions are a special kind of mental cause and that motive answers are descriptive causal law statements and intention answers are episodic statements of causal connections. We are not now concerned with whether such a theory gives answers that are appropriate to the various circumstances, which is the matter we have been dealing with; we now ask whether the theory is logically intelligible.

I have argued elsewhere[2] that such a theory is self-destructive if applied by the spectator to himself. But might not the spectator regard

---

[2] "Psychology and the Norms of Knowledge," *Philosophy and Phenomenological Research* XIV (1954), pp. 494-519. [Reprinted in this volume, pp. 57-72.]

answers (1) and (2) as mere illusions, and (1*a*), (2*a*) as half truths on the way to the fully true answers of type (4*a*) or (5*a*)? Let us see.

If the spectator says, "The man's intention to go to the bookstore caused him to cross the street," the answer is of form (4*a*) and "intention to go to the bookstore" is the name of an identifiable thing or event (mental cause) which regularly precedes crossing the street. But it obviously does not; there are many causes (or reasons) for doing anything, and the intention to go to a bookstore will be followed by my crossing a street only if many other specific conditions are present too. So we must say here, as we would in the case of any supposedly causal connection, "In circumstance C, the intention to do *y* is followed by doing *x*" "In circumstance C, the intention to *y* is followed by doing *x*," and so on; and to each we must add *ceteris paribus*. Now a man who sufficiently often intends *y* (going to a bookstore) and does an *x* that, under circumstances given, brings him to the bookstore, is said to be a booklover. His motive is said to be the love of books, which is a kind of substantialization or categorialization of the hypothetical connection between circumstance, desire, and appropriate action. A man is a booklover if, when near bookstores, he stops and looks; similarly, sugar is soluble if, when put in water, it disappears. "Bookloving" classifies the man, just as "soluble" classifies the sugar.

If this is a causal law about the man, we can replace the words "intends *y*" with some uninterpreted symbol D, and rephrase the law: "If C, then if D, then *x* *ceteris paribus*." For if D symbolizes the cause of *x*, *whatever* fits this schema in position D is a value of D and thus a cause of *x*; and it is a matter of brute fact what does fit the schema in position D. That "intention to *y*" is the only thing found which does fit it would be a matter of brute fact. But this is not the case; if "intention to *y*" is the only thing that fits, it is not a mere matter of fact, and our schema is not that of a causal law after all. "Intention to *y*" is not a cause of *x* if *x* is an intentional action, for the only thing that makes *x* an intentional action is that it does follow from "intention to *y*" and not from any other values that might be substituted for D. It is not a matter of brute empirical fact that we just find that men who intend *y* (our only evidence being that they say they desire it[3]) do *x;* it is not a matter

---

[3] There is a logical connection between saying we desire to go to bookstores and going to them, *ceteris paribus*. If a man always said he desired to go to bookstores but never did so even in the absence of obstacles, we would

of brute empirical fact that men who love books go to bookstores *ceteris paribus* and cross streets to get to them, as it is a matter of brute empirical fact that sugar when placed in water dissolves.

We do not discover the conditions under which the man goes to the bookstore in this way. We know immediately why we would cross the street, in the sense of knowing the connection between the love of books, the intention to go to the bookstore, and the act of going in that direction across the street with a goal in view. We use this information to establish, for each C, a family of *x, x', x"*... which will count as "ways of getting to the bookstore." We use this information in judging the other man's action; we answer the question, "Is he going to the bookstore?" not by looking for a mental or neural cause, but by asking, "Does he drop in at the library? Does he read? Does he purchase books?" Of course we may get the wrong answer. But this is the way we get both right and wrong answers.

There is, then, a logical relation between calling a mental state "the intention to go to the bookstore" and the action of going to it, *ceteris paribus*, which keeps us from calling "the intention to go to the bookstore" a cause of it, since a cause has no logical relations to its effect.[4] This logical relation establishes a domain of actions as

---

not say that he refuted the putatively causal law that we have stated but that he was lying about his desire or did not use the word "desire" or "bookstore" in the way that they are ordinarily used.

If "desire to go to the bookstore" were causally related to "going to the bookstore," then it would be necessary that we be able to define and identify the former without reference to the latter in order subsequently to establish a contingent relation between them. But the way we identify the desire that is related to going to the bookstore is not by finding some mental cause that always occurs prior to one's going to a bookstore so that we *subsequently* name this cause "desire to go to the bookstore." The fact is that we cannot identify the "cause" in question except by virtue of the fact that it is a desire to go to the bookstore, and thus the situation described as "desiring to go to the bookstore" stands in a logical and not a contingent relation to going to the bookstore, *ceteris paribus*.

[4] But the *name* we give to a cause may stand in a logical relation to the *name* we give to an effect. But here it is not a question of the name we give to the intention; it is a question of finding the thing itself independently of knowing what its effect will be. This is what I am denying to be possible in the case of intentions, following the arguments of Prichard and of Melden, *Free Action*.

appropriate to the intention, so that, given D, we can decide not which actions follow it but, more importantly, which actions go with it and follow *from* it. There is no such thing as an "*x* appropriate to D" if D is truly a cause. If D is truly a cause, then whatever happens right after it (etc.) is its effect. It is the logical relation between intention and appropriate action, not an empirically discovered relation between some unspecified but identifiable D and its actual effects (if it has any) which makes citing D, now specified as intention towards *y*, the appropriate response to questions asking for the reason for the *x* that does in fact take place. The D in question does not (except perhaps in the case of compulsions and what we have already agreed to call mental causes) produce *x*; it is a reason for *x*, which is to say that it serves to classify some possible members of the class of subsequent actions as appropriate and others as inappropriate to this D.

The conclusion of our argument is that if we are to render a causal account of a motivated or intentional action, the motive or the intention cited cannot be the cause we are looking for. But this is not equivalent to a refutation of determinism. Something else might be the cause of acts we believe are intentional. We shall now examine an argument designed to show this.

III

The causal relation, in ordinary speech, is transitive. If *m* is the cause of *n*, and *n* is the cause of *o*, then (under a few restrictive conditions which can easily be specified but are not here relevant), we say *m* is the cause of *o*. Conversely, if *n* is not the cause of *o*, but *m* is the cause of *n*, then, unless there is some other connection between *m* and *o*, *m* is not the cause of *o*. Hence if there is something that causes an intention or desire, but if the intention or desire is not the cause of the act (as we have just seen), it would follow that the cause of the former is not the cause of the latter. But at least one of the theses of causal determinism might thereby be saved.[5] And if there were some other route between the cause of the intention and the act, the act itself would be causally explained though the intention would not itself be in the causal chain as an intermediary between its cause and the action.

---

[5] Cf. n. 1, p. 159.

We may be more specific. If D is a consciously entertained intention or a desire, and A is a bodily action, and N is a state of the nervous system, epiphenomenalism holds that N causes both D and A, but that D is not itself a cause of A.[6] Hence we may safely ignore D and go directly from N to A. If we pay any attention to D at all, it will be to use it as the behaviourist uses verbal reports, *viz.* as a probe or symptom for the discovery of state N. To epiphenomenalism, accordingly, all motive and intention answers are reducible to physical cause answers, with perhaps mental cause answers as an intermediate stage in this reduction. That the agent is not willing or able to admit this reducibility with respect to his own motives and intentions is ascribed simply to his ignorance. The answer we are concerned with, therefore, is an answer of type (5a), not (5).

Here we are not troubled with the fact that there is a logical connection which gets mixed up with a causal relation, to the detriment of the latter. There is no logical relation between any N and any D or between any N and any A, though there may seem to be one between some D's and some A's (or, at least, we give them names as if there were such a connection).

But the difficulty with this theory arises, paradoxically, from the fact that there is not a logical relation where one is needed. For the events in N which produce D and A are not so related that D and A can be seen to be parts of one behavioural act which was to be explained. The only context in which the epiphenomenalist spectator permits himself

---

[6] With a strict regularity definition of causation, any specific *m* will be followed by some specific *n* and *o*, and there will be the same grounds for saying *n* causes *o* as for saying *m* causes *n* and *o*. Epiphenomenalism plus regularity theory of causation is thus indistinguishable from parallelism. We wish to avoid this short way with an interesting theory, so we admit the following quite possible situation. Given a total bodily state N, some ingredients of which will produce D and others A, it will follow that identical N's will be followed by identical D's and A's, whereas two merely highly similar N's might produce quite different D's and quite similar A's, or quite similar D's and very different A's. In general, epiphenomenalism needs to assume only that N's which produce like D's will usually produce like A's but it need not deny any of the many apparent exceptions. In fact, it will have to handle the exceptions in the way we have indicated; we shall see later how a non-causal theory of action will handle the exceptions to the generalization or norm that like intentions produce like actions.

to interrelate events is a causal one, not the intentionalistic context seen by the agent. But outside the context of the intentions and motives for the action, there is no action; there is no action, but merely bodily events, no crossing the street to go to the bookstore, but only contractions of muscles.

There is a sense in which crossing the street is a single action; there is no sense in which a chain of a million physiological events is a single physiological event. Only by tacitly using the concept of a single action—a concept requiring the awareness of intention—can the agent and spectator be aware of the same thing. Otherwise both their criteria for identification and the things they are talking about will be different. For the agent, it is an act immediately identifiable by his intention. He knows immediately what he is doing, *viz.* trying to get to the bookstore, and he knows this in complete ignorance of the nerves and muscles involved and of the causal laws which connect the behaviour of one with the other. For the spectator, what is happening is a series of muscular contractions during the time that and because of which the body moves across the street.

"Walking across the street" does not name an event that could have a cause if "cause" and "effect" refer to something physiological, for it does not name any physiological event at all. The events in question are singular neuromuscular events, followed by others. To explain walking across the street causally means to analyse what we ordinarily call crossing the street into a long series of bodily movements, each distinctly different from the others and each having a distinctly different cause, even if all the causes and effects are values to be inserted into physiological or physical laws. But "walking across the street" does not name one of the events in this series and is not a value of a term in any physiological or physical law.

There is another difficulty, of a more methodological nature. Let it be granted that tight causal connections hold between any two successive slices in the bodily behaviour as the body moves across the street. Such an analysis cannot, of course, be made in fact. Physiological laws would have to have so many variables in them that they could not be formulated and they could not be used for prediction of subsequent slices, since the body would have to be literally and not merely conceptually sliced to find the values for each variable. No one can be in a position to fill in more than one of the two schemata of explanation; the person who is in a position to say he intends to cross the street is not the person whose nerves have been put on microscope slides so that we can find and not merely speculate about his muscular contractions. There is a complementarity of descriptions which is as dependent upon experimental conditions here as in the physics laboratory. But it would be hazardous to suggest any point beyond which such analysis would not be successful or feasible, and it is a useful ideal in physiology to suppose that there is no such point. But such an attempt aims too high and hits too low. The spectator does not commit himself to explaining every physiological event occurring in the ten seconds it takes to cross the street, but only to explaining those events which are relevant to, or in some sense ingredient in or perhaps equivalent to, crossing the street. Then he must first select the events he is to explain, and he can do so only by reference to his own (and presumably the agent's) intentionalistic organization of the events of those ten seconds. If he denies the validity of intentionalistic thought, he cannot make this selection; that is why Kant said, on a very much simpler level, "There will never be a Newton of a blade of grass."

The epiphenomenalist spectator's programme, however, was one of excluding intentions from causal explanations, except as effects. But unless he makes reference to intentions he cannot relate the results of his analysis to what it was he wished to explain, viz. the agents' *soi disant* intentional act of crossing the street.

IV

Let us pause to review the path we have traversed and summarize our conclusions thus far. We have found that some human actions are explained by citing reasons for them; that these reasons lie in situations, intentions, and motives; and that the same reasons can be given by both agent and spectator. We have found other human actions which are not explained by giving reasons for them, but by citing their causes. We have found one difference between the agent's and the spectator's explanations in this form: the agent gives, as causes, mental events and some physical events which he directly experiences, while the spectator can cite either these or physical events which the agent does not know.

We next found that there are two intermediate kinds of explanations, which we called obstacle and compulsion answers to the question of why a man does what he does. Actions explained in these ways seem to have something in common with both intentional actions and actions whose explanation is causal. We found that explanations of these kinds can be given, and in the same way, by both agents and spectators. This suggested the possibility that there might be only one fundamental kind of explanation, the causal; that there might be a continuum of intentions and motives, through compulsions and responses to obstacles, to mental causes; and that the difference between the first and last might be a practical difference in the degree of appropriateness of causal explanations—ultimately a practical difference arising from the relations of the different kinds of answers to actions believed to be praiseworthy or blameworthy and those held to be innocent because done without a reason and hence not subject to deliberate control. And if this continuum could be extended a bit further, as the epiphenomenalist requires, so that mental cause explanations could be reduced to physical cause explanations, we should have a completely mechanistic determinism even of intentional actions.

But our analysis of the logical structure of causal explanations and explanations in terms of reasons showed such radically different structures that it seemed quite implausible to suggest that the difference between them rose solely from their diverse relations to the practical domain. A causally explicable situation is one in which there is a contingent relation between independently definable and observable events, while an intentionalistically explicable situation involves a logical relation by which specific actions are judged to be appropriate to specific motives or intentions and by which the motives and intentions are identified and defined. We found that when this logical structure is ignored, as it must be if intentions are to be considered a specific kind of cause, or if actions are to be explained without reference to intentions at all, the explicans (the action which was to be explained) disappeared. It disappeared not like a needle lost in a haystack, but, even worse, like a needle which changed into hay when put into the stack. Hence the theory of a continuum between intentional and causal explicata and between intentional and causal explanations had to be surrendered.

V

Now for the remaining chapter of our little story. The man is so agitated after his narrow escape from injury or death that he consults a psychiatrist. Eventually the following explanation of his action and his anxiety is formulated. Many years previously he had frequented the store because he had been fascinated by a clerk there. To escape the temptations thus presented, he finally avoided going into that neighbourhood for many years, and finally he forgot the very existence of the store and of the clerk. On this day, however, when he saw the bookstore, he was seized by his old desire, which he now mistook for the desire to browse in a bookstore. He acted on this desire only to be immediately threatened with punishment in the form of the automobile bearing down upon him. When he escaped this physical retribution, however, his old unappeased feelings of guilt about the clerk revived, and he became distraught and over-anxious long after the danger, which would have momentarily excited anyone, was passed. But when the man saw the true cause of his precipitate action—the desire for the girl—and of his anxiety, the anxiety diminished and he came to terms with his old hankering after forbidden fruit. So much for the little story.

If we accept this explanation which the man (agent) and psychiatrist (spectator) worked out together, as the man himself did, notice how many things we have previously said about him and his actions must be modified. For instance: (a) There was an intentional action (to see the clerk) which the agent did not understand as being due to this intention and its associated sexual motives, so that he honestly said he was trying to do one thing when in fact he was trying to do something else. (b) The action in question, while seeming to be a normal intentional action under deliberate control, was in fact like a compulsive action in that rational control was absent, absent because the action was not properly assessed as being the kind of action it was. (c) Hence the unconscious intention functioned like a cause of his action. (d) The cause of the action was a mental cause, though one known not to the agent but only to the spectator.

If we grant that the events in our story are properly explained (at least schematically), do not these differences, all of which are indicated in the language and therapeutic concepts and techniques of depth psychology, show that our previous conclusions about the differences between mental causes and intentions must be wrong? And if Freud's predilection for an epiphenomenalism even of unconscious mental processes[7] was justified, does it not follow that, in principle, physical cause explanations can be given for intentional actions when the agent's intentional explanation (reported in the first part of our study) is rejected but not replaced by answers of kind (4a)? The question, put into simpler terms, is this: Are there unconscious intentions, wishes, and the like, which unlike conscious intentions, etc., are causes of actions? Then unconscious motive explanations would be causal too.

Let it be said at once that we are not here discussing the empirical question as to whether there is some X (which the psychiatrist calls "unconscious wish") which is present in this man and in others like him which explains his behaviour and his anxiety, in the sense that it is present in him and his like and when removed from or modified in him and his like, behaviour and affect are changed. Of course there is; alcohol in his blood stream, though not called "unconscious wish," has these characteristics. So we have to add that we are dealing with a conceptual question: Can there be an X with the following characteristics? (a) It is a wish or intention or desire. (b) Its existence is known to the spectator but not to the agent. (c) It is a cause of some of the agent's acts and affects.

I shall argue that this combination of characteristics is impossible, in spite of the fact that the X is a construct in successful therapy. Just as (a) and (c) are incompatible with respect to conscious intentions, etc., they are incompatible even if (b) is inserted so as to reconcile them, as it were, and give them the name of "unconscious wishes," etc. I shall try to show that (c) is false, but that (a) and (b) are compatible in a way that seems excluded by our earlier arguments in Section I; but I shall try also to show that the psychoanalyst does not need (c) but only (a) and (b). That many or most psychoanalysts have held (c) seem to be due to a confusion of intentions with causes made for the sake of a scientific commitment to causal determinism, as if there could be no other kind of determinism or predictability in intentional actions. The combination of (a) with (b) gives the spectator a prerogative over the agent in the explanation of behaviour. Since the spectator alone attempts to give a completely causal explanation of actions according

---

[7] Cf. Ernest Jones, *The Life and Work of Sigmund Freud*, I, p. 368.

to (c), it seems to have been erroneously assumed that the transition from agent answers to spectator answers justified also a transition from the first pair of answers to the second pair of answers (i.e. from (1) and (2) to (4a) and (5a)). Much psychoanalytical talk is thus a hybrid offspring of two different sets of concepts and vocabularies. Its ancestry can be traced and understood only by seeing what it has inherited from each; when that is done, (c) can, I shall argue, be dispensed with. But we will then know how it came to seem to be in the family in the first place.

VI

We shall begin by examining the claim: The psychiatrist was talking about a wish which the agent did not know he had but which was a cause of his behaviour. In this sentence, the first clause is (a).

We call it unconscious simply because the agent was not conscious of it. There is no serious conceptual problem here, once we understand that "wish" is being used in a somewhat broader sense than usual, as "light" is when we call ultraviolet waves "invisible light." (And it is not even unusual usage now, so it seems to present little or no puzzle.)

But why do we call this X a wish at all? There seem to be two very good reasons for this. (1) Upon the completion of the therapy, it is acknowledged by the agent that he did indeed wish and intend to see the clerk, though he did not know this at the time he began to cross the street. The acknowledgment of this now helps him to "make sense" of his former action. He acknowledges it, perhaps reluctantly, but on the same kind of grounds he would formerly have acknowledged or claimed his motive to be the love of books even though he might not actually have thought "Oh for a book!" just prior to seeing the bookstore. But not every X which has characteristics (b) and (c) will be acknowledged in this way. We have already alluded to alcohol having characteristics (b) and (c). Suppose, for instance, that there were some peculiar physical process in his brain which the neurologist discovers but which the agent cannot be aware of more than he is aware of his hypothalamus, though it affects his behaviour; and suppose that its effects are such that the physiologist calls it the "bibliotropic nucleus" or the like. Now when the neurologist tells him that whoever has this physical process in his brain shows the peculiar behaviour called "bibliotropism" and points out to him that he shows signs of bibliotropism and the X-ray shows the bibliotropic nucleus, the agent will be convinced of the existence and effectiveness of the bibliotropic process. He has gained an unusually interesting piece of information about himself. But the acceptance of this knowledge is not equivalent to the confession of a love of books. Such knowledge is like any other knowledge of a surprising and unsuspected fact about himself, such as a new wrinkle or the onset of baldness. It is something that he would do well to take account of in anticipating future eventualities and happenings. In that way, his knowledge in the form of an answer (5a) may well be used in the control of his future behaviour in the vicinity of bookstores just as knowledge of a pathological condition may lead him to take precautions in the vicinity of bars.

The situation would be approximately the same if the existence of a mental cause were pointed out to him, though it is unlikely that one would need any help in discovering mental causes. (The occurrence of mental causes of inappropriate behaviour—*e.g.* the sight of a cat causing uncontrollable laughter—is likely to lead to investigation instead of terminating it.) But the psychiatrist does seem to be trying to discover and to make the patient aware of hitherto unknown mental causes, *viz.* unconscious wishes and intentions.

But, in fact, this is *not* what the psychoanalyst is doing; *he is not looking for causes.* And the patient does not appropriate what he discovers with the help of the psychiatrist in the same way that we have just seen he uses the knowledge of the bibliotropic process or the mental cause of silly laughter. Why? Because an intention is not a cause. The unconscious intentions, desires, and wishes, when brought to consciousness, have every characteristic of conscious intentions, desires, and wishes, except that the agent can truthfully say that he has acted on them without knowing he had them. Such knowledge leads him to make a re-classification of himself, to give new names to old ways of acting, and to set himself to deal with this intention or wish in the ways that he deals with those he always knew he had. He comes to terms with it by acknowledging and attempting to control it, through deliberation, choice, resolution, and decision, not by taking a pill for his bibliotropism or cacchination. As the agent comes to see his unconscious desires and wishes, he is not just learning a fact about this past; he is experiencing an enlargement of his sense of self[8] through taking something into his personal make-up whose existence he did not know or whose existence he regarded as something alien and external to himself. Until this kind of embracing of the motive or intention takes place, the agent simply does not believe what the psychiatrist tells him (or has not yet discovered what the psychiatrist wants him to discover about himself) and the therapy is ineffective. Knowledge of the unconscious intentions must become as direct as knowledge of the conscious ones when the agent overcomes the self-alienation implicit in being in the role of spectator to himself, preferring answers of type (4a) or (5a) to those of types (1), (2), or (3).

(2) Even before being acknowledged by the agent as an intention, this X serves the spectator in the same methodological way that a conscious intention of the agent would have served to explain actions not under therapeutic scrutiny. It is by reference to it, the spectator already suspecting its existence, that he is enabled to pick out certain strands of the agent's history as being connected with the desire for the clerk. It is not that he knows two things independently, to wit, that there is a desire for the clerk and that there are certain actions independently observed and that the first is related to the second by the contingent causal schema. Rather, he asks the same kinds of questions about this X that he unprofessionally asks about the motives and intentions of himself and his friends. He understands their motives and intentions (whether = X or conscious motives and intentions) through his understanding of what it means to have and to act upon a specific motive, intention, or wish. He may ask himself, "Given X, what would the man do?" and answer this question, at least in part, by considering what he would do if the motive or intention of which he was conscious were the same as this X, *mutatis mutandis*. Or he may ask himself, "If I did as the agent has done, what name would I and my friends give to the motives which led me to do it?" This is not the kind of question one asks about causal relations. One does not predict what sugar will do if put into water by asking, "What would I do if I were put into water?"

---

[8] On this phenomenon of the "enlargement" of the personal horizon, see S. Hampshire, *Thought and Action*, pp. 181-190; John Wilson, "Freedom and Compulsion," *Mind* LXVII (1958), pp. 60-89 at 68; Hinga Frette, "Psychoanalytic Perspectives on Moral Guilt and Responsibility," *Philosophy and Phenomenological Research* XVI (1955), pp. 18-29 at 28.

The contingency of the relation of causally related events requires independent observations and induction, not taking the role of another. Calling X an intention or wish thus provides the analyst with the guiding thread through the labyrinth of behaviour which he would not have had if he had thought of X merely as a cause.

VII

We turn now to characteristic (b): X is known to the spectator but not to the agent. Unconscious motive explanations and intention explanations can be only spectator answers to the question of why someone did so and so.

Here we meet with a certain peculiarity of intention and motive answers which we had occasion to comment upon only very briefly (p. 6). We have seen that there is a logical relation of appropriateness between most motive answers and most intention answers given by the agent or the spectator, respectively, so that given either we tacitly supply the other. But sometimes we do not infer the motive answer from the intention answer. When one feels constrained to ask explicitly, "What is your motive?"[9] this is evidence that the normal inference is not being made. To ask, "What is your motive?" is to show that the intention answer is not sufficient, and that there is some departure from the normally expected connection between motives and intentions. It indeed often suggests that while the intention sounds innocent, the motive may be improper, ignoble, or dishonourable. If the man were a booklover, his statement of intention to go to the bookstore would sufficiently explain why he crossed the street; if he is not a booklover, we should still want to know why he intended to do so, and thus look for another motive. (Similarly, but less interestingly, we may understand a man's motives but not be able to connect his actions with the motive, so we have to ask for his intentions. If the man is known to be a booklover we do not understand why he dashed

---

[9] When a rich father asks the suitor of his plain daughter, "What are your intentions?" he ought to ask, "What are your motives?" The intention is clear enough. If the father is poor and the daughter beautiful, however, perhaps "What is your intention?" is the right question for him to ask.

across a busy street if we think he knew that there was no bookstore on the other side.)

Psychoanalytical literature is filled with references to both unconscious intentions and unconscious motives. An unconscious motive can be the dispositional need to see the clerk; and we suspect its existence when a book-hater has the intention to browse in a bookstore where the clerk is. But given the unconscious motive, it does not automatically explain even the unconscious intention; there are perhaps more disparities in the unconscious motive-unconscious intention complex than in the conscious motive-conscious intention complex. His crossing the street may not indicate the unconscious motive of needing to see her, but of the need to be run over by the car so as not to see her, or to elicit her sympathy. We hypothesize other than obvious unconscious motives (*e.g.* guilt) by finding actions which do not follow from the intentions appropriate to the unconscious motives first postulated.

The spectator's evidence of unconscious motives and intentions, then, is the same as his evidence for conscious motives and intentions, though it is indubitably more obscure. The situation which elicits inquiry into unconscious motives is formally the same as that which occasions explicit inquiry into the conscious motive, *viz.* disparity between intentional acts and accredited motives and normal situational requirements. In each case, the intention may be known but is not thought to be adequately explanatory. This thought is based on three considerations. First, motives are dispositional; they must explain more than the present intention and act. If there were a one-to-one correspondence between motives and intentions, the motive would not, of course, explain the intention; such a motive answer is always uninstructive if not indeed impudent, *e.g.* "I did X because I'm the kind of man who does X." An intention answer, therefore, when inconsistent with other intention answers invites inquiry into motive. Second, the action itself may not be appropriate to the expressed intention, so we suspect another intention and, per corollary, another motive correlated with *it*. Notice, in our story, that the man *suddenly* crossed the street. Now to be sure one can suddenly dash across a busy street in order to browse at leisure in a bookstore, but does not it seem

an odd thing to do?[10] It suggests something other than the love of books
if we think of booklovers as being reflective and quiet chaps. *Cherchez
la femme.* Third, the affect can be inappropriate to the success or
failure of the action seen in the light of its expressed intention. In our
story, the clue to another motive was the lasting anxiety of the agent.
Great effort for trivial ends (trivial in terms of the enunciated
intention), great elation over trivial successes, great despondency over
trivial failures—all these indicate both to friends and psychiatrists some
inappropriateness that invites inquiry into the motive - intention - act -
affect constellation.

In such inquiries, the formal differences between the inquiries into
motives not directly known to the spectator but directly known to the
agent, and into those inferentially known to the spectator but not at all
to the agent, are not especially remarkable. We have already seen
instances, before we came to discuss depth phenomena, in which
dispositional motives are better known to acquaintances than to the
agents themselves. It may well be that where the connection of the
intention to the motive is not clear to the spectator it may be very clear
to the agent, no matter how queer the connection may be by standards
of the spectator and other members of the society. But the converse
may be true especially as motive is dispositional and classificatory. In
the latter case, the agent's intention answer may be inadequate or
puzzling in the light of the agent's own motive answer (as in the case in
which the agent said he had no motive but just did the action for the
hell of it or for no reason at all), but comprehensible to the spectator
who supplies the missing motive answer.

Why it should be the case that sometimes the spectator's motive
answer should be better than the agent's motive answer is a question
about the etiology of self-alienation, self-deception, rationalization, and
neurosis; and we are not here concerned with this empirical question.
It suffices to admit merely that this is sometimes the case, and to note
that the world did not have to wait for psychoanalysis to learn that it is
sometimes the case. My remarks are meant to show merely that while
the term "unconscious motive (wish, intention, and the like)" may seem

---

[10] I once had a student at Columbia University who asked to be excused
shortly before the end of my lecture each day at 117th Street in order to run
and not be late to the next class on 121st Street. I asked him what his next class
was, and he said, "A course in how to relax." I thought this odd.

to be an oxymoron, it is nevertheless a good name for a not uncommon phenomenon in our understanding of each other. For these answers can be given only by a spectator, or by the agent only when he stands back and looks at his past behaviour.

What depth psychology has contributed, along with its etiology of self-deception, its typology of unconscious motives, and its symbolology of conscious intentions and motives, is its technique of overcoming resistances that give a very different content to answers of type (1) and (2) in contrast to that of types (1a) and (2a), so that one can come to see himself as others see him and thus take steps to self-improvement he could not otherwise take.

VIII

The remaining characteristic of the X called "unconscious intention or wish" was that X was a cause of action. If our study of motives and intentions in the first part of this paper was correct in showing that motive statements are not cause statements and intentions are not causes, it would appear to be immaterial to our analysis whether the agent knows the motive and intention or not. If it is true that being an intention "*überhaupt*" suffices to show that what is called the intention cannot be the cause of the action, then its being unconscious, *i.e.* not known to the agent, will not make it a cause. And if the X were a cause, it does not seem that it could have the characteristic (*a*) even if we have been successful in showing that, whether intention or cause, it could have (*b*).

It is easy enough to document the use of causal language in referring to unconscious motives and intentions. This fact, however, proves almost nothing, since it is equally easy to find cases in which psychoanalysts call conscious motives causes too. That they call unconscious motives and intentions "causes" is a conceptual confusion. Let us then not go into the *ipsissima verba* of Freud, but examine the alleged causality of unconscious motives and intentions on its own merits.

The logical structure of the relation of an unconscious motive or intention to its manifestation is the same as that of the relation of a conscious dispositional motive or episodic intention to its manifestation, though in the former case the logical connection is discerned by the spectator only, and in the latter case by the agent as well as or instead of by the spectator. "The heart has its reasons the mind knows not of" was truly spoken of the mind of the agent, not of the spectator. If intentions were not reasons but causes, when brought to consciousness they would be recognized as mental causes and not as intentions at all. If they were causes, the guidance they give to analytical exploration and therapy would be lacking, since the only way, as causes, they could be got at would be by induction from independent observations. They are, on the contrary, in fact got at in the same way that the agent's conscious motives and intentions are discerned by both agent and spectator. That is, they are discovered by considering what motives would be appropriate for his expressed intentions and overt actions when the latter are not, as it were, almost self-explanatory.

Can we say, then, that (c) is indeed a false statement, and that the X we are looking for has only characteristics (a) and (b) which fully and completely justify its being called an "unconscious wish or motive or intention?" This would be a bold stroke, and it would be without hope of success against entrenched ways of thinking unless we could show, in the light of our positive and sympathetic analysis of psychoanalytic claims with respect to (a) and (b), why (c) has *seemed* to be true. I suggest two reasons for its seeming to be true. The first is, simply, that no careful logical analysis of such terms as "motive," "intention," "wish" and their relation to "cause" was available when psychoanalytic concepts were being formulated. Even Jones speaks of Freud's philosophical or logical naiveté; physiology and physical models won out in his mind over what he should have learned from Brentano. In this respect analytical philosophy may make some contribution to psychoanalytic theory.

The second, and far more interesting, reason is a practical one. It is this: in the therapeutic situation and in situations in which moral judgment is made and justice is to be dispensed, until the unconscious motive or intention is made manifest and embraced as a part of the agent's person and thus bravely faced and rejected, argument and moral judgment are misapplied and ineffective. "Unconsciousness" supplies an endless series of excuses just as causal explanations do. One does not argue with causes, but with reasons; one does not, either, argue with unconscious reasons, not because they are causes, but because they are not known to the person to whom the argument is addressed so that argument would be misdirected or, if properly directed, ineffective. If one cannot argue, it is easy to assume that what he has to put up with are causes and not reasons. Until reasons are known, they cannot be assessed and weighed and deliberated about and taken or rejected as policy statements or grounds of decision. The man in our story cannot be blamed for going to the bookstore to see the clerk, because he did not know that that was his purpose, any more than he could be praised for his bibliotropism, for praise and blame are effective in modifying behaviour only in so far as blame displaces one motive with another or the praise strengthens one we wish to nurture. It would be as silly to praise him for jumping from in front of the car as to blame him for going to the store, if the "Why did you do it?" question were answered in both cases, by both spectator and agent, with a causal answer, whether physical or mental.

Only when the intention is brought to the agent's consciousness as an intention, and not merely reported to him as if it were a cause (*e.g.* "People who have such and such experiences invariably do such and such things, and I have discovered that you have had such and such experiences; *ergo* ..."), can the intention and its associated motive be handled by the agent in the way in which motives and intentions are handled, *viz.* by deliberation and decision; only then does the reason for hunting for reasons emerge—for only when praise or blame is based upon insight into reasons is it likely to be effective. Until such a consciousness of motive is achieved, the man's actions are like effects of causes unknown to him; he understands his actions no better than he understands the symptoms of interest to the neurologist.

Until he acknowledges his effective motives, the logical relation of appropriateness among *conscious* motive, intention, action, and affect is as it were broken into as by an obstacle or by causal interference from without or by compulsion from within, all of which leads to inappropriate and not understood actions and affects. Only when this relation of appropriateness is obviously broken down, in fact, does one consult a psychiatrist. When this happens we expect different answers from the spectator and the agent. One does not go to a psychiatrist to ask what his motives are when the acknowledged intention, the action done, and the affect are appropriate to the situation and to each other. When they are not, the question "Why?" may be answered by the spectator who refers to a hidden motive which has its own *appropriate* intentions, actions, and affects, and which cannot be a mere cause with only *regular* consequent effects. And the agent's responsibility emerges when he accepts what seemed at first to be an alien cause as one of his own motives and begins to handle it in the way conscious motives are handled, and not as a cause in his brain or an obstacle outside would be handled.

If this account of the situation is correct, then characteristic (c) does not belong to X, and there is even better reason for calling X an unconscious motive or intention than there would have been if (c) had been correct. But I suggest that, just as significantly, our account has shown why it is erroneously believed that an unconscious motive or intention does function like a cause. All they have in common with causes is that they are effective whether known or not, and are therefore equally impervious to argument and persuasion. They are, then, in some circumstances best handled as if they *were* causes. But this does not shore up a complete causal explicability of intentional acts, which broke down in the context of conscious motives and intentions, for they are not causes of a peculiar kind which hinder, break in upon, or push intentional actions. They are motives and intentions in conflict with other motives and intentions—something you expect of motives and intentions. They are not causes. Knowledge of them contributes greatly to our ability to predict human action as well as to control our own. But the kind of prediction which we perform with the tools of depth psychology (unlike those of neurology) is not the causal prediction prevalent in the natural sciences.

7. Extraterrestrial Intelligent Life*¹

I must confess that I have a singular reason for being gratified at the privilege of delivering this paper as a presidential address - if it were not the presidential address I doubt that it would be accepted by the Program Committee. Our Association is not hospitable to cosmological speculations. I can avail myself only of presidential license in asking you to consider a perennial theme in philosophy which is neglected by philosophers at a time when it is most cherished by scientists. Many eminent philosophers—among others Aristotle,[2] Nicholas of Cusa, Giordano Bruno, Gassendi,[3] Locke,[4] Lambert,[5] Kant,[6] and William Whewell[7]—have believed that there is extraterrestrial life; yet I know of only one or two living professional philosophers writing in English[8] who have even discussed the question. This is unfortunate, since many of the problems our scientific

---

* Reprinted with permission from *Proceedings and Addresses of the American Philosophical Association* XLV (1971-2), pp. 5-21.

¹ Presidential address delivered before the Sixty-eighth Annual Eastern Meeting of the American Philosophical Association in New York City, December 28, 1971.

² *De Generatione Animalium* 761b; *De Motu Animaliurn* 699b19; see also *Metaphysics* 1074b1-14.

³ *Syntagma philosophicum*, Part II, Sect. 2, Book 1, ch. 6; in *Opera omnia* (1658) vol. I, pp. 524-530.

⁴ *Elements of Natural Philosophy* ch. 3, end.

⁵ *Cosmologische Briefe* (1761), esp. letters 6, 8, and 9 (pp. 62-65, 93, 103, 113, 119).

⁶ *Allgemeine Naturgeschichte und Theorie des Himmels* (1755), Part III (not in English translation).

⁷ *Astronomy and General Physics Considered with Reference to Natural Theology* (Bridgewater Treatise, 1833), pp. 206, 207, 214.

⁸ The most notable is Roland Puccetti, *Persons* (New York: Herder and Herder, 1969).

colleagues are raising, such as those of the criteria of life, mind, intelligence, and language, and the future viability of our civilization, are problems about which we philosophers have much to say. There are new sciences like exobiology whose foundations are in need of philosophical scrutiny. When the National Academy of Sciences explicitly calls attention to the philosophical dimensions and ramifications of the problem,[9] it seems to me we philosophers should relax our ban on cosmological speculation and think about possible worlds that may actually exist.

I

The belief that there are animate and superhuman beings inhabiting heavenly bodies, or that heavenly bodies are themselves animate and conscious—it is often difficult to know which—was very widespread in the ancient Mediterranean world. When many of the ancient Greek philosophers[10] asserted that the moon, planets, and stars are inhabited, they probably did so without great speculative venturesomeness; it might have been more idiosyncratic to have denied so commonplace a view. Though Aristotle believed that the moon is inhabited, the Aristotelian teaching of the uniqueness of the world put an end to easy assumptions.

The two ancient writings of most interest for our topic are those of Lucretius and Plutarch. That two writers having as little in common as they did came by very different arguments to much the same conclusion suggests that we have here to do with a myth or archetypal idea. Like the idea of God, to which it is not unrelated, the belief that we are not alone appeals on a prephilosophical level where men as different as Plutarch and Lucretius are at one. These two writers set the ground rules for all future speculation on extraterrestrial life. Let it be granted that they did not know even what little we know about the

---

[9] *A Review of Space Research* (National Academy of Sciences-National Research Council Publication 1079 [1962]), ch. 9, pp. 2-3.

[10] For example, Philolaos (Diels-Kranz [1964], p. 404); Anaxagoras (Kirk and Raven, p. 389); Democritus (*Ibid.*, p. 410); Epicurus (Diogenes Laertius, ix, 31); perhaps Anaximander (see Charles Mugler, *Devenir cyclique et pluralité des mondes* [Paris, 1953]); *Timaeus* 41E (see also *Laws* 967).

answers to their questions; but they knew the right questions to ask, and their questions and some of their answers have been repeated again and again.

Plutarch's thesis in *The Face that is in the Orb of the Moon* is that there are, or at least may be, men in the moon. He reaches this conclusion from four premises. (1) The earth has no privileged position in the universe (925 E-926 C). (2) The earth and heavenly bodies are not where they should be in accordance with the doctrine of natural positions and movements; hence the matter of the universe has been distributed by an intelligence working by design (926 F-927 F, 928 C-D). (3) The moon is sufficiently like the earth to support life (937 C-D). (4) If the moon did not support life, it would exist to no purpose, and this is inconsistent with the premise of intelligent design (937 E). From these it is supposed to follow that there are living beings on the moon.

Lucretius' *De rerum natura* was written before Plutarch's dialogue, but it may best be considered as if it were a criticism of it, for Lucretian reactions take place repeatedly against a long line of Plutarchean arguments. Lucretius accepts only two of the four premises of Plutarch's argument, namely the first and the third. There is an infinity of empty space with atoms jostling about, and here and there are "gatherings of matter" (II, 1044 ff) some of which are other worlds with their own skies and races of men and beasts (II, 1067 ff) which have originated in natural ways, have undergone divergent natural selection in diverse environments, and have developed diverse civilizations (V, 774 ff). There is no design; the celestial bodies do not exist for the sake of their inhabitants; their inhabitants exist by chance. Lucretius does not stop with the paltry question of whether the moon is sufficiently earth-like to support life; he says that there must be innumerable worlds in all degrees of likeness and unlikeness, and therefore there must be worlds which have inhabitants some like us and some unlike.

These speculations by Plutarch and Lucretius set up the ways of arguing for two thousand years. New astronomical and biological information has been repeatedly put into these two forms. The Plutarchean argument became a part of the natural theology of Christianity after the Copernican revolution; the Lucretian argument came into its own after the Darwinian. But no successful elaboration of these promising beginnings, which we cannot help admiring even today, was made for fourteen centuries. St. Augustine exercised his great authority against the plurality of worlds,[11] in the eighth century a bishop was removed from office for affirming plurality; and it was formally declared heretical in the eleventh.[12] When the teachings of Aristotle were introduced in Paris in the thirteenth century, added weight was given to the dogma of the uniqueness of the world, so much weight indeed that it threatened the dogma of the power of God to go against the natural Aristotelian order. So in the Condemnation of 1277 it was forbidden to teach that God could not have created a plurality of worlds (Article 27). This was not done in defense of the thesis of an actual plurality, but only in defense of the omnipotence of God. Both Albertus Magnus and St. Thomas Aquinas had already held it to be in the power of God to create more worlds than one, but had denied, on good Platonic and Aristotelian grounds, that He had in fact done so.[13]

While the normal form of teleology in the Middle Ages had been man-centered or God-centered, the doctrine of the plurality of worlds based upon Copernicus broadened the teleological framework. While every part of the universe was designed for a purpose or at least had a purpose in the organic and spiritual unity of nature—no one denied that—man and our own earth were no longer seen as the sole purpose. When it was decided that the earth is a planet and the sun a star, the pervasive teleological conviction implied that there are other living beings for whose benefit the planets and stars exist. Nicholas of Cusa drew this Plutarchean inference even before Copernicus. Both he and Bruno rejected the craft-handiwork conception of a teleology of design in favor of the animistic neo-Platonic principle of the plenitude of being, holding that the perfection of each heavenly body requires that it support spiritual life. "[Other worlds] are not required for the perfection and subsistence of our own world, but ... for the subsistence and perfection of our universe itself an infinity of worlds is necessary," wrote Bruno.[14]

---

[11] *City of God*, XII, ch. 11, 12.
[12] Grant McColley, "The Seventeenth-Century Doctrine of a Plurality of Worlds," *Annals of Science* I (1936), pp. 385-430 at 395.
[13] *Summa theologica* I, Quest. 47, art. 3; see also Quest. 70, art. 3.
[14] Bruno, *Of the Infinite Universe and the Worlds*, Fifth Dialogue (Singer transl.), p. 376; similarly, Nicholas of Cusa, *Of Learned Ignorance*, II, 13.

By the seventeenth and eighteenth centuries, the belief had become a commonplace. It was supported sometimes by neo-Platonic, sometimes by deistic, and occasionally by materialistic arguments which followed the Plutarchean or Lucretian paradigms.[15] The most important sources of the received opinion were works of Thomas Wilkins,[16] Christian Huyghens,[17] and Bernard de Foritenelle.[18] While Montaigne,[19] Milton,[20] and Pope[21] urged men to give more thought to mundane problems, others like Campanella,[22] Swift,[23] and Voltaire[24] followed Lucian[25] in using the imaginary inhabitants of other worlds as critics of or as models for condemning and attempting to rectify the follies of mankind. Throughout Europe astrobiology was an important part of the "evidences of Christianity"; only a few men, such as Thomas Paine,[26] thought that the plurality of worlds rendered Christianity "little and ridiculous, and scatters it in the mind like feathers in the air." But on one point all were agreed: the universe was full of life, man was not alone.

---

[15] Good historical accounts will be found in McColley, *op. cit.*; A.O. Lovejoy, *The Great Chain of Being*, ch. 4; Marjorie Hope Nicolson, *The World in the Moon* (Smith College Studies in Modern Languages, XVII [1936]) and *Voyages to the Moon* (New York, 1948); and R. V. Chamberlin, *Life on Other Worlds, A Study in the History of Opinion* (Bulletin of the University of Utah, 22, no. 3 [1936]).

[16] *The Discovery of a New World, or A Discourse Tending to Prove* (*It is Probable*) *There May be Another Inhabitable World in the Moon* (1638) in *Mathematical and Philosophical Works of the Rt. Rev. John Wilkins* (1802, reprint, London, 1970).

[17] *The Celestial Worlds Discover'd* (1698).

[18] *Entretiens sur la pluralité des mondes* (1686).

[19] *Essays*, Book II, xii (London, 1891), p. 226.

[20] *Paradise Lost* VIII, lines 100-105.

[21] *An Essay on Man*, Epistle I, lines 21-22 *et passim*.

[22] *Civitas soli* (1623).

[23] *Gulliver's Travels*, Book III, "Voyage to Laputa."

[24] *Micromégas* (1752).

[25] See Lucian's *Icaromennipus or the Sky-Man* as well as his better known *A True History*.

[26] *The Age of Reason* (Liberal Arts Press, 1948), p. 44.

The first detailed scientific criticism of the doctrine appeared in an anonymous work published in 1854 by William Whewell, *The Plurality of Worlds*. This book, by the eminent historian and philosopher of science well acquainted with the latest advances in geology, biology, and astronomy, is a criticism of the classical English formulation of pluralism as an evidence of Christianity, the writings of Bishop Thomas Chalmers.[27] It is also a silent renunciation—perhaps this explains its anonymity—of conjectures about extraterrestrial life which he had permitted himself in his Bridgewater Treatise[28] twenty years earlier.

From his imposing astronomical and geological learning Whewell inferred that the universe has only a small number of planetary systems and that the earth is uniquely able to support life.[29] He concluded:

> The belief that other planets, as well as our own, are the seats of habitation of living beings has been entertained in general, not in consequence of physical reasons, but in spite of physical reasons; and because there were conceived to be other reasons, of another kind, theological and philosophical, for such a belief.[30]

These "other reasons," however, no longer existed for Whewell—not because he doubted the validity of arguments from design but because he held that arguments from design pointed to the opposite conclusion. The world would be imperfectly designed if the incarnation of Christ were only terrestrial while there were unredeemable souls elsewhere in the universe.[31]

---

[27] *Discourses on the Christian Revelation Viewed in Connection with Modern Astronomy* (1818) in *Works* (New York, 1850), IV, pp. 362-414.

[28] Cited in footnote 6, *supra*.

[29] *The Plurality of Worlds*, pp. 161, 172, 186.

[30] *Ibid.*, p. 234.

[31] *Ibid.*, pp. 282-287. The same problem led both Augustine (*loc. cit.*) and Melanchthon (*Initia doctrinae physicae*, in *Corpus Reformatortun* XIII, columns 220-221) to deny the plurality of worlds. More imaginative solutions have appealed to some modern theologians; see the survey of (mostly German) literature in Wolfgang Müller, *Man Among the Stars* (New York, 1957), ch. 13.

Whewell's book caused a great stir in Victorian theological and astronomical circles and was severely criticized.[32] Hume's objection to the argument from design was not repeated by Whewell, but he was arguing as if he remembered Hume's words:

> The religious hypothesis ... must be considered only as a particular method for accounting for the visible phenomena of the universe; but no just reasoner will ever presume to infer from it any single fact, or alter or add to the phenomena, any single particular.[33]

While one might argue from extraterrestrial life to the purposive design of parts of the universe indifferent to man, Hume would forbid us to argue from the assumption of pervasive design to the existence of unobserved life. But I do not think anyone remembered Hume at this juncture; the argument from design was threatened much closer to home. It was considered more important to preserve the argument from design against Darwin, Huxley, and Wallace[34] to show that man is uniquely the purpose of terrestrial arrangements than it was to use the argument to show that he is *not* unique in the cosmic order.

There were soon two new scientific considerations which strengthened Whewell's case. The first was the refutation of the theory of spontaneous generation. Lucretius had believed that from the primal aggregations of matter life would spontaneously arise; now it seemed certain, on the best experimental evidence, that it would not. The second was the objections raised against the Kant-Laplace nebular hypothesis about the origin of the solar system. As long as this theory had been accepted, there had been ground for believing that all stars have planets. By the end of the century the evidence turned against it, and it was replaced in astronomical orthodoxy by the explanation of

---

[32] For example, by Sir David Brewster, *More Worlds than One* (1854) and Richard Anthony Proctor, *Other Worlds than Ours* (1870) and *Our Place Among the Infinites* (1875).

[33] *Enquiry Concerning Human Understanding*, sect. 11.

[34] Wallace's *Man's Place in Nature* (1893) is important not only for its conclusions against the doctrine of plurality, but because of its Lucretian rejection of teleological considerations which had been the principal bulwark of the theory before that time. It is the first treatment of the problem that reads like modern science. See J.M. Drachman, *Studies in the Literature of Natural Science* (New York, 1930), ch. 23.

solar systems as results of close approaches of stars to each other. Since such approaches can occur only seldom, planetary systems and hence life must be extremely rare.

With the rejection of both the Plutarchean premise of design and the Lucretian premises of innumerable worlds and the natural generation of life, the ancient doctrine temporarily disappeared from both astronomy and theology; the "canals" of Mars had only a *succès de scandale.* Yet now once again we find the belief widespread, embraced by eminent astronomers and biologists and supported by taxpayers. Old ideas like this never die. When one argument fails, another will be found. Now it is an inference from non-anthropocentric naturalism. This Lucretian thought, filled out by the work of Copernicus, Darwin, and Marx,[35] provides the philosophical basis for contemporary exobiology. But it is not the only one which motivates it, as we shall see.

II

The contemporary Lucretian argument stands on two legs, one astronomical and one biological. The astronomical is the hypothesis that the earth is not anomalous. Once again it seems that the occurrence of planetary systems can best be explained by a modification of the Kant-Laplace hypothesis, the implication being that many suns support families of planets. While the problem of the infinity of the universe is not as clear to us as it appeared to Lucretius, it seems that the universe gets larger with every advance in astrophysics. There are 10^{21} stars in the observable universe, and this is quite enough for highly improbable events to have occurred many times. Even if only one out of a million stars has at least one planet, there are 10^{15} planets in the universe. Actually the probability derived from astronomical theory and a few delicate observations (e.g., of Barnard's Star) is much higher than one out of a million, so in all probability the number of planetary systems is much larger than 10^{15}.

The biological premise is likewise the rehabilitation of a theory rejected in the nineteenth century. Once again it is believed that life arises spontaneously when conditions are "right." It was conjectured

---

[35] See S.A. Kaplan, ed., *Extraterrestrial Civilizations* (Israel Program for Scientific Translations, Jerusalem, 1971), p. 257n. (A very sophisticated book.)

what the conditions were on the primitive earth, and then it was found in the laboratory that under these conditions organic molecules necessary for life are produced. One of the conditions we cannot replicate in the laboratory is their duration for billions of years, during which these compounds might polymerize and associate into simple living systems from which the evolutionary process might begin. But according to strong scientific dogma this did occur on earth, and under like conditions elsewhere it is highly probable that the same process occurs there too.

But how alike do these conditions have to be? No one knows, for at most only one case is known, and there is no well-established theory of the transition of complex organic molecules to simple living systems from which the requisite degree of similarity and the probabilities might be deduced. If only one sun in a million has a planet, and only one planet in a million supports life, there are a thousand million abodes of life in the universe. This line of thought, however dear to popular science writers, implies nothing about the actual universe unless we know whether the second of these fractions—one out of a million—is of the right order of magnitude. It is, to be sure, a small fraction, but for all we know it may be much too large. The chemistry underlying exobiology now provides only conjectures about what may perhaps be the necessary conditions of life; it says nothing about the sufficient conditions, or how probable is their occurrence.

The connecting link between the new astronomical and new biochemical arguments lies in recent empirical discoveries. There are organic materials in meteorites and in interstellar space, and the gases occluded in moon-rocks suggest that the conditions *necessary* for the origin of life were not confined to the primitive earth. But absolutely nothing is known of what the *sufficient* conditions are, or how pervasive or local they may be.

No one now expects to find advanced life elsewhere in the solar system. But in a few years we may know whether there is primitive life on Mars. A microorganism on Mars will convert "the miracle of life" on earth into a "mere statistic." It will contribute markedly to the argument that advanced life is present outside the solar system.

III

Space travel, or even the sending of instrumental probes, to other solar systems is so far beyond human reach that it is not worthwhile discussing at a sober philosophical cocktail party. Nor do I think it promising to hope or fear that we will get evidence of the existence of superior beings by their visiting us. The only even moderately realistic hope for evidence lies in receiving and interpreting signals from extraterrestrial societies.[36] The technology required presents no insurmountable obstacles; what stands in the way of using it is human unimaginativeness and impatience and the instability of human civilization.

In the idea of interstellar communication, however, all the anthropomorphism so painfully eliminated with the Plutarchian argument insidiously reappears. To entertain hope of such converse requires that we believe that a pattern of evolution like ours, from simple organisms to advanced civilization, has been repeated within signaling distance and synchronously with our own development. It requires that the citizens of heavenly cities be sufficiently like us to reciprocate our curiosity and to take the same measures we would take to signal to them, and sufficiently unlike us to have managed a technological project which probably exceeds our resources of

---

[36] See A.G.W. Cameron, ed., *Interstellar Communication* (New York: Benjamin, 1963); I.S. Shklovskii and Carl Sagan, *Intelligent Life in the Universe* (New York: Delta, 1964), ch. 27-35; S.A. Kaplan, *op. cit.*, pp. 1-212; Walter Sullivan, *We Are Not Alone* (New York: McGraw Hill, 1964), ch. 13-15. I cannot take seriously the possibility of establishing the existence of extraterrestrial civilizations by the observation of artifacts other than signals (e.g., "Dyson spheres") because it seems to me we would be irresistibly tempted by Occam's Razor to explain them as natural products. Only if we had "direct" evidence (through intelligible signals) of the existence of extraterrestrial civilizations would an artificial origin of *other* artifacts appear to be a plausibly simple explanation. But I grant that the comparative simplicity of two hypotheses like these is an inexact notion, and one of them may appear more plausible at one time and the other at another. The fate of the "canals" on Mars, however, does not inspire confidence in gross artifacts as evidence of intelligent design.

curiosity, patience, and stability. All of these assumptions are highly speculative, but we must make them or else give up the game.

If we are to suppose that those creatures are enough like us to make communication from them possible, we may have to suppose that their biochemical base is more like ours than we have any conclusive reason to believe;[37] but even assuming the same biochemistry we do not have any good reason to believe that the courses of the two evolutions would go in the same direction.[38] We do not even know whether conscious intelligence, at least in its higher forms, is in the long run biologically advantageous or not even on earth, let alone elsewhere. Speaking against this optimistic assumption is the fact that the only species on earth which prides itself on its intelligence is the only one with the intelligence necessary, and possibly sufficient, to render itself extinct tomorrow. We do not know whether the development of human-like species leads to species-suicide here or elsewhere; we do not know whether evolution elsewhere is likely to be progressive in terrestrial terms or not. We cannot assume that our evolution is both typical and non-lethal for any other reason than that not to assume it puts a sudden end to our research.

Even if we assume a common neurological base and evolutionary history, the cultural and technological aspects of human life are so loosely determined biologically that we must acknowledge the probability of widely divergent and perhaps unrecognizable manifestations of communal intelligence. We see this even on earth; why not expect it in the heavens? But everything that makes exotic extraterrestrial societies different from us reduces the probability of their disclosure. The feasible methods of interstellar communication are filters which will keep out evidence of the existence of beings whose logic, grammar, and technology, if they have such, are radically

---

[37] On alternative biochemistries see V.A. Firsoff, *Life Beyond the Earth* (London: Hutchinson, 1963), pp. 106-146. On "silicon life" see the remarks by Bergson in *Creative Evolution* (New York, 1911), pp. 256-257.

[38] Compare the contrasting views of George Gaylord Simpson, "The Non-Prevalence of Humanoids," *Science* 143 (1964), pp. 769-775, and A.E. Slater, "The Probability of Intelligent Life Evolving on a Planet," *Proceedings of the VIIth International Astronautical Congress* (Barcelona, 1957), pp. 395-402, with R. Bieri, "Humanoids on Other Planets," *The American Scientist* 52 (1964), pp. 452-458.

different from our own. To hope for evidence of living beings with radically different technologies based upon exotic sciences and logics is in principle vain. To believe that there are societies elsewhere bent upon and capable of communicating with us is not only to be anthropomorphic; even worse, it is to believe that civilizations elsewhere are like *one* civilization that has existed on only a small portion of this earth for only a few hundred years.

But for the sake of getting on with our work, let us grant that all these unlikely conditions may be fulfilled somewhere. But when? We run into the problem of synchrony. In order to communicate with each other, two planetary populations have to be alike at the same time.[39] One limiting factor is the density of civilizations in space, but an equally severe constraint is their density in time. The life-time of civilizations determines the probability of their having overlapping durations. Given optimistic estimates of their absolute densities in space (say two within a hundred light years of each other), the average life-time if they are to have signal-competency at the same time must be of the order of 10 million years.[40] In that length of time, biological change will predominate over cultural evolution. Suppose, however, that species and civilizations can survive long enough to overlap to a significant degree. We, being a "young" technological civilization, must expect any other civilization with which we establish contact to be much older, technologically more advanced, and socially more stable than we are. But then we run into another limiting factor. The longevity of a technology is much less than that of a civilization. Out of perhaps a half million years of human life, we have had a radiomagnetic competency for 50 years, and fifty years from now it may be obsolete even if we still exist. Simultaneously existing civilizations are unlikely at any moment to possess compatible technologies of communication.

---

[39] "At the same time" is ambiguous. More precisely, the receiving civilization must at the time of reception be in the same technological stage as the sending civilization at the time of sending. Since stars are not all of the same age, the logic of the argument is not affected by the elapsed time of signal transport.

[40] Compare the independent calculations of Shklovskii and Sagan (*op. cit.*, pp. 413, 418, 450) with those of Sebastian von Hoerner in Cameron (*op. cit.*, p. 275).

Thus our conjectures concerning history, especially the future history, of mankind are important variables in estimating our chances of finding out if we are alone. One has to be exceedingly optimistic about the future of mankind to be even moderately confident of getting an answer to our old question. Personally I do not feel such optimism, but let me talk a bit as if I did.

IV

Let us suppose that radio astronomers aiming their dish at a nearby star pick up a modulated radio signal that seems to have come from a planet. What will we do? How will we read it?

In the absence of collateral information, the necessary but not sufficient condition for knowing that something is a message is to know what it says.[41] Since the necessary collateral information will be lacking, we must guess that it is a message, guess what it says, and then try to see if the signal can convey that message. Since we cannot know what encipherment has been used, we must make conjectures about that too on an anthropomorphic model. We must ask what message we would send and what encipherment we would use if we were they. Plausible candidates are: a binary encipherment of the series of prime numbers, the expansion of e, or simple arithmetic truths which will contextually exhibit logical constants and operators.[42] It should be possible to match signals against such paradigms and look for a fit which would provide the necessary condition for deciding that a message had been received. But it would not be a sufficient condition, for the signal could have been produced by natural processes. To find out if it is an artifact of intelligence, we would follow Descartes'

---

[41] This denies that "interstellar eavesdropping" (see J.A. Webb, in Cameron, *op. cit.*, ch. 18) will give us the desired evidence. The detection of signals meant for domestic consumption on a heavenly body is more probable than the detection of unidirectional signals beamed to us; but since the former cannot, in all probability, be deciphered, the evidence that they are intelligently modulated will be unavailable.

[42] Hans Freudenthal, *Lincos, Design of a Language for Cosmic Intercourse* (Amsterdam, 1960), vol. I (all published); Lancelot Hogben, "Astroglossa" in *Science in Authority* (London, 1963).

teaching that a machine can "speak" but cannot "discourse." We would try to answer the putative message by continuing it and waiting the appropriate number of years or decades or centuries to see if the series is correctly continued still further.

If it is, we shall have as much proof as we can reasonably hope for. But there are an infinite number of rules by which a finite series of marks can be continued. Human imagination must limit the number of rules to be tried; and it is precisely the fact that this imagination is human which may be fatal to our hopes. If there is a sender, he may not recognize our return signal as an intelligent response, and we will have received a message without ever knowing it.

Let us suppose, however, that we pass the first test and establish the existence of an intelligent sender. That will be much, a very great deal, but not all we want. We want a vocabulary of denotative words. Professor Quine[43] has made us familiar with a problem we meet here in extreme form. For us to know that a string of marks is in a language, there must be observable objects or actions with which we know it to be correlated. But we do not know what facts extraterrestrial messages are to be about, since we do not know what kinds of things are up there to be talked about. We do not expect them to talk about rabbits as we do, but we don't even know whether "undetached parts of rabbits"[44] are there to be talked about in strange ways.

Two means of providing the denotative components have been proposed. The messages might contain ostensive references to something we both can see, e.g., variations in the intensity of the sun.[45] By scanning all likely fields of empirical information available to both of us we could try to match the putatively denotative content of the messages with them.

---

[43] *Word and Object*, p. 26: "...it is to [nonverbal] stimulation that we must look for whatever empirical content there may be" in a language.

[44] *Ibid.*, p. 52.

[45] Suggested by Everett Hafner, "Techniques of Interstellar Communication," in *Exobiology* (Astronautical Society Publication no. 19 [1969]), pp. 37-68 at 60. Similar ideas in Hogben, *op. cit.*

Another means is superficially more promising: that they use television signals and supply us with a vocabulary.[46] This is not technically impossible, provided we use the word "television" loosely. But there is an epistemological barrier which may be insurmountable. We do not know what things are up there and don't know how they will make themselves known to the sender. Therefore we have no way of knowing whether the pictorial array we achieve will correspond to any extraterrestrial fact. If their sensory channels are different from ours, as may well be the case, what is image for them will be snow for us. Only if the things they think worth talking about look to them in much the same way things we are interested in look to us can we correctly believe that we have received the picture they sent.[47]

V

I have emphasized, but I do not believe I have exaggerated, some difficulties in establishing the existence of intelligent extraterrestrial life. I have emphasized them because most of those now writing on the problem seem to me to minimize them. They have invariably assigned favorable probabilities to unknown but limiting conditions. Though they have insistently warned against the dangers of anthropomorphism, their models have been inescapably anthropomorphic. Their assumptions have not been made irresponsibly; they have been made as the minimum price for responsible speculation. But I want to ask in

---

[46] Suggested by Philip Morrison in Cameron, *op. cit.*, pp. 266-270; Sullivan, *op. cit.*, ch. 18. The idea was developed by Fred Hoyle in his novel, *The Black Cloud.*

[47] Underlying the applicability of television is an anthropomorphic assumption that the information input of the sender of the message is like that of us human receivers, and there is not the slightest reason for believing this to be the case. Suppose, on the contrary, that his principal information channel is a sense organ unknown to us; or, for purpose of simplication, suppose it to be olfactory. In the latter case he identifies an apple by the distribution, spatial or temporal, of smells. He will then send a tele-olfaction image which we will interpret as a television image. But since the olfactory image he has is different from the optical image we receive, we will not recognize the latter as the image of an apple. (This assumes, furthermore, that there are things like apples up there.)

conclusion, why do almost all their speculations now point in the same direction? I have two answers, one cynical and one sentimental.

The cynic will say it is not accidental that the belief is held most strongly at a time when it is at last within the range of technology to discover if it is true. One of the reasons for our space program is to find out if there is extraterrestrial life; but unless the estimated probabilities of success are high, they cannot be used in justifying the enormous costs involved. What more natural, then, that those who have to justify the costs or go out of the business of exobiology should strongly believe in the possibility, nay the probability, of success? I am not accusing anyone of dishonesty or even of disingenuousness; I am merely reminding you that nothing succeeds without hope of success, and that in general the antecedent credulity with which an interesting hypothesis is held varies directly with the costs incurred in establishing it.

The other answer is more speculative. While the old argument from design is heard no more, I suspect that deep-seated philosophical, religious, and existential commitments which once availed themselves of the argument from design are still silently effective in guiding the Lucretian argument and keeping alive the archetypal idea that man is not alone.[48]

Myth, religion, and now science-fiction with their tales of benevolent and malevolent extraterrestrial beings are commentaries on the human condition. I believe even responsible scientific speculation and expensive technology of space exploration in search for other life are the peculiarly modern equivalent of angelology and Utopia or of demonology and apocalypse.

In the sixteenth and seventeenth centuries there was a deep pessimism about the decline of nature, polluted by the sins of man.[49] Nature was redeemed if there were higher beings in the universe, so all was not lost even though man and earth were corrupt. There was the silence of infinite space which frightened Pascal; he suffered a

---

[48] For somewhat similar ideas see Carl G. Jung, *Flying Saucers* (New York, 1969), and Robert Plank, *The Emotional Significance of Imaginary Beings* (Charles C. Thomas Co., 1968), esp. pp. 149-150.

[49] See Victor Harris, *All Coherence Gone* (Chicago, 1949), esp. pp. 95, 104, and Marjorie Hope Nicolson, *The Breaking of the Circle* (Evanston, 1950), ch. 3 and 4.

"Brunonian shock"[50] upon moving out of a friendly sphere into a lifeless infinite mechanism. This shock could be ameliorated by seeing the stars as other homes, and the universe as friendly to life after all. We are now suffering from technological shock, destroying by radiological and chemical, if not moral, pollution the only abode of life we know. Are we not enough like our ancestors to respond with the same desperate hope they did? *Exobiology recapitulates eschatology.* The eschatological hope of help from heaven revives when the heavens of modern astronomy replace the Heaven of religion. That we can learn from more advanced societies in the skies the secret of survival is the eschatological hope which motivates, or at least is used to justify, the work of exobiologists.[51] But somewhat like people who object to spending money needed in the ghettoes on exploring the moon, I think the best hope for our survival is to be based on understanding human predicaments here on earth, not on expecting a saving message from super-human beings in the skies.

Thinking about and even hoping to find extraterrestrial civilizations, however, sharpen our search for and appreciation of the peculiar virtues and vices of the only form of life we know. Exobiology and other exo-sciences cannot proceed merely by generalization from terrestrial experience; they must construct models of a more abstract nature of which terrestrial life and society are specifications. In that way hypotheses about extraterrestrial situations may throw light on the terrestrial, while the illumination of the extraterrestrial by hard facts about life on earth is at best dim and wavering. What Peter Winch has said about anthropology, we may say about exo-sociology: "Seriously to study another way of life is necessarily to seek to extend our own— not simply to bring the other way within the already existing boundaries of our own..."[52] Even if the exo-sciences fail to attain their prime goal, here is a valuable by-product. The quest for other, and better, forms of life, society, technology, ethics, and law may not reveal that they are actual elsewhere; but it may in the long run help us make some of them actual on earth.

---

[50] Wolfgang Philip, *Das Zeitalter der Aufklärung* (Bremen, 1963), xxvii.

[51] For example, Gösta Ehrensvaard, *Man on Another World* (University of Chicago Press, 1965), pp. 7-9, 168 *et passim*; Puccetti, *op. cit.*, pp. 113 ff.

[52] "Understanding a Primitive Society," *American Philosophical Quarterly* I (1964), pp. 307-324 at 317-18.

Yet after all there is some glimmer of hope for an answer. As long as it exists—and I think it will exist as long as we do—it would be a mistake to let niggardliness, skepticism, and despair inhibit the search. Many more harmful things can be done with our technology than listening for another civilization. If it should be successful, probably nothing is more worth using it for. So we have to ask, how should we proceed, and what shall we do if we succeed?

To the first, there are two simple and prudent answers. Let us give more thought to possible worlds so as to prepare ourselves to interpret any evidence we get that they are actual. Here is work for disciplined science-fiction writers, astronomers, biologists, psychologists, sociologists, and linguisticians. I venture to believe that even philosophers might be of some help.

Second, let there be world-wide sharing of resources of radio observatories. If all appropriate observatories devote some time to a systematic project of this kind, the costs in other more efficient research can be equitably spread.[53] But it must be remembered that the search is not worth undertaking unless it is planned to last decades, centuries, or even forever. Such cooperation would be a small step in bringing about the discovery of how much enlightened intelligence there is on one planet at least, our own.

And what if we succeed? I have two conjectures. First, after a few weeks *it will be forgotten*, just as the details of the first moon landing have already been forgotten by most people. We are so well prepared by popular science and science-fiction for signals from outer space[54] that success will be just another nine-day's wonder like Orson Wells' "Invasion from Mars" or the "Great Moon Hoax" which shocked New York City in 1837.[55]

My second conjecture is: *it will never be forgotten*. For what is important is not a single discovery, but the beginning of an endless

---

[53] Progress was made in this direction at the Byurakan Soviet-American Conference on Communication with Extraterrestrial Intelligence; see *News Report* (National Academy of Sciences) October, 1971, pp. 1, 4-5.

[54] According to the Gallup Poll, 53% of the people listed in *International Who's Who* believe in the existence of extraterrestrial life. *New York Times*, June 13, 1971.

[55] Richard Adams Locke, *The Great Moon Hoax, or a Discovery that the Moon has a Vast Population of Human Beings* (New York, 1859).

series of discoveries which will change everything in unforeseeable ways. We will be well prepared for the initial discovery since we have to know what it will be to know when it has occurred. We are not prepared for the next discovery and the discovery after that; we have no idea what they will be. But if they are made, there is no limit to what in coming centuries we may learn about other creatures and, more portentously, about ourselves. Compared to such advances in knowledge, the Copernican and Darwinian Revolutions and the discovery of the New World[56] have been but minor preludes.

---

[56] Responses to the discovery of America which was unanticipated, give, in spite of this difference, some clues to what may be reactions to the discovery of other worlds. For example, the question as to whether American aboriginees had souls and whether they were under natural law was discussed in terms not wholly unlike those in which our ethical and political relation to other beings are now discussed. See J.H. Eliott, *The Old World and the New, 1492-1650* (Cambridge University Press, 1970), especially chapter ii.

8. World Enough, and Time*

Mr. Shandy, in the act of begetting Tristram, terminates his carnal intercourse with his wife in order to wind the clock. Rousseau, expecting death, sells his clock, exulting, "I shall never have to know the time again." These two *beaux gestes* symbolize two extreme attitudes towards time in the eighteenth century.

When Plato defined time as "the moving image of eternity," he set a perennial problem for philosophy. It was a special, and an especially difficult, formulation of the wider problem of the relation of appearance to reality. While no philosopher can entirely avoid this problem and probably none can solve it, the urgency of the problem can be reduced by directing the attention to one or the other of the two polar opposites and forgetting, or at least neglecting, the other. The history of the philosophy of time shows alterations in where the focus of attention falls, either in eternity as ontologically real and basic, or in time as empirically experienced and quantified appearance. It does not solve the problem of their relation to attend to only one of them, but where the attention rests emphasizes the relative tractableness and importance of one or the other of the two. Philosophical weight is given to what one sees as the proper vehicle or receptacle of knowledge and aspiration. Seeing things under the aspect of eternity and seeing them under the aspect of time are usually symptoms of an other-worldly and a this-worldly orientation respectively. Finding *this* world quite enough is a characteristic trend of the Enlightenment, which nurtured the growth of time at the expense of eternity. This essay will attempt to chronicle this development in a few representative philosophers of the century.

There are few genuinely new ideas in the philosophy of time in the eighteenth century. Many of the ideas which the student of the history

* Reprinted with permission from *Probability, Time, and Space in Eighteenth Century Literature* ed. Paula Backscheider, pp. 113-139. New York: AMS Press, 1979.

of ideas identifies as "Newtonian," "Lockean," "Leibnizian," and "Kantian" are named after only their most prominent eighteenth-century proponents; but most of the component ideas (though not the complex ideas made up of them) can be found in earlier philosophers such as Plotinus, St. Augustine, Nicholas of Cusa, Telesio, Bruno, Galileo, Descartes, and Gassendi. But for the purposes of this brief essay on the eighteenth century, may I be allowed to write, for the most part, as if the eighteenth century got its ideas of time from Newton, Leibniz, and Locke?

I. Newton

Aristotle had defined time as the number, or measure, of motion, by which he understood any kind of change. He recognized that rapid and slow motions may occupy, and be measures of, the same amount of time,[1] and hence that motions are measures of time but not time itself, in which the motions occur. In this he was followed by Descartes, for whom time was only "a mode of thinking" adding nothing to what is being thought about, which he calls duration.[2] This duration is a distant descendant of Plato's eternity and an almost immediate progenitor of Newton's absolute time.

Newton contrasts absolute with relative time (sc. Descartes' time) as follows:

> Absolute, true, and mathematical time, of itself, and from its own nature, flows equably without regard to anything external, and by another name is called duration: relative, apparent, and common time, is some sensible and external (whether accurate or unequable) measure of duration by means of motion, which is commonly used instead of true time; such as an hour, a month, a year.[3]

After giving his equally famous definition of two kinds of space, Newton distinguishes absolute from relative motion, the former being change of absolute place in absolute time. He then argues that from the

---

[1] *Physics* IV, 14.

[2] *Principles of Philosophy*, I §57.

[3] *Mathematical Principles of Natural Philosophy*, Definition VIII, Scholium (Motte translation, New York, 1846, p. 77).

position of bodies "in our regions" it is impossible to determine whether they are at absolute rest or not. But from the inertial forces which belong to bodies only by virtue of their absolute motion, he argues that it is possible to show that a twirling bucket of water is in absolute motion while the fixed stars (which, assuming the bucket to be the geometrical point of origin, are in relative motion) are not in absolute motion. This is because a force must have been impressed upon the water, since it recedes from the axis of rotation.[4] From the bucket experiment, so-called, Newton concludes that the "relative quantities [of motion] are not the quantities themselves, whose name they bear, but those sensible measures of them (either accurate or inaccurate) which are commonly used instead of the measured quantities [of absolute space and time] themselves."[5] If we knew the forces acting upon the heavenly bodies, which it is Newton's purpose to discover, we could then determine their real and not merely their relative motions. These forces are gravitational and inertial, and given the laws of motion and impressed forces, Newton believed absolute motions, and hence positions in absolute time and space, could be discovered. These locations and quantities may be very different from what they appear to be in our frameworks of relative space and time, and Newton warns against confusing the measures, which are relative, with what is measured, which is absolute. "They do strain the sacred writings, who there interpret those words for their measured quantities; nor do those less defile the purity of mathematical and philosophical truths, who confound real quantities themselves with their relations and vulgar measures."[6]

Newton is more explicit about absolute space than about absolute time: and this is characteristic of most philosophers. It is infinitely easier to think about and to talk about space than time; there is something at least imaginably thing-like about space, but this is not true of time; whether right or wrong, it seems to make sense to speak of space as existing, whereas the existence of time is a much more obscure notion since, it may be thought, only part of time, viz. the present, "really" exists. After generations of Newtonism, we have learned to think about absolute space, and without any Pascalian

---

[4] *Ibid.*, p. 81.
[5] *Ibid.*, p. 81.
[6] *Ibid.*, p. 81.

horror; but we have hardly learned to think about absolute time—the time that would have flowed equably in the absence of anything *in* time, in the absence of anything happening. Yet to understand Newton we must make a double effort: to understand his novel notion of absolute space—a task difficult enough when he wrote, but speciously easy now—and to understand his conception of absolute time. Perhaps in his own day the latter was easier because it was less mystifying to those who thought they had a cogent conception of eternity.[7]

The best we can do, perhaps, is to apply, by analogy, what he says about absolute space to absolute time; for his two definitions are parallel. Both space and time are absolute in the sense of requiring nothing external for their existence. It is an accident of both that there are things in space and things which last through intervals of time. Space and time are empty receptacles into which God put the matter he created; but they would have existed exactly as they are had no body been created to occupy them. They are infinite and infinitely divisible; but whereas space is isotropic, time has a sense, flowing from future to past. They meet the requirements which philosophers at that time put upon substance: they exist without being dependent upon the existence of anything else, and they can be conceived without requiring the conception of existence of anything else. They are ontologically primitive and epistemologically objective.

Leibniz, as we shall see, saw seeds of infidelity and atheism in such a substantial conception of space and time. Here were two substances God did not create, waiting for him to fill them. Spinoza, just shortly before this time, had called extension (roughly, space) an attribute of substance (God), and Samuel Clarke, Newton's disciple, called space (and presumably time) a property of God.[8] We do not know what Newton thought on these matters; he did say that absolute space is "the sensorium of God," and he adumbrates the notion that absolute time is God's eternal duration. When Leibniz, Berkeley, and finally Kant show

---

[7] The *Encyclopédie* (art., Eternité, ed. 1778, vol. 6, p. 45) says rather acidly that it has reported on the scholastic debates about eternity rather fully "because they serve to show into what labyrinths one is hurled when one wants to reason about something one cannot conceive."

[8] *The Leibniz-Clarke Correspondence*, Clarke's Fourth Paper, §10. *Philosophical Papers and Letters*, translated by L. E. Loemker (Chicago, 1956), vol. II, p. 1127.

ontologically objective and absolute space and time to be unintelligible and to be no longer needed in cosmology, divine support for them, which was sought by Newton and Clarke, is no longer required. The world is enough for time.

A subtle shift has occurred. Eternity had been, metaphysically, conceived as timelessness. Time was irrelevant to reality and to God; we speak only in human terms (all we have) when we refer to the everlastingness of God, and we can hardly avoid ascribing a history—albeit a beginningless and endless history—to God. But Newton temporalizes eternity itself; eternity is for him the infinite mathematical time that was before the world and will last after the world is destroyed, but coeval with God.[9] All this belongs more to Newton's theology than to his cosmology, but never before or since, I think, has the eternal and the cosmically temporal been brought into so close a union. If absolute time is needed in the understanding of the world, then eternity is needed; Newton warns against confusing absolute and relative time, as we have seen, because that will "strain the sacred writings," i.e., will mix up ordinary temporal measurements with eternity. With every cosmological or metaphysical or epistemological step away from time's absoluteness there is a step towards making the world itself enough for time.

II. Locke

John Locke called himself "an underlaborour in clearing the ground a little, and removing some of the rubbish that lies in the way of knowledge" in "an age that produces such masters as the great Huygenius and the incomparable Mr. Newton." Locke provided an epistemology to ground Newton's cosmology, but we shall see how much rubbish he removed in Newton's own theory of time.

Locke discusses time as a simple mode of duration. Duration corresponds to "expansion," which is the name he prefers to "space" or "extension" when speaking of Newton's absolute space independent of the existence of bodies in it. "Duration, antecedent to all bodies and

---

[9] See Werner Gent, *Die Philosophie des Raumes und der Zeit* (Hildesheim, second ed., 1962), Vol. I, p. 165.

motions which it is measured by"[10] is the Lockean counterpart to
Newton's duration which, we have seen, becomes first absolute time
and then, through its infinity and equability, eventually either eternity
or a substitute for it. "Expansion and duration do mutually embrace and
comprehend each other, every part of space being in every part of
duration, and every part of duration in every part of expansion."[11] That
is, every part of space exists at all times, and conversely. The place of a
body is that part of expansion it occupies, and time is that part of
duration lying between two things or between the beginning and end of
a thing.—So much for Locke's ontology of duration, which is like but
perhaps less "mystical" than Newton's.

By a simple mode Locke means "a modification of the same
[simple] idea which the mind either finds in things existing, or is able
to make within itself without the help of any extrinsic object, or any
foreign suggestion."[12] Examples of simple modes are number ("the
simple idea of an unit repeated") and space and time. The simple idea
underlying time is that of duration, and the modes are "any different
lengths" of it whereof we have distinct ideas, as hours, days, years, etc.,
time and eternity."[13] (Note especially that he says eternity is a mode of
time; this is not the language of Plato, or the theologians.) To
understand time, we must first consider the simple idea of duration.

One is aware of "a train of ideas which constantly succeed one
another in his understanding," and reflection on this furnishes him with
the idea of succession, the idea of his own duration during this
succession, the idea of the duration of other things co-existing with his
own thinking, and, finally, "the idea of the duration of things which
exist while he does not think."[14]

Like St. Augustine, therefore, Locke finds the origin of our temporal
ideas not in motion per se, but in one motion only, viz., the motion
(change) observed in a sequence of ideas. It is not even the observation
of change, but the change of observation, that generates our sense of
succession and time. There is, as it were, an internal clock by which

---

[10] *Essay Concerning Human Understanding*, Book II, ch. xv, § 4. (edited
by John W. Yolton, Everyman ed., vol. I, p. 161).
[11] *Ibid.*, § 12 (p. 167).
[12] *Ibid.*, ch. 13, §1 (p. 133).
[13] *Ibid.*, ch. 14, §1 (p. 146).
[14] *Ibid.*, §5 (p. 147).

motion itself is measured, and motion which is too rapid or too slow to cause a sequence of noticeably different ideas does not measure time. "The constant and regular succession of ideas in a waking man, is, as it were, the measure and standard of all other successions."[15] But this standard is observable only by the individual; hence some motions "constant, regular, and universally observable by all mankind and supposed equal to one another, have with reason been made use of for the measure of duration."[16]

But, Locke reminds us, in a passage reminiscent of Newton, "We must carefully distinguish betwixt the duration itself, and the measure we make use of to judge of its length;"[17] but he makes this remark for a quite different purpose. Duration is, for him, the lastingness of things; there is no talk in Locke about an empty, eternal duration whether there are things enduring or not; but it is time, not duration understood as lastingness of things, which is infinite. Time, which is like number, can be extrapolated beyond the duration of things that exist, and just as there is no greatest number, so there is no maximum of time. Time is infinite; duration need not be and, because of the creation of the world, is not. Hence Locke can attach a quite precise meaning to applying "the measure of a year to the duration before the creation." It is the infinite extendability of the measure, not of what is measured, which gives rise to the conception of infinite time independent of the answer to the question about the beginning or end of the world. For eternity, we are given a mathematical property of a continuous infinite series.[18]

Locke thus supplies an epistemology for Newton's cosmology, but not for his theology and metaphysics or for those parts of his cosmology which depend upon absolute time considered as eternity. While Newton gives no argument for the infinity of absolute time and thus none for the eternity of God's duration—piety is no argument— Locke's theory does contain an argument based on the analogy of numbers as the measures of duration or motion with numbers which are indifferent to the nature and existence of things numbered, the latter being infinitely extendable.[19] Eternity was always something thought of

---

[15] *Ibid.*, §12 (p. 150).
[16] *Ibid.*, §19 (p. 152).
[17] *Ibid.*, §21 (p. 154).
[18] *Ibid.*, §31 (p. 159).
[19] *Ibid.*, §30 (p. 158).

as given, though beyond human comprehension; now it, or its substitute infinite time, is something constructed by human thought from human experience. Not that Locke drew any unusual theological consequences from this fundamental shift in his conceptual arrangements; he just as confidently as Newton ascribed his temporal concepts to "that Being which must necessarily have always existed."[20]

Before leaving Locke, I wish to mention two criticisms to which he was subjected. Berkeley objects to both Newton and Locke on the point that the time they speak of (both relative and absolute) is an abstract idea. He agrees with Locke that the simple mode (he calls it "simple idea") of time has its root in the succession of ideas in the mind, but when "abstracted" from that and ascribed the properties of flowing uniformly, of being participated in by all things, and of being infinitely divisible he finds himself (really Locke and Newton) "lost and embrangled in inextricable difficulties." Time is nothing if "abstracted from the succession of ideas in our minds;"[21] that is what time is, and not "only the sensible measure thereof, as Mr. Locke and others think."[22]

The reader of Locke is often baffled by the ease with which Locke moves from a simple idea to the simple and complex modes of it. To be sure, without the experience of succession it is difficult to see how one would gain the idea of time; but the properties of time are so different from the properties of any experienced succession that it is unclear how the latter could *originate* in the former. This is Leibniz's repeated complaint about Locke's derivations—that he leaves out the work of, and the predispositions of the intellect involved in, the movement from a simple idea to the simple and complex modes and ideas of substance. Thus he criticizes Locke: "A succession of perceptions awakens in us the idea of duration, but it does not make it.... Changing perceptions furnish us with the occasion of thinking of time, and we measure it by uniform changes."[23] Fully to understand and to weigh this criticism,

---

[20] *Ibid.*, §31 (p. 159).

[21] *Treatise Concerning the Principles of Human Knowledge*, §98.

[22] Letter to Samuel Johnson, March 24, 1730, in *Principles, Dialogues, and Correspondence*, edited by Colin M. Turbayne (Indianapolis, 1965), p. 240.

[23] *New Essays Concerning Human Understanding*, translated by A.G. Langley (LaSalle, 1949), p. 156.

however, requires that we understand Leibniz's positive doctrine of time.

III. Leibniz

Leibniz was the most unashamed metaphysician of the philosophers studied in this paper. Not for him any silent or reticent piety and acknowledgment of the mystery of God; Leibniz sometimes writes as if he were as privy to the councils of God as he was to those of Hanover. He speaks with as much rational assurance about God as about mathematics, physics, logic, history, and diplomacy. In this metaphysical assurance, he is perhaps more characteristic of the seventeenth than of the eighteenth century; but it is necessary to speak of him after Newton and Locke since he was an explicit critic of them.

Against Newton and his metaphysical disciple Samuel Clarke, Leibniz argues that Newton cannot distinguish between absolute and relative space and time, because he cannot establish absolute motion through the study of forces. (In this he would have agreed with Berkeley, and modern physics since Mach and Einstein has sided with them as over against Newton.) Hence the concept of an absolute time, independent of the things and happenings that occur in it, is a useless conception in physics. But, worse still, he finds the concept of absolute time to be metaphysically and theologically dangerous. If there is an absolute time, the following question is intelligible and demands an answer: why did God create the world at the moment (in absolute time) that he did, and not earlier or later? But this question cannot *in principle* be answered, because in absolute time one moment is exactly like any other moment; by Leibniz's principle of the identity of indiscernibles, moments in absolute time are identical, and God therefore could have had no reason to create the world at one moment rather than another. But, granting that there is absolute time, He did so, therefore He did something without a sufficient reason, which is against His rationality. Therefore there is no absolute time. [24]

Leibniz has another reason for rejecting absolute time, this one being a logical instead of a theological reason. Everything that really exists

---

[24] *Leibniz-Clarke Correspondence*, Leibniz's Third Paper, 13 (Loemker, II, 1109).

(i.e., every substance, or monad) is an individual with attributes (properties and changes of properties) which inhere in it. All propositions about substances are propositions in which the predicates inhere in the substance and in the concept of the substance if that concept be complete. Real predicates are one-place predicates, dependent only on the subject of which they are predicated; and all true affirmative judgments are, either implicitly or explicitly, analytical of the subject-concept. Another way of saying this is: What is true of a single substance would be true of it if it were the only thing in the universe. Temporal predicates, such as "before..." and "at the same time as...," are two-place predicates; they cannot be true of a thing taken in isolation. They express relations, and relations are not a part of the ultimate ontological furniture of the universe, which consists exclusively of active substances and their states existing independently of, but in a pre-established harmony with, all other things. Each monad is essentially and dynamically unrelated to all the others, but each is a "living mirror" of the universe, reflecting it from its own point of view.

Thus, for Leibniz, there is no absolute time and space as ontological primitives; even relative time and space are not metaphysical realities. He says they are not real, but ideal; that is, they are representations in single monads of the order of their states and the states of the other monads. As representations, not true realities, they are phenomena; but the spatial and temporal locations assigned to things in each monad's reflection of the world are determined by what is genuinely real, and hence they are not illusory (unless taken to be more than they are). The illusion arises from thinking that the monads are physically real, extended things and therefore material; while in truth they are unextended spiritual agents. But correctly taken as phenomena without further pretensions, they are *phenomena bene fundata*.

It is therefore incumbent upon Leibniz to show what there is in the system of monads which is not spatio-temporal but which serves as the foundation of the phenomenal appearance of the world, which is under the condition of relative time and space. He says that time is the "order of possible inconsistents" or of non-compossible possibilities.[25] That is, two propositions which are mutually exclusive may both be true under one condition only, viz., that they are true at different times; two

---

[25] *Leibniz's Correspondence with De Voider*, and "The Metaphysical Foundations of Mathematics" (Loemker, II, 865, 1083).

things which could not coexist (e.g., my youth and my old age) may nevertheless exist if there is time, a time when I was young and a time when I am old. Now God could have created a world (perhaps like Spinoza's "block universe," as William James called it) in which everything was logically consistent but in which the number of possibilities to be realized was limited by its instantaneous or permanent, unchanging character. But God in creating the best of all possible worlds created that one in which there would be a maximum of realized possibilities, and the condition under which this maximum is achieved is that they are realized, or at least represented, as occurring one after another. (Space is the order of incompatible things existing simultaneously—they exist at different places; time is the order of incompatibles existing at the same place—but at different times).

It is quite clear from this that God himself must have envisaged the world *sub specie temporis* as well as *aeternitatis*; he created a world in which non-compossible possibilities would be realized. That shows that there is nothing necessarily illusory about temporality, though God (as Augustine says) must have surveyed instantaneously or eternally what we men experience only under the form of time. Leibniz at least once says that space and time do not depend upon the actuality of things, but only upon their possibility; and without an actual world, space and time would be only ideas in God's mind.[26] More usually, however, Leibniz writes as if space and time are only the ways by which finite monads interpret relations between things which are not intrinsically spatio-temporal at all. For example, a state of a monad which is *logically* prior to another state is seen as *temporally* prior. Time is a phenomenal mapping of the ontological and logical relations between the states of a monad which are, in turn, reflections of the state of the entire universe. Loemker describes Leibniz's physics as "a phenomenal commentary on his metaphysics." The realm of nature (spatio-temporal) is an ectype of the realm of grace. Time is a moving image of eternity, in which what is ontologically necessary appears to be phenomenally contingent.

The idea of "mapping" logical or ontological relations phenomenally is easier to represent by a spatial than a temporal model. Ruth Saw's

---

[26] *Leibniz-Clarke Correspondence*, Leibniz's fourth paper, §41. (Loemker, II, 1123).

lucid model[27] is that of a cross-word puzzle. The logical relations are: The second letter in a nine-letter word meaning "elephant" is the last letter in the name of a great desert, the third letter is the initial letter in the name of the Greek god of time, etc. Such a "program" is logically independent of the spatial representation on the grid of a cross-word puzzle, but the latter is the more perspicuous representation of it for us men. Perhaps a graph in which one of the coordinates is marked "time" will serve as a model for the spatio-temporal representation of a mathematical function in which the values of one of the variables is logically ("eternally") fixed by the values of another.

Like Descartes and Newton, Leibniz distinguishes between duration and time, which is its relative metric and well-founded phenomenon. Duration is essential to substances, which persist and, according to Leibniz, cannot be destroyed. This means that there is a set of durational predicates which belong to each substance and not just to its phenomenal presentation. While it is literally true that God, the *monas monadum*, exists at all times, because he is coeval with the temporal world which is a manifestation of his choice of the best of all possible worlds, there is a constant danger of subreption, of a "category mistake" in using temporal predicates or durational predicates in describing the world in Leibniz's metaphysics.[28] Though without the attribution of time-like predicates to substances, his theory is unintelligible; in the phenomenal world where his theory of time is most at home, he has no more use for metaphysical duration than for absolute time.

IV. Kant

Kant agreed with Newton that time and space are absolute, that is, independent of the things and events which occupy them. But he

---

[27] Ruth Lydia Shaw, *Leibniz* (Penguin Books, 1954), p. 109.

[28] The great complexity of the problem led Bertrand Russell to discern three inconsistent theories of time in Leibniz, only two of which I have alluded to. See *Critical Exposition of the Philosophy of Leibniz* (London, 1900), §74. In *Early German Philosophy* (Cambridge, 1969) p. 270, I have discussed Wolff's theory of time and the appropriateness of Kant's tendency to ascribe Wolff's views to his master, Leibniz.

agreed with Leibniz that time and space are not metaphysically objective, that is, more than well-grounded phenomena. Absoluteness and objectivity had not been clearly distinguished from each other before Kant, and it is not unusual to find even today, in popular scientific articles about the theory of relativity, the confusion which Kant was the first to remove. When reading about the theory of relativity, the reader often does not know whether it is relativity in the sense of relationality or relativity in the sense of subjectivity, i.e., relation to the knowing mind, that is being expounded; perhaps sometimes the author himself does not know.

For Kant, the question as to whether time is objective (real) and the question as to whether it is absolute (not relative) must be answered by quite distinct inquiries. We shall discuss Kant's theory of time under five somewhat overlapping rubrics in order to keep these two questions as distinct as possible.

1. *The metaphysical unreality of time.* Kant teaches the "transcendental ideality," not the "transcendental reality," of time.[29] Time is *only* a form of experience and does not pertain to reality as it is in itself, about which we know and can know nothing. In his *Inaugural Dissertation of 1770*, he sees the purpose of his critical philosophy to be the isolation of the forms and principles of the sensible world (which are space and time) from the forms and principles of the intelligible world (which in 1770 he thought to be the categories of classical ontology). It is essential to prevent the use of the former in discussing the intelligible world, since Kant believed that most of the failures of classical metaphysics were a consequence of the "subreptitious" use of time and space as if they were forms of things in general instead of merely forms of human experience.

Kant's reason for believing that they are forms of experience instead of independent objects of experience is found in the pattern of his thought called his "Copernican Revolution." According to this, the necessary and imprescriptable features of what we know must be features determined by the operations of the mind independently of what happens to be the content or object of the experience. If time were real, and if it were experienced as a content or object (as it would be if it were real), we could at most say: Everything I have experienced has had a date, therefore in all probability everything I will ever experience

---

[29] *Critique of Pure Reason*, A 35/B 52.

will have a date. Our knowledge of time would be inductive and empirical.[30] But we do not say any such thing: We know *a priori* (i.e., we know it to be necessarily and unexceptionably true) that all experiences and all objects of experience will be temporal. Now all the other philosophers we have discussed knew this, but only for Kant did it pose a problem: How do we know something about every experience (viz., that it will be temporal) before we have it?

The term *a priori* is equivocal. It may describe what we know necessarily and universally to be the case. But it may also refer to what makes such knowledge possible. In this sense it refers to our "knowing apparatus," as it were, indicating that the universal and necessary form of knowledge "must lie ready for our sensations *a priori* [in the second sense] and so must allow of being considered apart from all sensations."[31] In this second sense (and only in this sense) Kant's theory resembles Descartes' theory of innate ideas, more especially in the modified form of it which Leibniz defended against Locke's attack. All our knowledge begins with experience, Kant and Leibniz say in apparent agreement with Locke; but not all of it arises out of experience,[32] and what does not arise out of experience is precisely that which we know *a priori* (in the first sense) because it is *a priori* (in the second sense).

Kant argues that if we think away all the temporal content, time itself, instead of disappearing along with that from which Locke thought it was an abstraction, cannot itself be thought away. The form of our perception, in the absence of any empirical content, becomes itself an object of a pure (not an empirical) intuition. Thus Kant concludes that time is (a) the form of all our experience and (b) the object of a particular kind of experience he calls pure intuition.[33]

2. *The absoluteness of time.* In the previous sentence I have anticipated this Kantian thesis: time is an *object* (though not an empirical object, like a dog, who makes his presence known by causing sensations in us) and not merely a relation between objects (for it subsists and can be known even when it is considered as if it were

---

[30] *Ibid.*, A 40/B 57.

[31] *Ibid.*, A 20/B 34.

[32] Compare the first paragraph of the Introduction to the *Critique of Pure Reason* with Leibniz's *New Essays*, Book II, Ch. 1 (Langley, p. 111).

[33] *Critique of Pure Reason*, A 31/B 46; A 32-4/B 49-51.

empty of objects and events). Time is a very peculiar thing, differing from all other things except space in that it is not empirically known; but it is like every other thing in the world in that it is an *individual*. That is, there is one time, and what we call "times" are mere parts or limitations in it.[34] It is not a concept like that of man, for we can understand the concept of man without knowing whether there are any individual men and without knowing how many men there are. But we know that there is one time, since any two events are related to each other as either successive or not, and of any two events which are not simultaneous, one is before the other. All events are therefore in one time; and Kant says time is given as an infinite magnitude.

Kant gives another proof of the absoluteness of space which we may adapt, by analogy, for a proof of the absoluteness of time.[35] The space-argument is known as the argument from non-congruent counterparts. If space is merely a relation between things, as Leibniz believed, then when the relations among the parts of two things are identical, there should be no discernible spatial difference between them. But this is not the case. The relations between the fingers of a glove and the fingers of the hand that the glove fits are identical; but the relations between the fingers of a right hand and those between the fingers of a left hand are identical; therefore a left-hand glove should fit a right hand. But it does not. In order to explain this phenomenon, Kant says, we must relate the hand and the glove "to the whole of space." Since we easily make the distinction between left and right, and since this distinction is not a matter of abstract geometrical relations but something which must be seen or directly experienced or ostensively defined, we must have a notion of the whole of space which is independent of the things in it.

The preceding argument says that left and right are not analyzable without remainder into the mutual relations of the things occupying space; we must know also how things are oriented in absolute space. A similar argument can be contrived for time. Time has a *sense* which is not captured by Leibniz's relational analysis into the condition under which non-compossibles become possible, for this relation is the same whether one of the non-compossibles is earlier or later than the other. World history might as well have run backwards, so far as Leibniz's

[34] *Ibid.*, A 32/B 47.
[35] *Prolegomena to any Future Metaphysics*, §13.

analysis of time is concerned; in fact, to Leibniz there would be no discernible difference—granting his relational analysis—between a world running one way and a world running the other. By analogy to the space argument, we can attribute to Kant the view that the difference between one direction and the opposite direction of time can be discerned only by relating temporal series to the one absolute time as an infinite given magnitude.

3. *Time sensible, not conceptual.* All our knowledge of existing things is the application of general predicates (universals) to particulars. We must be able to say something general about a particular, and we must bring any particular under some general concepts. The particular, to which we may refer as a "this," is the thing which we are talking about, and the general concept gives us information about the "this" by predicating of it that it is like or unlike something else. Concepts are the work of thought, but the identification of what they are about is the work of our senses. I *see* a this; I *think* about it.

There are logical forms (categories) which are our rules of thinking about things and expressing our knowledge of them in judgments which attribute a predicate to a subject. These categories are *a priori* and are related to logic. But Kant discovered a philosophical problem in identifying a particular to which the conceptual predicates are attributed. He asks: What are the *a priori* forms of our sensing particulars, analogous in function to the categories which are *a priori* forms for our thought about them? And he answers: Space and time are the two necessary forms of individuation, of identification of a "this," and of re-identification in two experiences of the same thing. Leibniz had held that two objects having all their properties in common would be indiscernible and therefore identical; Kant adds that though there could be (though there probably are not) things having all one-place predicates in common, they would still not be identical because they would be in different locations in space and time. He concludes:

> Time is not something that exists of itself, or which inheres in things as an objective determination.... Time is nothing but the subjective condition under which alone [knowledge of particular existing things] can take place in us. For that being so, this form

[of knowledge] can be represented prior to the objects, and therefore *a priori*.[36]

Kant has said much the same about space, which he interprets as absolute but not as ontologically real, as a form of phenomena and therefore not as conceptually analyzable without remainder. But now Kant introduces an important difference between the two. Space, he says, is the form of our outer sense, while time is the form of our inner sense. This much is in agreement with Locke; and, as Locke saw, outer things and motions come under the form of time only by being represented in our inner sense, in our awareness of changes in our stream of consciousness. Hence Kant adds to the statement that "time is nothing but the form of inner sense" the statement: "Time is the formal *a priori* condition of all [phenomena] whatsoever."[37] Locke, in his naiveté, had not seen the problem involved in how we move from the awareness of the time of the passage of our ideas to the dating of events in the physical world which we perceive. Kant must show how we construct a public, objective time-series out of data which are private and, presumably, different for every observer.

Before we narrate Kant's efforts in this direction, however, we must take note of Kant's repeated use of the word "our" in referring to inner and outer sense. Unlike the categories, which are logically necessary, Kant holds that there is nothing logically necessary in our having the forms of sensibility which we do have. We can easily imagine that the inhabitants of other planets (whom Kant believed to exist) and angels (whom he did not believe to exist) and perhaps intelligent animals have quite different ways of identifying and re-identifying particulars, though we cannot imagine what these other forms and ways of particularizing may be. For all we know, space and time may be nothing more than forms of *human* sensibility and knowledge. It is only a short step from this view to the more extreme view that space and time are culturally determined, and that their study belongs in the sociology of knowledge. This is a step Kant did not take, and probably would have resisted had he thought about it. But those who argue that time as Western man understands it is not a necessary human form of organizing experience, and that other ways of organizing experience

---

[36] *Critique of Pure Reason*, A 32-3/B 49.

[37] *Ibid.*, A 34/B 50.

actually exist and are manifested in different linguistic and artistic and explanatory structures are only going one step beyond Kant along a path he first opened.

4. *The rehabilitation of relative time.* The problem in the penultimate paragraph of the previous section is that of moving from time as the form of inner sense to time as one of the forms of the physical world. In a happy example, Kant illustrates the process he is attempting to understand. I first see the basement and then the roof of a house; and I first see a ship pass under one bridge and then see it pass under a different bridge. Both of these pairs of experiences are temporally related: Each is one experience after another. But of the first I say that the house had a roof at the *same* time that it had a basement, and of the second I say that the ship was under one bridge and under another at *different* times. How do we do this? It would be easy if we could perceive (and not merely have a pure intuition of) absolute time; for then each thing we experience could be dated, and we would find the dates of roof and basement the same, and the date of passage under one bridge earlier than that of passage under the other. Since we cannot do that, we must be content to fix their dates only in relation to each other, but in a public time in which their relations may or may not be the same as the relations among the private experiences themselves. (Another example: I see the flash of a gun, and one second later hear the explosion; you see the flash, and hear the explosion two seconds later. What *a priori* principles are involved in our decision, confirmed by experiment, that the two occurred at the same time?)

Kant's answer to these questions is given in the most important, and probably the most difficult, chapter of the *Critique of Pure Reason*, entitled "The Second Analogy of Experience." What follows here will be a gross over-simplification of that chapter but will not, I hope, substantially misrepresent it. In brief, we attach temporal predicates to objects not just by seeing them in time as the form of our *inner* experience, but by conceptualizing the kinds of objects we are seeing. It is only because of a vast background of empirical concepts and laws of nature that we say that the roof of a house (in all probability) does not exist without the continuing existence of its foundation; the fact that we happen to see the roof before we see the basement is dismissed as irrelevant to what the situation in the world is. For similar reasons we know that an unanchored ship (in all probability) moves down-stream, and this knowledge leads us not to ignore the order in which we see it in different positions. If I saw the roof first and then the basement, I would draw the same conclusion that I would from seeing the basement and then the roof. But if I see the ship under bridge one and then under bridge two, I do *not* draw the conclusion I would draw were I to see it first under bridge two and then under bridge one: In one case, I say the boat is moving downstream, in the other, upstream.

Now in these examples, it is mostly empirical knowledge about houses, ships, streams, and bridges that permits us to draw the conclusions we do. But Kant argues that all this empirical knowledge is content for *a priori categorial* forms which are "schematized," i.e., manifested as *a priori* patterns of time. In the case of the house, there is the *a priori* category of substance as the permanent in time; in the case of the ship, the *a priori* category of causality which is a necessary sequence in the states of a thing. Each of these *a priori* categorial principles appears in a slightly different form in Newton's physics, for which Kant supplies an epistemological foundation far sounder than that provided by Locke.

5. *Time and the language of faith.* Kant appears to have had to pay a very high price for this solution to the problems he inherited from Newton, Leibniz, and Locke. He has had to give up any application of temporal predicates to reality (e.g., to God, to the soul, and to things as they are in themselves apart from their appearances to human beings). The history of creation, the eternity of God, the immortality of the soul, and other favorite topics of the theologian and metaphysician are unattainably beyond the reach of human knowledge. It seems, even, that it does not make sense even to talk about them, much less to claim to know any truths about them. Claims to know about them are not only unfounded; but in giving them up, we have paid no high price. On the contrary, they are dangerous, because, Kant says, *if* such talk were well-grounded, the metaphysical world could only be an extension of the spatio-temporal causal world of our scientific experience, and the other world of metaphysics would be just the same old Newtonian world, only vaster. In the Newtonian world, or in its metaphysical duplicate, there would be no place for the assumptions which Kant thought we have to make in order to take moral concerns as valid. In spite of what Newton said, in a Newtonian world there is no place for God; in a world of matter in space and of motion in time, there is no place for an immaterial substance (the soul) and its temporal predicate of immortality; no way in which an event can occur without being

determined, according to the laws of motion, by a temporally earlier event, and hence no freedom of the will, hence no morality.

But all of these dire consequences are ruled out once we realize that the form of time applies only to the world of phenomena, and that our knowledge is restricted to this. "I ... found it necessary," Kant says, "to deny knowledge in order to make room for faith.[38]

Two points in this famous sentence are worth noting. (A) Kant says he found it *necessary* to deny knowledge. But this does not mean that he called upon faith, *ab extra*, to limit or to supplement knowledge. Kant is not fideistic. Rather he has shown that the conditions of *a priori* knowledge can be met only if knowledge is confined to the appearances of things, and does not reach their reality *an sich*. The conditions that make knowledge *possible* also restrict its scope. (B) Kant says he found it necessary to deny *knowledge*. Kant is not in the long line of Christian apologists who denied reason in order to make way for faith, who appealed, in James' expression, to a *will* to believe against or beyond the evidence. Rather Kant insists that reason has two functions, one in knowing (theoretical reason) and one in guiding conduct (practical reason); it is the *same* reason in two functions, and it is as possible, and as necessary, to be reasonable in the conduct of life as it is to be reasonable in the conduct of inquiry. We cannot *know* that the will is free, or that God exists, or that the soul is immortal; but Kant thinks that it is reasonable to believe that they are in order to use reason in the conduct of our lives; hence these beliefs are articles of rational faith.

But it is only enthusiasm (*Schwärmerei*) to claim knowledge of them, and *Schwärmerei* is morally corrupting:

> Assuming that [nature] had indulged our wish and had provided us with that power of insight or enlightenment which we would like to possess or which some erroneously believe they do possess, what would be the consequence so far as we can discern it?... God and eternity in their awful majesty would stand unceasingly before our eyes... Transgression of the law would be shunned.... [But] most actions conforming to the [moral] law would be done from fear,

---

[38] *Ibid.*, B xxx.

few would be done from hope, none from duty. The moral worth of actions... would not exist at all.[39]

But, of course, human beings cannot be silent about the things they believe really exist, though they cannot know them (and most religious-minded people probably do not know that they cannot know them). They must talk a religious or metaphysical language using temporal and spatial metaphors in which they ascribe to God everlastingness and omnipresence and to the soul a future life. This is inevitable, and it is not dangerous if we take such locutions as symbolical expressions of faith and not as knowledge-claims. Thus men can talk an appropriate language of eternity;[40] but all their knowledge is of things in time and space.

V. Conclusion

I have written brief accounts of the theories of time formulated by four eminent philosophers of the eighteenth century, and written it as if Locke, Leibniz, and Kant were doing nothing but working over a system left in an unsatisfactory state by Newton. This, of course, is a fiction. Each of the three later philosophers had access to all the traditional treatments of time that were available to Newton, and perhaps made better use of them; and each of them was sensitive, to a degree to which Newton was not, to what was going on in the world outside the laboratories and halls of philosophy. I do not think it very fruitful to see great philosophers as if they were mere spokesmen for their times (though this may be effective when trying to understand second-raters), for they are more likely to be disposed to criticize than to celebrate the climate of opinion in which they live. Still, each philosopher is a child of his times, and I do not think it too far-fetched to see the general trend from Newton's to Kant's philosophy of time as at least obscurely reflecting some of the major shifts in the thinking of

---

[39] *Critique of Practical Reason*, translated by L. W. Beck (Chicago, 1949), p. 248.

[40] *The End of All Things* in *Kant on History*, edited by L. W. Beck (Indianapolis, 1963), p. 76.

the Enlightenment about man and his place in the world and in world-history.

There is a sentence in Finnegan's Wake which reads: "Shake eternity, and lick creation." I do not know what this sentence means in the context of that book, but in isolation it suggests to me that man can master the world ("lick creation") if he breaks up the solid, static, Eleatic world ("shake eternity") of which the world of his knowledge and action was thought to be only a moving image—perhaps not exactly an illusory image, but at least one lacking the ontological dignity and perfection of true reality. Every one of our philosophers admits the eternal; Newton, and especially Leibniz, seem to be intimately acquainted with it, while for Kant it is only an object for rational faith and plays no part in the understanding of the world or our experience. Locke alone seems sincerely uninterested in it, though he too pays lip-service to it. If the Enlightenment can be characterized as a period of growing secularization, of decreasing need for other-worldly revelation and succour, of finding this world sufficiently rich in human challenges and opportunities, then we can say that the Enlightenment in general was bent upon shaking eternity so that it could lick creation. Human conceptions replace divine conceptions; the *sensorium dei* of Newton becomes the Kantian form of *human* sense.

There are at least two trends of thought in the eighteenth century as a consequence of which human time replaces divine eternity as the proper object and concern of man.

The first is what Lovejoy called "the temporalization of the great chain of being."[41] At the beginning of the century, the great chain was vertical; at the end, horizontal or perhaps gently sloping upward. At the beginning, the chain was suspended from a static eternity, and every link in it was characterized by its vertical distance from God. Thus does the great chain appear in Pope's *Essay on Man*. But there was empirical, scientific evidence against this conception of the great chain, in that occupants could not be found for every stage. The gaps, however, had once been filled (as we know from the fossil record). The plenitude of being is not representable by a chain hanging at rest, but by a temporal process in which some of the stages of being were occupied only in the past and some are to be occupied only in the future. The historicisation of nature develops into an eschatology of

---

[41] *The Great Chain of Being* (Cambridge, 1936), Chapter 9.

progress, in which time is itself almost a creative force begetting new forms of natural beings and new social arrangements among mankind and trending to a goal which is not eternally present but an ever-receding end. The heavenly city becomes the future city. Eternity had been shaken, and creation was in course of being licked. Hegel writes: "Enlightenment, proclaiming itself as the pure and true, here turns what is held to be eternal life and a holy spirit into a concrete passing thing of sense, and contaminates it with what belongs to sense-certainty [i.e., perception under the form of space and time]."[42]

The second is a vast increase in the amount of time available for the explanation of the present situation and for the pursuit of human goals.[43] There is something a little pitiable, to me at least, in Sir Isaac Newton, perhaps the greatest mathematical genius who ever lived, spending his time trying to calculate, from Biblical texts, the time of the ending of the world. The age of the world is sufficiently short for him to think that the world did not come, in time, to its present state but was formed in its present state by the hand of the Creator. Locke (in an aside, and by way of illustrating something else) appears to think that 5,639 years is a plausible conjecture, but he mentions a Chinese estimate of 3,269,000 years which he does not believe is true.[44] Kant, on the other hand, speaks of the age of the world in "millions of years or centuries," and gives calculations of tidal friction to determine how long the day was at various periods in the very distant past. For him, the universe at large is in a "steady state"—the material which once formed one solar system will be dissipated again into primordial chaotic dust from which new nebulae and solar systems will be formed, and formed by the slow inexorable processes of attraction and repulsion governed by Newton's laws. For Kant, there is world enough and time to explain all the present and all the different past and future states of the universe without appealing to an act of creation or special providence of the kind Newton believed was necessary for the establishment and stabilization of the solar system. Closer to the earth, Hutton, the founder of modern geology, held that there was in the

---

[42] *Phenomenology of Mind* (Baillie translation), p. 571.

[43] See Stephen Toulmin and June Goodfield, *The Discovery of Time* (London, 1965), chapters 4, 5, and 6.

[44] *Essay Concerning Human Understanding*, Bk. II, Ch. xiv, §29 (Yolton, I, 158).

geological record "no vestige of a beginning," nor even any sign of catastrophic changes which had had to be assumed when it was believed that the age of the earth was small. [45]

The history of mankind likewise requires more time than is allowed by Biblical chronology, and Enlightenment historiography gets along well without divine guidance and intervention; just think of the contrast between Bossuet and Gibbon! When the slow-moving processes of civil history are not allowed enough time to effect the treat changes which the new study of antiquities showed must have occurred, it was easy, nay necessary, to appeal to another world, which is timeless, to account for this one. But when it is discovered that there is time enough, this appeal to eternity becomes less and less importunate.

So eternity was shaken, shaken out of the philosophy of nature and the philosophy of man. Its place was taken by a human phenomenon or invention, time. We were left with the time without any pretensions to eternity; time was quite enough.

---

[45] James Hutton, "Theory of the Earth, or an Investigation of the Laws Observable in the Composition, Dissolution, and Restoration of Land upon the Globe," *Transactions of the Royal Society of Edinburgh*, vol. i, part ii, pp. 209-304 (1788), at p. 304. Reprinted in *James Hutton's System of the Earth, 1785; Theory of the Earth, 1788; Observations on Granite, 1794*; together with *Playfair's Biography of Hutton*, with Introduction by V.A. Eyles (*Contributions to the History of Geology*, ed. G. W. White, vol. 5. New York: Hafner Press, 1973), p. 128.

9. Philosophy As Literature*

My choice of the topic, "Philosophy as Literature," is a result of experiences which I do not believe are unique to me, yet which have been largely ignored by both philosophers and students of polite letters.[1] The experiences are those of aesthetic satisfaction upon reading many a fine work of philosophy, a gratification comparable in kind, and sometimes in degree, to that which I have upon reading a good novel, play, or poem. For me, philosophy is, among other things, a genre of literature.

Yet if it is literature, it is literature neglected by critics and ignored by most people who love literature. The student of English literature of the eighteenth century is told that Locke's influence upon it is pervasive, and that he cannot understand *Tom Jones* and *Tristram Shandy* unless he knows the *Essay Concerning the Human Understanding*. So he dutifully learns about the *Essay*. He may even read it, but never, I think, with any other motive than to understand the "real" literature. He does not think the *Essay* is itself literature, a work to be approached with the canons of literary criticism or with the joyous anticipation he feels when he comes to the works of Swift, Addison, and Johnson.

My choice of Locke is perhaps not entirely fair to the student of letters, for there are a few authors whom he reads as literature and whom the philosopher reads as philosophy. Notable examples are

---

* Reprinted with permission from *Philosophical Style* ed. B. Lang, pp. 234-258. Chicago: Nielson Hall, 1980.

[1] While there is a small amount of writing which deals with the topic, the only formal and explicit full treatment I know is William Charlton, "Is Philosophy a Form of Literature?," *British Journal of Aesthetics* 14 (1974), pp. 3-16. His answer is affirmative, but is reached by quite a different route from the one I follow here. Since writing this essay several articles dealing explicitly with the topic have come to my attention: Berel Lang, "Space, Time, and Philosophical Style," *Critical Inquiry* II, pp. 263-280; and see footnote 27.

Plato and Nietzsche. What the philosopher finds and admires most in them is rather different from what the student of literature and the educated general reader most admire. The philosopher prefers *The Will to Power*, the litterateur *Zarathustra*. The philosopher prefers the *Sophist*, *Theaetetus*, and *Parmenides*, while the man of letters prefers the *Phaedrus*, *Phaedo*, and *Symposium*. But they are at one in their devotion to one book of Plato's: the *Republic*, paradoxically the one book in which Plato is most hostile to the poet, the hero of the student of letters. At the end of the *Republic*, Plato recounts the "ancient quarrel between philosophy and poetry" and banishes the poet from the ideal city because the poet may mislead the citizen by the sweetness of his song. The poet makes illusion attractive, and takes the mind away from truth, the realm of the philosopher. But the existence of the *Republic* is itself an argument against banishing the poets. It is itself a work of art, and had Plato succeeded in establishing an earthly city according to its pattern, it would have been a tribute to his writing literature of power, not literature of knowledge. I cited Plato as a counter-example to my statement that men of letters have neglected philosophical writings; but I did so with the assurance that Plato is the best example I can cite for my thesis that works of philosophy *can* be works of literature too.

Other counter-examples are not as clear as that of Plato. I refer to some closer to home, namely Emerson and Carlyle. Consider Emerson. I will be told, correctly, that students of American literature have a far deeper love and better understanding of Emerson than professional philosophers do. Precisely. What professional ever thought of Emerson as one of theirs? American literature is welcome to him. This attitude may be unjust to Emerson, and it may be question-begging in a dispute over whether literary scholars study real philosophers. So I must make clear how, at least at the beginning of this essay, I am going to use the words "philosophy" and "literature."

The source books assigned by professors of English and other languages constitute Literature with a capital L. The source books in the syllabi of professors of philosophy constitute Philosophy with a capital P. There is little overlap between the two sets of books. My thesis is that this is not due to any inherent lack of literary quality in all the works called Philosophy, or of philosophical merit in all the works called Literature.

This is an offer, and a plea. It offers to the student of literature an almost virgin field for his critical exploration. And it is a plea to the sensitive student of literature to furnish the rest of us with imaginative insights into the literature of philosophy, to teach philosophers the crafts of criticism and techniques for the articulation of literary taste in philosophy, and to make the literary experience of philosophy more understandable.

But before I expatiate on philosophy as literature, there are two other topics I must touch upon. They are: philosophy *of* Literature, and philosophy *in* Literature.

I. Philosophy of Literature²

I have given a rough-and-ready description of what I mean by Literature. But in a serious philosophical discourse I must try to explain why professors of literature choose just the books they do for their students to study. Why, I am asking, are *David Copperfield, Hamlet, Paradise Lost, The Antiquities and Natural History of Selborne,* and *Holy Living and Holy Dying* chosen as Literature with a capital L, while Locke's *Essay,* Hobbes' *Leviathan* and Mill's *Utilitarianism* are not chosen? I will now try to answer that question.

Literature, like any art, is jealous of the attention we pay to other things. It holds attention to itself, and it rewards the single-minded attention we give it, delighting us if we take it exactly as it is. It concentrates into a single vision what we may see piece-meal on scattered occasions; and it may embody what we would never see had we not been helped to see it by the artist's vivid presentation of it.

Literature, however, is unlike any other art in its most important feature, which I shall try to make salient by comparing it with music and painting. Music is not normally *about* anything. It is tone and rhythm and pattern to be enjoyed for themselves; its ideas, if there are any, are musical ideas. Only rarely, and then not very successfully, does it tell a story, present a philosophy, or imitate anything that is not

---

² In this section, I have to deal briefly with the classical problem of 'truth' in the arts, a problem which is once again in the center of interest of critics and aestheticians. I hope the brevity of my treatment will not be mistaken for dogmatism.

music. Painting is sometimes like music in that tone and rhythm and pattern of light and color hold our attention, but usually it is also like literature in that it is a painting *of* something.

Literature, however, is *always* about something. The surface-values of the physical text are not like beautiful tones and colors, and if the spoken text has beauty of rhythm, consonance, and tone this is always parasitic upon its meaning. Euphonious nonsense syllables do not make poetry.

Here lies the paradox of the art of literature. Like any art, it is jealous of the attention we pay to other things, yet the personalities depicted, the events narrated, the emotions aroused or recollected in tranquillity, and the ideas conveyed by literature do get our attention. How, then, can we give literature the undivided focal attention which any art-work demands, and yet experience facts and values which are not visible on the surface of the text?

The paradox arises from an ambiguity in the word "about." Literature is about something that does not take our attention away from the text. Compare *The Origin of Species*, which is about the life of plants and animals, with *Ulysses*, which is about a day in the life of Leopold Bloom. The two "abouts" function very differently. One is a "reportorial about," and the other a "fictive about."[3] *The Origin of Species* is about plants and animals; Darwin studied them, his writing refers to them, and the worth of his writing is the precise degree to which he told the truth about them. Darwin had no other relevant purpose than to reveal and explain these antecedent facts. His success is not that he wrote a book one loves to read, or whose style one admires, but that he wrote a book that instructs us about plants and animals. The meaning of *The Origin of Species*, what it is reportorially about, is meaning in the mode of *semantic transparency*. The rich ambiguity, the over-determination, and the invitation to diverse levels of interpretation which rivet our attention to a literary text would be faults in a scientific treatise.

Briefly, his point is as follows. "Dr. Johnson was a lexicographer" is about Johnson, and about is a semantic two-place predicate, (...) is

---

[3] The ambiguities in "about" and the paradoxes arising from them are well known to philosophers. Very generally, I am here following a suggestion by Nelson Goodman ("About," *Mind* LXX (1961), pp. 1-24 at p. 18) in his discussion of "rhetorically about" (like my "fictive about").

about (...), the blanks to be filled by an existing sentence and the name of an existing man. "Dr. Grantly was an archdeacon" is about Grantly; but here about is a syntactic one-place predicate, (...) is about Grantly, where the blank is to be filled by a sentence Trollope wrote, and the predicate "is about Grantly" tells us what kind of sentence it is; Goodman calls it a "Grantly-about" sentence, and it is to be distinguished from another sentence which Trollope wrote which is a "Harding-about" sentence. Ordinary syntax does not differentiate between these one-place and two-place predicates, but once this is done the difference between the reportorial and the fictive about is evident.

We do not ordinarily give devoted and single-minded attention to the medium of Darwin's message—we see *through it* to the biological facts and theories he is talking about. The semantic transparency of the reportorial about puts a constraint on freedom of interpretation of *The Origin of Species*. To the extent that Darwin was successful, there is one right way of reading his book.[4]

None of this is true of literature. Transparency to antecedent fact is here not controlling. The literary "fictive about" is not transparent to antecedent fact; there may indeed be no antecedent fact. The author of a work of literature may create what it is about by creating that which seems to be about it. There was no Barchester until Trollope created it. Even if there is an antecedent fact, the transparent truth about it is not what is important, as it was for Darwin: "what is said" may be more interesting than whatever it is "about which it is said." Boswell attempted to report the truth about Dr. Johnson, whom he knew but did not create. But Boswell created the Johnson whom we know. Boswell's *Life of Samuel Johnson* as a work of literature is not depreciated by a more accurate biography; in fact, a more accurate one may make us more aware than we were of Boswell's literary power. *The Life of Johnson* would cease to be biography, but would remain literature, even if it should turn out, *mirabile dictu*, that Dr. Johnson never existed.

---

[4] This seems *prima facie* to be true, or at least far more nearly true of *The Origin of Species* than it is of, say, *The Wasteland*. Later I shall indicate at least some modifications that may need to be made.

All this is summarized when I say that the fictive about is a mode of semantic arrest,[5] in contrast to the semantic transparency of the nonliterary text with its reportorial about. But there are different degrees of semantic arrest. It may be almost total, as in *Finnegan's Wake*; almost absent, as in *The Natural History of Selborne*. In Trollope, the semantic arrest is much greater than in Boswell, for there never was an Archdeacon Grantly about whom Trollope wrote. Yet we do not miss him! The medium has become the message; in Denys de Rougement's metaphor, it is "a trap for attention." The Archdeacon is literally a creation of Trollope's, while at most we can say not quite literally that Johnson was Boswell's creation.

Trollope gives his created world whatever power or reality it has by arresting our attention at the medium in which he created it. We do not, like early readers of *Utopia*, look for it on a map. We love the book, *Barchester Towers*, which exists, not the city, which does not exist. Our attention is arrested by those qualities which pervade the medium through which (better: in which) we seem to see what Trollope seems to be talking *about*. But there is, literally, nothing, no existing thing, he is reporting the truth about.

Yet even in what is officially called fiction, there is no creation *ex nihilo*. Had Trollope created the book and the town of Barchester *out of nothing*, we could [not] understand it. Trollope lived, along with us, in a world he never made; he transformed parts of it into a world he did make. The constraint on Trollope's creation was not antecedent facts *about* Barchester which he had to report truly, but antecedent facts about life, to which he wanted to be true.

In a work of literary art, *truth to* must be distinguished from *truth about*,[6] especially since, as I have been arguing, much literature is not the truth *about* anything. *Truth about* is the achievement of the reportorial about; but *truth to* does not perfectly correspond to the fictive about, though the fictive about depends upon *truth to*. "Trollope

---

[5] I formulated this concept first in "Judgments of Meaning in Art," *Journal of Philosophy* XLI (1944), pp. 169-178. [Reprinted in this volume, pp. 45-55.] A similar concept under the title "intransitive attention" was subsequently developed by Eliseo Vivas in *Problems of Aesthetics*, pp. 406-411.

[6] See John Hospers, *Meaning and Truth in the Arts* (University of North Carolina Press, 1947), p. 163.

is true to life" does not mean that his sentences are the truth about real life in real Barchester, because there is no real Barchester. It means, rather, that what he says fictively about Barchester coheres with the truth about life which he knew as the background of his creation and which we know as the apperceptive mass enabling us to understand his creation. The life *to* which he was true is not the life which he is talking *about*, for he is talking about Barchester which, unlike the cathedral towns he and you and I know, never existed. But it is only because we know something about real cathedral towns that we can easily move back and forth between those to which he was true and the one which he created.

The interpretation of life and that of literature differ in one important respect, however much they overlap in other respects. Even if the life discovered in literature is brutely factual, tediously repetitious, and is dispersively disorganized, it can be and by successful literature is changed, made lucid and redeemed. None of the tedium and fortuitousness and chaos of real life is changed, made lucid, or redeemed by fine talk in real life. Literature, while still true to what we know about this life, can effect this organization, elucidation, and redemption by creating an image of another life.

II. Philosophy in Literature

The literary artist creates, but he does not create out of nothing. What he knows of human nature and history and of what people have felt and thought are the materials he uses in building another world. Only because of this can that new world delineate and illuminate the features of the old world. "We can learn from texts," writes Peter Jones, "by using them for the construction of propositions applicable to the world we live in."[7] It is for this reason that Aristotle said tragedy is more philosophical than history.

Perhaps the most important facts about the world which are transmuted into literature are human beliefs. High literature contains ideas and beliefs and doubts which have traditionally been the subject matter of philosophy: fate and freedom, nature and convention, truth and illusion, man and God, the one and the many, what is and what

---

[7] *Philosophy in the Novel* (Oxford, 1975), p. 194.

ought to be, vice and virtue, happiness and misery. High literature almost always deals with such ideas, and where it does not do so explicitly, it nevertheless shows that it has been shaped by them. Students of literature are ignorant of philosophy at their own peril, even when not dealing with what they themselves call "philosophical literature."

There is a spectrum of philosophical literature, stretching from what I shall call "philosophical quotation" to "philosophical exhibition." These are pure types, but most philosophical literature lies somewhere in between.

By philosophical quotation I mean the explicit and didactic use of philosophical ideas, the author's own or more often those he has learned from others. The two best known examples of this occur in *De rerum natura* and *The Essay on Man*. Lucretius is disarmingly frank about the quotations in his poem. The ideas come from Epicurus, and he compares his verse to the honey which Roman mothers would rub on the lip of a vessel from which the child was to drink a noxious-tasting medicine:

> "...by such method haply I might hold
> The mind of thee upon these lines of ours."[8]

Were this a just description of his poem, it would not be great poetry but metrical philosophy, and the metre would be meretricious decoration. The genius of Lucretius consists in the way he rendered into genuine poetry a system of philosophy to which the sensuous charm of verse would seem to be most impervious.

Pope's *Essay on Man* came under close philosophical scrutiny in 1751 when the Berlin Academy offered a prize for the best essay on "Pope's System, comprised in the sentence, 'Whatever is, is right'."[9] Lessing and Mendelssohn did not compete for the prize, but wrote a polemic against both Pope and the Academy under the title *Pope a Metaphysician*. They attacked the academicians' thought that Pope had a system or, as a poet, could have one.

---

[8] *Lucretius* I, lines 960-961.
[9] The Academy misquoted: "Whatever is, is good."

The philosopher who climbs Parnassus and the poet who descends to the plain and gives out quiet wisdom meet each other half way; they meet, exchange costume, and return to where they started. Each brings the other's appearance with him, but nothing more. The poet has become a philosophical poet, and the philosopher a poetical philosopher. But the philosophical poet isn't for that reason a philosopher, and a poetical philosopher isn't a poet.[10]

The reason why the poet cannot be a philosopher and the philosopher a poet lies in the style and function of philosophy and poetry. A philosopher has to prove, and each of the twenty-one steps in his proof is equally important, no matter how tedious it may be. The poet, a light and winged creature, will not get entangled in proofs. So what does he do with what he has learned from the philosopher? He quotes, approximately. He quotes Epicurus in favor of pleasure and Epictetus in praise of virtue, but he cannot make a system out of these antithetical quotations—only a poem. Lessing and Mendelssohn make sport looking for these inconsistent quotations which Pope had strung together from Leibniz, Plato, Shaftesbury, Spinoza, and King's *De origine mali.*

It was to such "philosophical poetry," I think, that George Boas was referring when he said, "The ideas of poetry are usually stale and often false, and no one older than sixteen would find it worth his while to read poetry merely for what it says."[11]

But what about the great philosophical poets who did not just quote—Dante, Milton, Goethe, Wordsworth, Hardy? Their mode of poetically philosophising is not quoting, but exhibiting.[12] They embody philosophical stances in situations and character so that the reader can see philosophical models instead of having to think about abstract philosophical concepts. Theirs is a logic of images, not of concepts. The eighteenth century is full of such philosophical

---

[10] *Lessings Werke* (Petersen u.v. Olshausen, eds.), vol. 24, p. 100.

[11] *Philosophy and Poetry* (Norton, Mass., 1932), p. 9.

[12] Corresponding to Wittgenstein's distinction between saying and showing, *Tractatus* 4.022; and to Eliot's ideas "as matter for argument" and "as matter for inspection" (*The Sacred Wood* [1928], p. 162). But the distinction is an older one. Philip Sidney wrote, "Whatsoever the Philosopher sayth shoulde be doone, hee [the poet] giveth a perfect picture of it in someone, by whom he supposeth it was doone" (*Apologie*).

exhibition: I mention only *Candide* and *Rameau's Nephew*. In *The Magic Mountain* there is the conflict between Settembrini and Naphta, who incarnate opposing philosophies; the reader *sees* the price that must be paid for embracing either. In *Middlemarch*, in Peter Jones' interpretation,[13] we see a conflict between two forms of egoism which are consequences of different functionings of the imagination, each with its history in philosophy, but each here embodied in single characters in opposition to others. One of the most abstruse philosophical problems is that of personal identity. Locke, Hume, and Kant tried to solve it conceptually, but Conrad takes the problem out of the study and exhibits alternative trials at its solution in Lord Jim's attempts to come to terms with his fatal mistake.[14]

My favorite philosophical exhibition is the scene in *Huckleberry Finn* where Huck decides not to turn Jim in. He believes he is sinning, and that he will be damned, yet at the same time he knows he is doing the right thing. The philosophical ideas here are the same as in Plato's *Euthyphro*, yet Mark Twain exhibits the conflict in a man we admire whereas Plato recounts it in an explicit conceptual argument between Socrates and a prig. The same ideas are presented once in the mode of what De Quincy called the literature of power, and once in the mode of the literature of knowledge.

III. Philosophy as Literature

In saying that literature exists in the mode of semantic arrest, I may have rendered it impossible to regard philosophy as literature. At least it appears to degrade the claim that philosophy is literature to two trivialities. These are: (a) that there are, in many philosophical writings, passages that merit the approbative adjective "literary"; (b) that there are a few whole books of philosophy that can be read with literary delight. I shall comment upon each.

(a) Just as there are philosophical quotations in literature, there are literary interludes in philosophical works. These interludes may occur in the most unexpected places; there are several even in that book aptly

---

[13] *Op. cit.*, ch. i.

[14] See Bruce Johnson, *Conrad's Metaphors of the Mind* (Minneapolis, 1971), pp. 6, 91.

called "a literary wasteland," the *Critique of Pure Reason*.[15] There are one or two in Spinoza, many in Descartes, Berkeley, and Hume, one even in Hegel. In general, however, modern philosophy has characteristically eschewed literary decoration in favor of "the plain, historical method" and imitated the language which Thomas Sprat, in his *History of the Royal Society*, recommended as the language of science: "a close, naked, natural way of speaking." Contenting himself with being "an humble underlabourer" in the garden cultivated "by the incomparable Mr. Newton," Locke, who was a fellow of the Royal Society, was unlikely to affect a style which was passing out in science though still prevalent in philosophy (e.g., in Shaftesbury). He tried to put an end to the time when "Philosophy, which is nothing but the true Knowledge of Things, was thought unfit, or uncapable to be brought into well-bred Company, and polite Conversation."[16] With him, English philosophy set its course firmly in the direction of the literature of knowledge and away from the literature of power which, in De Quincy's words, "move[s]...through affections and pleasure and sympathy."

After an exuberant emancipation from scholastic restraint and the full exploitation of the stylistic elegance of the humanists, philosophy returned to a style close to that of scholasticism. (We should not allow difference in typography to hide resemblance of style.) It is a style of definition, analysis, and proof, a style which makes no apologies for being unedifying and often boring. The model for modern philosophy has been Locke and Hobbes, not Shaftesbury and Pascal. A few passages of poetry, a few of the more sensuous rhetorical tropes, may occasionally lighten the burden of heavy and dry impersonal philosophical work; but they do not convert philosophy into literature.

(b) Yet the stylistic splendours of literature are sometimes evident in philosophical writings about ideas. There have been philosophers like Nietzsche writing philosophy as if they were writing literature of power to charm or coerce the reader into agreement. (Everyone remembers the quip about Henry and William James.) Everyone can take delight in Schopenhauer's misery and agony with as purely a literary attitude as one brings to *The Sorrows of Young Werther*. The eighteenth century

---

[15] David Tarbet, "The Fabric of Metaphor in the *Critique of Pure Reason*," *Journal of the History of Philosophy* VI (1968), pp. 357-370.

[16] *Essay Concerning the Human Understanding*, "Epistle to the Reader."

had great philosophical stylists who can be, and have been, poorly imitated since then: in Germany, Mendelssohn; in France, Diderot; in England, Berkeley and Hume. Russell at his best, which is not in his purplest passages, reminds us of these Enlightenment philosophers with his clarity, economy, and wit. Bergson and Santayana, on the other hand, are warnings to other philosophers not to write too well. Their lush style is as evocative as Swinburne, and the richness of their imagery exhibits philosophical ideas when the reader has a right to demand analysis and proof, an argument and not an aphorism.

Of course, there is nothing wrong with a philosopher's writing attractively and well; Brand Blanshard has written a book, *On Philosophical Style*, urging him to do so. But in exhibition which gives philosophy the power of literature lies a threat to philosophy which wants to be more than a commentary on and guide to life. Philosophy can pretend to be a guide to life only because it professes to tell the truth about the most pervasive features of reality and our knowledge of it. Therefore no philosopher wants his book to be read under the conditions of semantic arrest. He may want his message to be persuasive and use his skill to make it so; but to the extent that he depends upon his rhetorical skill at persuasion, his persuasiveness will distract from the philosophical work of testing what he says. Kant complained about Rousseau for this very thing; he said he must read Rousseau "until the beauty of his expression no longer distracts me at all, and only then can I survey him with reason."[17] A too obvious artistry produces semantic arrest in a book which the author wanted to be semantically transparent; when this happens, the philosophical reader will dismiss it contemptuously as "mere literature."

But I think we know enough about philosophy, and enough about "about," not to believe that philosophy is about all time and all existence in the same way that *The Origin of Species* is about all plants and animals. Semantic arrest exists also in philosophy, though it is not usually engendered by the charm of the medium. There is a deeper reason why philosophy is not simply reportorial. Modern philosophy begins with Descartes' *cogito, ergo sum*. Descartes erected a system of truths about the world which derived their inferential certainty from the intuitive certainty he had of himself as thinker. The primary task of reporting on the world, without constant reminder that our knowledge

---

[17] *Fragmente aus dem Nachlasse* (Hartenstein ed.), p. 315.

of it depends as much on ourselves as on the world, has been taken over by the scientist little troubled by epistemological scruples. Almost all modern philosophy is predicated on the Cartesian thesis of the priority of the cognitive consciousness.

This much Cartesianism underlies Kant's Copernican Revolution in philosophy. Kant taught that the world which can be known is constituted by laws whose original legislation lay not with God or nature but with the knower. The world, even the world of science and mathematics as well as that of history and ethics, is a human world. It may not be a part of, or even a reflection of, things as they are. It is created by constructive operations of the mind. For Kant, the human world is necessarily as it appears to be—Euclidean and Newtonian— because that is the only way the mind can "spell appearances in order that they may be read as experience" of objects.[18] The transcendental imagination constructs the world, but the Kantian transcendental imagination is rigorously controlled by the rules of understanding.

But the imagination did not long remain in this subordinate position, and Kant's construction of a unique universal human world was pluralized by the romanticists, led by Herder and Coleridge. This pluralization was later made more radical by Nietzsche, Dilthey, and Cassirer. More recently, Pepper and Turbayne[19] have explored the ways in which the choice of metaphors within a single language gives shape to entire systems of philosophy. But Kant based his metaphor of spelling and reading on the eighteenth-century theory of universal grammar. When this doctrine was rejected by his disciple von Humboldt, who saw irreducible differences in the tongues of men and saw each language as in part reflecting and in part determining a form of life, these philosophers interpreted the variety of readings that philosophers had made of the world as the product of creative acts of the imagination determined by the varieties of temperament, language, and culture. They saw the thinking and speaking of the philosopher as one act of creativity comparable to that of artists. Nietzsche says: "Gradually it has become clear to me what every great philosophy has

---

[18] *Critique of Pure Reason*, B 371.

[19] *World Hypothesis* (University of California Press, 1942), *The Myth of Metaphor* (Yale University Press, 1962).

been: namely, the personal confession of its author, and a kind of involuntary and unconscious memoir."[20]

One effect of this has been the increasing attention that philosophers have given to communication and expression. How could philosophy fail to be exceedingly "linguistic" in our century? Why indeed should it try not to be, when the understanding of the linguistic process is as central a concern to our century as discovering the laws of motion was to the seventeenth? Philosophy, says Whitehead, is an attitude of mind towards doctrines ignorantly entertained, a critique of the abstractions current in one's culture.[21] Language is the abstraction dominant in our culture today. Language and communication theory have supplied models and metaphors which are pervasive in almost all modern thought from genetics to theology. Linguistic philosophy is an effort to become self-conscious and critical about them. Linguistic philosophy is reflexive meta-philosophy, and philosophy and its expression have become problematic.

"The limits of my language," says Wittgenstein,[22] "are [*bedeuten*] the limits of my world." But notice: this is parallel to what I have been saying about literature, that its meaning and value are not located in antecedent and independent fact about which it reports, but that it hedges its value and meaning in itself through semantic arrest. The limits of the world of Barchester are the limits of Trollope's language. Philosophy is as much a "language-game" as a mathematical system, a crossword puzzle, a novel or poem is. Whitehead said, "In the real world it is more important that a proposition be interesting than that it be true,"[23] and Archibald MacLeish wrote:

A poem should be equal to:
Not true
• • •
A poem should not mean
But be[24]

---

[20] *Beyond Good and Evil*, §6.

[21] *Modes of Thought* (New York, 1938), p. 233.

[22] *Tractatus* 5.6.

[23] *Process and Reality*, pp. 395-396

[24] "Ars Poetica," in *MacLeish's Poems, 1924-1933* (Houghton-Mifflin, 1933), pp. 122-123.

To see Philosophy in this light is offensive to those who adhere to the ideal of perennial philosophy, to those who believe that philosophical truth is like scientific truth and not at all like the values of literature. Most philosophers can bring themselves to see philosophies they think are wrong in this way, but not their own. Philosophy may be read as literature; but it is not written that way.

Not only philosophy is seen to be human-all-too-human; even the truth of science has lost some of its inhuman luster. We see science not as a photographic report on nature, but as an image refracted through human temperament standardized by human institutions. The paradigms and metaphors of science[25] are not exclusively reportorial about nature, but are imaginative models the construction of which is comparable to the act of the writer who converts a mere chronicle into a history or vague feelings into a lyric. In both science and philosophy we discern operations of the mind which have previously been regarded as operative only in the creation of art and literature.

***

My time is almost up, and I cannot go into detail about what follows from regarding philosophy as literature, e.g., about the canons for judging philosophy as literature. I will speak of only one problem, namely that of genre. What are the proper relations of substance to form in philosophical writing? I once jotted down fifty-three generic names of kinds of philosophical writings. They ranged from aphorisms and apologies at the beginning of the alphabet, through meditations and quodlibetal questions, to term papers and treatises at the end. Of each it may be asked: what relations obtain, or ought to obtain, between the content of a philosophy and its literary expression? Rather than discuss this vast question *in abstracto*, let me raise two specific questions which may be more easily answered and which may throw some light on the more general question.

---

[25] See Thomas Kuhn, *The Structure of Scientific Revolutions* (Chicago, 1962) and C. M. Turbayne, *op. cit.* Earlier, in discussing *The Origin of Species* I intentionally ignored this aspect of scientific theory-construction and writing, for I wished to use a common-sense foil to bring out the peculiar strength of the artistic imagination. I cannot here explore this feature.

(1) Why is Nietzsche's style aphoristic instead of systematic? It is not that Nietzsche could not sustain a long philosophical argument. It is, rather, that his perspectivism in epistemology makes him think that reality can be grasped better by a quick glance (in an apercu) than with the use of a deductive apparatus. The will to systematic thought, he wrote, is a symptom of lack of integrity.[26] And why did Hegel not write aphorisms? Because in the structure of his world all things are related essentially to all others, and truth is the whole.

(2) Second, why did Plato write dialogues? Did he have the same reasons that Boethius, Hume, and Fontenelle did? Why did Leibniz call his commentary on Locke *New Essays*, yet write them in dialogue form? Why did Berkeley write almost exactly the same philosophy twice, once in the *Treatise* and once in the *Three Dialogues*? Why is the philosophical outcome of Hume's *Dialogues* so obscure?

I cannot answer all these questions.[27] I shall conclude, however, with an attempt to answer the question about Plato. Was the dialogue form just a literary decoration, or was it inherently related to the world-view of which it was the vehicle? External reasons—the infamous litigiousness of the Athenian character, Plato's desire to celebrate Socrates—have been given; but these answers are superficial. There is a deeper philosophical reason which *required* the dialogue genre. Both Plato and Socrates believed that genuine knowledge is knowledge of the universal, of the form common to many things and the idea common to many minds. Dialogue is the method of eliminating the accidents and transiencies of private experiences of particular things. Dialogue leaves in the mind a common denominator of the diverse experiences of each participant. It is the outward dramatic form of dialectic, which Socrates defined as the discourse of the soul with itself.

In his old age there was a marked change in Plato's style. Though the *Timaeus* and the *Critias* are called dialogues, that seems hardly the right name. Timaeus speaks uninterruptedly for 64 pages, and Critias

---

[26] *Twilight of the Idols*, §26.

[27] But most of them have been answered by Albert William Levi in an article published since the completion of this paper: "Philosophy as Literature: The Dialogue," *Philosophy and Rhetoric* 9 (1976) 1-20. On Hume see John Bricke, "On the Interpretation of Hume's Dialogues," *Religious Studies* II, pp. 1-18.

is still going strong when, after 13 pages without interruption, the fragment breaks off. One thinks Plato might have done better to give up the conventional dialogue form present in the first few pages of each work. Do we still have the perfect matching of style and content, of expression and method, which was perfected in the dialogues of the early and middle periods?

Obviously not, if we take dialogue to be only the outward form of dialectic. But dialogue has other functions too. It can create an artificial voice for which the author does not have to take full public responsibility. A character in a dialogue (even when he talks without interruption for 64 pages) can say things which the author, or the protagonist with whom he is identified, does not dare say in *propria persona*. Though the philosophical substance of the *Timaeus* is not itself presented in dialogue, it is in a dialogic frame. In the short and graceful natural dialogue at the beginning, a stage is set for an "entertainment" (*Tim.* 17) in which legends, travelers' tales, and a man's recollection of his grandfather's stories are to be narrated. The speakers bid for forbearance and indulgence from the hearers; Critias appeals for help from the muse of memory (*Crit.* 108), as well he might. When Timaeus' main speech begins, he reminds the others that "I who am the speaker, and you who are the hearers, are only mortal men, and we ought to accept a tale (or myth) which is likely and enquire no further" (*Tim.* 29D). For Socrates, who had been skeptical of cosmology since reading Anaxagoras, the proper vehicle for cosmology is tale, fable, and myth. The dialogic medium under the rubric of "entertainment" provides insulation against his dialectical questioning, his trusted instrument in the search for truth which is above and beyond likelihood and "noble fiction."[28]

---

[28] I am indebted to Professor Colin M. Turbayne and Professor Russell Peck for advice especially on this last paragraph.

10. Kant on the Uniformity of Nature*

I

In the *Treatise of Human Nature*[1] Hume discusses two principles which underlie our causal inferences. The first is the principle of the universal validity of the causal connection. According to it, everything that begins to exist necessarily has a cause.

The second principle reads: every particular cause necessarily has a particular effect. This, however, is ambiguous. One can find in it two meanings which Hume himself did not clearly separate. First of all, if *this A* causes *this B* (e.g., if *this* lightning causes *this* thunder), then there stands between *this* case of *A* and *this* case of *B* a necessary relation, such that *this A* could not (*ceteris paribus*) have been followed by a case of non-*B*. But it would still be possible, *ceteris paribus*, that another case of lightning might not be followed by a case of thunder, despite the fact that *this* lightning was *vera causa* of *this* thunder. Though every causal relation which does obtain obtains necessarily, this principle does not exclude the possibility that every such connection is unique; there could be causality without causal law.

Second, this principle can also mean that like causes necessarily have like effects. For example, if lightning ever causes thunder, then, *ceteris paribus* lightning always causes thunder. This reading of the principle is that of the generalizability of each specific causal connection, and on it is based the possibility of discovering causal laws by induction.

---

* Reprinted with permission from *Synthese*, volume XLVII (1981), pp. 449-464.
[1] *Treatise of Human Nature* (Selby-Bigge, ed.), p. 78.

The truth-value of the last-formulated principle is independent of the truth or falsity of the two previous principles;[2] at least Hume claims to have established this principle purely inductively.   These three mutually independent principles—of the universal validity, the necessity, and the generalizability of the causal connection—are the presuppositions of the theory of the thoroughgoing causal determinism of nature.

In spite of the reciprocal logical independence of the principles, Hume saw deep-lying psychological connections among them. According to Hume the empirical data which support the third are sufficient to explain also the human belief in the necessity—perhaps also the belief in the universal validity—of the causal connection.   In this argument Hume does not assume the truth of the second principle, that of necessity; here and there he denies this principle. It suffices him to show why the principle of the necessity of the connection is unavoidably believed by us men.   He is of the opinion that this principle does not express a necessity *in re*, but only a psychological disposition of belief, which can have originated only out of the association of ideas of repeated pairs of impressions. The repetition of several pairs of similar things or impressions, which constitutes the observation ground for the generalizability, creates in us an expectation of the second thing (thunder) when the first (lightning) occurs.   The psychological ground of this expectation is misinterpreted as an objective causal ground *in re*.[3]   One adjoins the principle of necessity to that of generalizability in order to give some foundation to the latter, that is, in order to posit a reason why future occurrences will be connected just as past occurrences were. But this is in vain, for the necessity is only a subjective one.

Occasionally Hume also opines that an answer to the question of the origin of our assent to the generalizability principle serves also to explain the origin of our belief in the principle of universal validity, i.e., of the unexceptionable scope of causal connections. Consequently

---

[2] More exactly: The truth of the third does not depend upon the truth of the second provided that cases falling only under the second are not regarded as exceptions to laws. The second could be true even though there were no laws.

[3] *Treatise of Human Nature*, pp. 65, 84, 88.

he says that he will "sink"[4] the effort to ground the first principle in his investigation into the grounds of the generalizability principle. As a consequence of that, he never discusses the first principle at length; he makes only occasional remarks about it, which have almost universally been neglected or misunderstood. But one can easily imagine how he could most simply have explained the origin of our assent to the first principle; and it is quite easily understood, and pardonable, that Kant, who was not able to read the *Treatise*, should have been led to believe (presumably by Beattie) that Hume had in fact offered such an explanation.

Kant interprets Hume as if one observed many things in what are regarded as causal relations and from them made the inductive inference that all things are pair-wise related to others. But this argument is not to be found in Hume. Instead of this simple inductive explanation, Hume—unknown to Kant—sketched a kind of answer which is astonishingly like Kant's own.[5] Hume saw in the human demand for coherence in experience the roots of a fictive, not an inductive, belief in the unexceptionability of the causal relation in general. Correspondingly, he explained that we expect unobserved connections to resemble observed connections, especially in the case (e.g., of the butler's bringing the letter[6]) where strictly inductive inferences from accidentally observed facts would be misleading. In ignorance of this anticipation of his own explanation and justification of the unexceptionability of causal relations, Kant wrote: "Hume falsely inferred from the contingency of our determination in accordance with the law the contingency of the law itself" (A 766/B 794).

Kant had already long conceded to Hume that every specific causal connection is to be discovered only empirically, and that no logical necessity or intuitive status is to be ascribed to it. He can have learned this from Hume's *Inquiry* (though more likely he learned it from Crusius), and even in 1763 he wrote: "Rain does not follow wind

---

[4] *Ibid.*, p. 82.

[5] I have undertaken to show this in "Prussian Hume and a Scottish Kant," *Essays on Kant and Hume* (Yale University Press, 1978), pp. 121-124.

[6] *Treatise of Human Nature*, p. 196.

because of the law of identity."[7] Only much later did he discover, presumably through Beattie, that Hume had questioned the causal principle itself; and in this questioning, Kant could no longer follow him. The Second Analogy of Experience attacked Hume's view (at least Kant's conception or misconception of that view) concerning the principles of the universal validity and the necessity of causality. Even so, the Humean scope of the generalizability principle (i.e., of the generalizability of any specific causal connection) remained unaffected; but its logical status was changed. According to Hume, the generalizability principle is an induction out of naive and raw experience, independent of the other principles. According to Kant, on the contrary, the generalizability principle epistemologically presupposes the other principles.[8]

It appears, Kant wrote, that this

> contradicts all that has hitherto been taught in regard to the procedure of our understanding ... [to wit] that only through the perception and comparison of events repeatedly following in a uniform (*übereinstimmend*) manner upon preceding appearances are we enabled to discover a rule according to which certain events always follow upon certain appearances, and that this is the way in which we are first led to construct for ourselves the concept of cause (A 195-6/B 240-1).

On the contrary, Kant says, in order to perceive events as objective changes in the world (and not to observe mere changes in our consciousness), it is necessary that we first "place" (*legen*) causal relations between events in experience to enable us to have knowledge of objective spatial changes, among pairs of which we may later discover specific causal connections and, by induction, specific causal laws.

This is Kant's answer to Hume. Most succinctly: (1) Kant concedes to Hume that repeating pairs of resembling events are to be found in experience, and that we inductively infer from them that similar pairs will be found in the future because they are probably connected causally. Kant and Hume agree that we cannot know without

---

[7] *Versuch den Begriff negativer Grössen in die Weltweisheit einzuführen*, Akademie ed. II, p. 203.

[8] "Once more unto the breach," *Essays on Kant and Hume*, pp. 130-135.

experience what specific objective events are connected with specific other objective events.

(2) By the ship-house example, Kant explains that we are able to interpret some subjective sequences of representations as revealing objective changes, and to distinguish them from other subjective sequences of representations in which no reference to objective changes is to be found. Naturally Hume, like any other normal man, had been drawing this distinction without any need of philosophical instruction. Here is the common premise for Kant and Hume.

(3) But Kant attempts to show that this difference is not presuppositionless. It cannot be drawn without presupposing that objective changes are causally related. This is the main burden of the Second Analogy.

(4) In order to carry through the Humean program for the empirical establishment of particular causal laws, therefore, one must already accept the Second Analogy. This is Kant's answer to Hume: it contains no *petitio principii*, because it takes its origin from a Humean premise that we know objective changes.[9] According to Kant's argument, Hume assumed implicitly and unknowingly the principle of the unexceptionable validity of the causal connection *before* he could draw the inductive inference that like causes have like effects.

This polemic against Hume appears to me to be valid, and in my opinion refutes the theory of the derivation of the belief in the principle of universal validity which Kant, and almost everyone since, have erroneously ascribed to Hume. But it leaves open the question whether Kant himself has established the principles of the universality and necessity of the causal connection, or has only scored a debating point against Hume. Kant showed that Hume had had to assume implicitly the principle of universality; but how does it stand with the premise itself that like pairs of events repeat themselves, without which premise inductive inferences to empirical laws could not get started? In order to give a transcendental proof of the causal principle in its entire scope,

---

[9] Here I must take exception to the position of Peter Rohs (*Transzendentale Logik*, pp. 253-254). He rejects the "fact of experience" as a valid premise "if by experience we understand *gesetzmässige* experience." In my interpretation of the argument the common premise for both Kant and Hume is the fact of an objective sequence of states of an object. From this fact Kant, but not Hume, derives their causal dependency.

it would not be sufficient merely to take over from Hume this observation of repetition of like pairs; it would have to be deduced or justified.

It is possible that Kant believed that, in the Second Analogy, he had proved not only the universality and necessity of the causal connection, but also its generalizability. Kant's usual word for the uniformity of natural events is "regularity" (*Regelmässigkeit*). There is an ambiguity in the word "rule" (*Regel*) to which Kant appears not always to have attended. In the first edition, the Second Analogy reads: "Everything which happens (comes to be) presupposes something which it follows according to a rule (*nach einer Regel*)"(A 189). Here the word "rule" refers to the necessity (and, per corollary, the universality in the sense of unexceptionability) of the causal connection. We use the word "rule" in this sense when we say, for example. "The integers of π follow one another according to a rule," and it is only for this reason that the calculation of π always leads to the same string of numbers. In the *Prolegomena* Kant says: "a rule permits us to represent a series of ideas as necessary."[10]

But "as a rule" and "regularly" (*regelmässig)* can also refer to "the usual thing," as in the sentences "As a rule he arrives early," or "He regularly arrives early."[11] In this sense, the "regular" means the maximally-usual, whether it be necessary or brought about by adherence to a rule, or not. In accordance with this usage, Kant writes: "Rules can have merely general validity"[12] (*Gemeingultigkeit*, not *Allgemeingultigkeit*). But Kant appears to have sometimes confused

---

[10] *Prolegomena* §23 (Akademie ed. IV, p. 305).

[11] The difference between the two meanings of regularity is somewhat like that between the two meanings of lawfulness in Kant's moral philosophy, namely that between moral and legal lawfulness. See *Kritik der praktischen Vernunft*, Akademie ed. V, p. 71. It is perhaps well here to elaborate on the different meanings of "regularity." Because the etymology of this word and that of "rule" do not obviously overlap, "regularity" in English usually has only the second of the meanings which *Regelmässigkeit* has in German. Since *Regelmässigkeit* is derived from *Regel* (= rule), it may have the two meanings indicated, viz., that something happens as a rule (= generally) and that something happens *because of a rule*. To keep these meanings distinct I have sometimes used such expressions as "uniformity" and "generalizability" where the German would be *Regelmässigkeit*.

[12] *Reflexion* 5226.

these two meanings: for example, he says, "Every rule requires a uniformity (*Gleichformigkeit*) of effects, which grounds the concept of cause" (A 549/B 577; also A 536/B 564). But there are more places which show that the rule mentioned in the formula of the Second Analogy in the A Edition is that of the rule-governed necessity that pairs of events be causally related, and not that of the uniformity of effects of like causes.

Consequently, it is often objected[13] that the Second Analogy says nothing towards the justification of the principle of like causes having like effects. Certainly it must be admitted that in the text of the Analogy no proof of the existence of causal laws can be found; Lauener has clearly shown this.[14] But implicitly there is in it the hint of such a proof. This is argued by a student of mine, Jeffrey R. Dodge, in a paper entitled "Uniformity of Empirical Cause-Effect Relations in the Second Analogy," which will soon appear in *Kant-Studien*. According to Dodge, if the regularity (in the second sense, viz., generalizability, uniformity) of the causal connection is not assumed, Kant would not be able to distinguish between merely preceding events and causally determining events; and then Schopenhauer would have been right when he objected that, according to Kant, "We can perceive no sequence in time as objective with the exception of the cause-effect sequence."[15] In order to avoid this common objection, Kant ought to

---

[13] For example, by A.O. Lovejoy, "On Kant's reply to Hume," reprinted in M.S. Gram's *Kant: Disputed Questions*, pp. 300-302. Even more sweepingly, Peter Sachta has objected that "in the framework of the Kantian system it cannot be seen why appearances of the same kind, which are considered by the understanding to be causes, must always be coupled with the same appearances as effects" (*Die Theorie der Kausalität in Kants Kritik der reinen Vernunft*, p. 139). But other, more sympathetic, commentators concede that the Second Analogy does not support inductive generality (see, for example, Wrynn Smith, "Kant and the general law of causality," *Philosophical Studies* XXXII (1977), pp. 113-128; and Gerd Buchdal, "Causality, causal laws, and scientific theory in the philosophy of Kant," *British Journal for the Philosophy of Science* XVI (1965), pp. 187-208); but they reject the assumption that it was the business of the Second Analogy to do this, and find the establishment of this aspect of causality elsewhere in the Kantian corpus (as I myself do).

[14] Henri Lauener, *Hume und Kant*, pp. 117-119.

[15] *Über die vierfache Wurzel des Satzes vom zureichenden Grunde*, §23.

have argued as follows. After he had drawn the distinction between objective and subjective sequences of appearances, he ought to have drawn, within the objective sequences, still another distinction, namely:

(a) A pair of objective events which are (because objective) in some manner causally determined (as both the house and the ship are causally determined), but the causes of which are not themselves directly observed. (For example, in the case of the causally determined motion of the ship, which can move either up or down the river, the movement in either of these directions is causally determined, but the observed position up-river is not the cause of the subsequently observed position down-river, because the ship, moved by unobserved causes, can also at another time move up-stream.)

(b) A pair of objective events of which the first is regarded as the cause of the second, both of which (respectively cause and effect) are observed.

In order to refute Schopenhauer's objection, we must justify the distinction between cases *(a)* and *(b)*. It depends obviously upon the uniformity of the pair described in *(b)*, which we call the cause-effect pair. In this it is contrasted with the non-uniform (irregular) sequence of the events in pair *(a)*, which, because they are objective, are in some manner causally determined, but are not causally connected *with each other*. Only the *(b)* pair is regarded as a cause-effect pair, and that means that regularity (uniformity, generalizability) is a necessary condition for the recognition of the causal connection in the Second Analogy itself. Hence according to the Copernican Revolution, we have a right to say that objective causal connections are not only necessary and omnipresent, but are regular (uniform, generalisable).

If Kant had attempted to justify this distinction (which he implicitly makes), in Dodge's opinion he would have given a transcendental deduction of the generalizability principle and not merely of the principle of necessity and universality. I cannot here go into Dodge's paper in more detail, but I mention the fact that Dodge does not claim that Kant himself followed this line of thought. Consequently at the end of the Second Analogy the question still remains open for him whether the principle of the uniformity of causal connections holds *a priori* or not. Without this, however, the schema is lacking for the category of causality, and the category is lacking *Sinn und Bedeutung* (B 155).

II

Kant was aware of this problem. He sets it forth in §13: "Appearances could very well be so constituted, that the understanding could not find them to be in accordance with the conditions of its unity; and everything might lie in such confusion that, for example, in the series of appearances nothing should present itself which might yield a rule of synthesis and thus correspond to the concept of cause and effect, so that this concept would be wholly empty, nugatory and meaningless" (A 90/B 123). The Deduction of the Categories and the section on the Principles have as their goal the refutation of this possibility. But it is questionable whether they succeed.

Unfortunately it is not sufficient, as many commentators think, to regard the whole movement of the "Transcendental Analytic" as the solution to this problem. Looking upon the Analytic as a solution might give the following brief argument: in order to be able to determine my existence in time, I must possess consciousness of objects outside me (B275): I can have such consciousness only if I can draw a distinction between the sequence of my representations and the sequence of objective states of affairs (A 191/B 236); I can do this only by presupposing the Second Analogy of Experience. But, as we have seen, the Second Analogy does not give a proof of the regularity (= generalizability, uniformity) of specific causal connections.

Kant's efforts at arguments more directly pointing to the uniformity of nature are to be found in his two accounts of the concept of affinity.

(1) The Theory of Affinity in the A Deduction

Man has the capacity to reproduce his representations in ways described by empirical psychological laws of association. If representation *A* frequently occurs along with representation *B*, an occurrence of *A* causes a transition of consciousness to representation *B*. Such association in the manifold of representations is a precondition of the unity of self-consciousness. This unity requires the regular (*regelmässige*) reproduction of representations, in the absence of which reproduction the representations would belong to no experience and would be only a "blind play, less even than a dream" (A112). But this capacity, without which we would have neither the perception of any object nor a unitary consciousness, would lie in us "dead and unknown" if A and B did not in fact so often occur together that the imagination was empowered to associate A with B instead of with C, D, etc. The representation A must in every case, or at least very often, have occurred together with B, since our imagination is in actual fact led to associate A with B. There must be a ground for A's and B's occurring together, and it must lie in the object of the associated perceptions A and B. "This objective ground of all association of appearances I call the affinity of the appearances" (A122; cf. *Anthropologie*, §31C).

If the object were a thing in itself, Kant's theory of affinity would be a gross dogmatism, almost a theory of pre-established harmony between things in themselves and our cognitive syntheses. In a subtle philosophical joke Hume suggests this,[16] but Kant could not do so without surrendering his entire philosophy. The object of which Kant is here speaking is a complex of appearances, the formal affinity of which is the product of synthetic activities of the knowing consciousness. In a piece of cinnobar there is an affinity of empirical properties, which are consequences of force (*Kraft*) as the "causality of a substance" (A 648/B 676).[17] This empirical affinity is, according to Kant, a consequence of the transcendental affinity of the *object in general* (A114). Therefore the world of appearances must consist of constant things (like cinnobar) and uniform sequences of its properties as changes of a substance.

This line of thought, however, does not lead to the goal. For, as Allison[18] has shown, there is a fatal ambiguity in the concept of "appearance." First, it means "object," i.e., an empirically perceived thing in space outside me, for example, cinnobar; and the required affinity must lie in this object and its empirical properties such as red color, heavy weight, and so forth. But "appearance" also means "representation," and the transcendentally necessary affinity of appearances in this sense is only the formal unity of their apperception. Regardless of the specific empirical characters evinced, *all*

[16] *Enquiry Concerning Human Understanding* (Selby-Bigge, ed.), p. 54.

[17] See Karen Gloy, *Die Kantische Theorie der Naturwissenschaft*, p. 60.

[18] Henry E. Allison, "Transcendental affinity, Kant's answer to Hume," *Proceedings of the Third International Kant Congress*, 1970, pp. 203-211.

representations in one consciousness have this kind of affinity. The empirical affinity of the *a posteriori* properties cannot, therefore, be a mere consequence of the transcendental affinity of their representations. Kant's argument could, at most, prove that if there is such an object as cinnobar, its empirical characteristics are necessarily to be found together—but this is an analytical judgment. One cannot by such an argument prove that empirically observed red color and heavy weight are so bound together by affinity that they are necessarily to be found together.

Hence in spite of the theory of affinity in the first edition, it would be possible for the world to be regulated by the categories and analogies without presenting empirically constant *Gestalten* of qualities and repetitions of empirically resembling pairs of states of affairs.[19] In order to guarantee these empirical regularities the *necessary* condition of which is transcendental affinity, one would have to add another condition. Perhaps it would be that of a noumenal regularity. Kant does not, of course, avail himself of this in the first *Critique*;[20] perhaps we can see here a reason why there is no mention of affinity in the Deduction in the second edition.

(2) Affinity in the Methodology and First Introduction to the Critique Of Judgment.

In the Methodology of the first *Critique* Kant discusses the idea of a system of empirical concepts; with only slight change, this can be extended to the idea of a system of empirical laws. Reason puts at the disposal of the understanding a law of the affinity of all empirical concepts (A 657/B 685) which Heimsoeth[21] describes as follows:

> this kind of affinity (*Sachverwandschaft*), which makes possible the classification of things, properties, forces, and lawful connections (*Gesetzlichkeiten*), can only be *thought* a priori; we

---

[19] Thus Paton in *Kant's Metaphysic of Experience*, I, p. 448.

[20] But A.C. Ewing ascribes to Kant himself "a dependence upon unknown noumenal conditions" in *Kant's Treatment of Causality*, p. 59, also p. 100n.

[21] Heinz Heimsoeth, *Transzendentale Dialektik*, p. 579.

can *know* this kind of relation only by meeting with corresponding facts from time to time, by receiving answers to questions which we methodically put to nature.

Affinity of this sort stands as a regulative idea of the relation between specific *given* empirical concepts (or laws). For that reason, it has to presuppose that there are in fact empirical genera and regularities (A 650/B 678). Kant assumes them here[22] but that is precisely our question.

In the *First Introduction to the Critique of Judgment,* however, Kant widens the regulative idea of the affinity of genera and uniformities to include the idea of the affinity of specific perceptions under generic concepts and laws—something he had merely assumed in the Methodology. "...In groping about among natural forms, whose mutual agreement with common empirical but higher laws would be seen by our judgment as entirely fortuitous," he says,[23] "it would be still more fortuitous if particular perceptions [were] fortunately qualified to stand under empirical laws." The regulative idea of the technic of nature is what removes both contingencies.

Here Kant holds that the sought for regularity (uniformity) of the causal connection has another source, and a lower authority, than the unexceptionable universality of causality in general. The latter is a constitutive categorial condition of possible experience, and is independent of the empirical affinity of appearances. The former is a rule of reflective judgment and the expression of a regulative idea. It expresses a demand which we make on every empirical causal explanation, but not a condition which nature itself must fulfill.

Another interpretation of the situation is, however, possible; and there are a few signs that Kant was sympathetic to it. According to this reading, the distinction between constitutive and regulative principles, and accordingly that between determinant and reflective judgment, is

---

[22] Admittedly Kant in two places (A 654/B 682; more specifically, Akademie ed. III, p. 433, lines 22 and 28) mentions affinity as a condition for any single empirical concept, but does not develop the thought. He may have meant affinity in the sense of the A Deduction.

[23] *Erste Einleitung in die Kritik der Urtheilskraft,* Akademie ed. XX, 210; Lehmann ed., p. 17.

not to be drawn very sharply.[24] The principle of the Second Analogy (in one sense already called "regulative" at A 179/B 222) is interpreted as a maxim of judgment in *Critique of Judgment*, §70. According to the constitutive principle of the Second Analogy, all objects and occurrences of possible experience stand necessarily in causal relations. But according to the regulative maxim of the Second Analogy, one is to find these connections under the guidance of the schema of succession of the manifold *in so far as* it is subjected to a rule of uniformity and repeatability (A 144/B 183). But whether, or to what extent, one can find such connections—that is always in question. Assuming this interpretation, one finds in Kant the primordial form of the modern imperativistic conception of the concept of causality, as it has been developed in our own day especially by the Vienna School.[25]

III

Hume's second principle reads: every particular cause has necessarily a particular effect. If we emphasize "necessarily," this is an analytic judgment, because "causal condition" means a "necessitating condition." The question is not whether things in causal connection are necessarily connected, but whether there are in fact such connections. Hume pretended to doubt that, and explained the almost instinctive belief according to which a repeating connection is a necessary connection. Between things Hume found only repeating connections, not necessary connections; therefore he sequestered the imagined necessary connection in the human mind. In this, Kant says, he was right,[26] in so far as he regarded things as things in themselves.

But since for Kant things are appearances, it was not necessary for him to separate ontologically the causal connections and the things

---

[24] See Frederick P. Van De Pitte, "Is Kant's distinction between reflective and determinant judgment valid?," *Akten des IV. Internationalen Kant-Kongresses* (1974), pp. 445-451.

[25] Arthur Pap so interprets Kant (*The A Priori in Physical Theory*, pp. 39, 68); also Stephan Körner, *Kant*, pp. 103-104.

[26] *Kritik der praktischen Vernunft*, Akademie ed. V, p. 53; cf. Lauener, *op. cit.*, p. 119.

connected by them. On the contrary, the appearances (= objects) stand *a priori* under the causal conditions of their possible experience.

But the question arises again for Kant concerning the necessity of the temporal connections between two things which we *subsequently* discover to be cause and effect. For how can we know not merely that every thing stands in a necessary connection with something else, but that any thing *A* stands in a necessary connection to some specific *B* such that we can *empirically* discover that *A*'s cause *B*'s? Only experience can teach us that lightning is the cause of thunder, but experience teaches us only what happens, not what must necessarily happen. It is absurd to try to discover without experience any synthetic necessary connection; but it is equally absurd to try to confirm the necessity of connections through experiences.

We must, therefore, attempt to understand in what senses Kant regarded empirical regularities as necessary. He differentiates three levels of natural laws, each of which presents a specific degree of necessity. (1) The fundamental principles (*Grundsatze*) such as the Analogies of Experience, which Kant occasionally calls "universal laws of nature," are *a priori*, i.e., universal and necessary. Without them experience in the sense of empirical knowledge of objects is impossible. We may refer to this as formal, but not as logical, necessity.

(2) The natural laws which constitute "rational cosmology" (*rationale Weltlehre*) are known *a priori* and are thereby distinct from mere empirical laws.[27] They are the three Newtonian laws of mechanics.[28] These laws depend respectively upon the three Analogies plus a single empirical concept, that of the existence of movable matter. "One seeks the scope of knowledge which the reason is capable of having about these objects" of outer sense;[29] reason is capable of such knowledge to the extent that the intuition of the movement of objects is *a priori* constructable.

(3) The laws (more exactly: the rules) of experimental science (*Experimentallehre*) or of a systematic art (like chemistry) are empirical. Concerning them, Kant says: "Certainly empirical laws as

---

[27] *Metaphysische Anfangsgründe der Naturwissenschaft*, Akademie ed. V, p. 468.

[28] *Ibid.*, pp. 541-548; also p. 534.

[29] *Ibid.*, p. 470.

such can by no means take their origin from the pure understanding. ...But all empirical laws are only particular determinations of the pure laws of the understanding, under which and according to the norm of which they are at all possible" (A127-8; cf. also B 165). This does not mean, however, that we can have insight into the necessity of specific empirical laws of nature.

There are two kinds of necessity involved in empirical laws: first, formal necessity, the necessity that every explanation conform to the Analogies of Experience; and second, a material necessity, i.e., the necessity *in re* of specific empirically discovered but general connections which are regarded as causal. The first can stand without the second; the first kind obtains even when a statement of the second kind is false. It is in the formal sense of necessity that every judgment of experience is necessary (= universally valid) even though our knowledge of it is merely empirical and arises and remains *a posteriori* (A 104).[30]

We must here remember that not every regularity (*Regelmässigkeit*) is lawlike (*gesetzmässig*). Earlier I have distinguished between two meanings of regularity. Empirically, it means merely a constant sequence of changes or a constant coexistence of the properties of an object. Transcendentally, it means: necessary according to a rule. Occasionally Kant attempts to hold these two meanings terminologically separate, and when he does so he calls a rule exclusively the assertion of an empirically known repeating sequence of facts, and by law he means only a *necessary* rule.[31] Only under the assumption of the necessity of a rule do we use a rule as an explanation of a fact; in order to make explanatory use of a statement of empirical regularity, we read the modality of necessity into it, implicitly or explicitly. Without this addition of the concept of necessity, a merely enumerative generalization does not explain anything, for without the modality of necessity it cannot support a contrafactual subjunctive. For this reason Kant asserts that in spite of their empirical origin, natural laws carry with them "an expression of necessity, and hence at least the suggestion of a determination from grounds which are valid *a priori*

---

[30] *Prolegomena* §20, Akademie ed. V, p. 300. Gordon G. Brittan, Jr. makes the following analogy: judgment of experience: judgment of perception = empirical law: accidental generalization (*Kant's Theory of Science*, p. 183).

[31] A 113. Other documentation in Gloy, *op. cit.*, p. 19.

and prior to all experience" (A 159/B 298; see also *Critique of Judgment*, Akademie ed. V, p. 180).

A regularity which is not derivable from a transcendental principle has the value of a law only if we subsume it under the concept of necessity. It remains an empirical question whether in any specific case we are correct in doing so. But if the inductive generalization is carefully performed, "one always assumes that the rules of nature are necessary, for it is for this reason that there is nature and that the rules can be understood *a priori*; therefore one calls them laws, *anticipando*.[32] It is the idea of the coherence of the experience of nature as a system which leads us to think into the empirical uniformities of nature a necessitation by grounds unknown to us.

IV

In conclusion I summarize the results of this study.

(1) As an answer to the first of Hume's questions, Kant attempts to prove in the Second Analogy that every change in the states of a substance necessarily has a cause, and that we know this *a priori*.

(2) The Second Analogy does not show what is the cause of any particular change;

(3) Nor prove that like causes always have like effects. (But new and not yet published investigations by Dodge seem to show that the regularity of the causal connection can be proved as part of the Second Analogy.)

(4) By the letter of the text, however, Hume's third principle, that of regularity, remains in Kant a regulative principle.

(5) There are three levels of necessity in Kant's conception of the lawfulness of nature: *(a)* the transcendental necessity of the principles proved in the Analytic, including the Analogies of Experience; *(b)* the necessity of the principles of pure cosmology, which he thinks can be derived from transcendental principles and a priori constructable intuitions; *(c)* the regulative necessity of empirical regularities, which are subsequently to be brought under the idea of a system and unity of the several causal laws.

---

[32] *Reflexion* 5414. See also *Logik Vorlesungen* §84 (Akademie ed. IX, p. 133).

(6) In the third *Critique* Kant hints that the chasm between regulative and constitutive necessity of the causal principles can be bridged.

With the exception of the explicit argumentation of the Second Analogy, I do not find the differences between the Humean and the Kantian conceptions of the regularity of nature to be as great and as sharp as has generally been believed.

11. Five Concepts of Freedom in Kant[*]

In Kant's works I can distinguish at least five important conceptions of freedom. In part they overlap, some are inconsistent with others, and some presuppose others. Kant's nomenclature for them is variable, and for some of them he has no name at all. Three of them appear to me to be untenable, and the others which are more promising are hardly more than merely adumbrated by Kant. In *The Actor and the Spectator* I gave a fuller development of these latter conceptions, and though I briefly indicated their Kantian character I did not show their Kantian provenance. After briefly presenting the better-known Kantian conceptions of freedom, I shall devote the remainder of the paper to documenting, elaborating, and defending the fifth conception, and showing its relation to Stephan Körner's.

1. The Empirical Concept of Freedom

The first concept of freedom is empirical, since empirical considerations are decisive for the question whether a specific act was freely done. The kind of freedom involved is called by Kant the comparative, the psychological, and the practical.[1]

It is an empirical question whether, and to what extent, a specific person in a particular case acted freely. "Freely" here means voluntarily, not coerced. Aristotle[2] formulated criteria of freedom in this sense, and today there are specific juridical criteria of it. In deciding whether to impute responsibility to a lawbreaker, one raises

---

[*] Reprinted with permission from *Stephan Körner—Philosophical Analysis and Reconstruction* ed. J.T.J. Srzednick, pp. 35-51. Dordrecht: Martinus Nijhoff, 1987.

[1] *Critique of Pure Reason*, A 802/B 830; *Critique of Practical Reason*, Akademie ed., V, pp. 96-97.

[2] *Nicomachean Ethics*, Book III, ch.1.

181

empirical, not metaphysical, questions. We want to know, for instance, whether he was driven by an uncontrollable passion. When we decide that a particular person was free in doing a particular action, we say nothing about men in general and freedom in general. A man may be free today, but not free tomorrow. It is not this concept of freedom, but solely its moral sufficiency[3] which Kant later rejected. In the *Critique of Practical Reason* he calls it, as a foundation of morality, a "wretched subterfuge" (*elender Behelf*) which grounds only the "freedom of a turnspit."[4]

2. The Concept of Moral Freedom

It is the task of the *Critique of Practical Reason* to confirm freedom in the transcendental sense. But since I have not yet discussed this concept of freedom, I must say here in only a preliminary way: the concept of freedom in the second *Critique* is the concept of a freedom which cannot be empirically established and which is not, like the freedom Kant calls comparative, a peculiar kind of natural causality. The *Critique of Pure Reason* had proved, Kant thought, the possibility of transcendental freedom; in the second *Critique* he attempted to show its actuality. The freedom whose actuality is necessary for morality is transcendental freedom. But the ultimate identification of moral with transcendental freedom is not self-evident on the surface; in themselves they appear to be independent of each other. Only after I have developed the concept of moral freedom will I come to the concept of transcendental freedom in its own right and show the relationship between them.

The main steps in the proof of moral freedom are as follows. Granted the moral phenomenon, "the fact of reason"; i.e. assume that the ground of moral action is a pure law. If this law and the decision to act out of respect for it were links in an empirical temporal chain of natural causes, the moral phenomenon as described would be

---

[3] See *Critique of Pure Reason* A 803/B 831. On different interpretations of this passage, see my *Commentary on Kant's Critique of Practical Reason*, p.190, note 40.

[4] *Critique of Practical Reason*, pp. 96, 97.

impossible. But moral action as described is not impossible; therefore moral action cannot be an effect of natural causes.[5]

The moral law is the *ratio cognoscendi* of freedom, and freedom is the *ratio essendi* of moral responsibility.[6] A free will and an unconditionally commanding practical law presuppose each other.[7] The mere independence of the will from the incentives of sense and feeling is freedom in the negative sense, and it, like empirical freedom, is a precondition of freedom in the positive sense, namely the effectiveness of the legislation of pure practical reason and the ability to undertake actions in accordance with and because of (out of respect for) this law. Freedom in this positive sense is called *autonomy*.[8] The situation, however, is more complicated than it appears in the second *Critique*. In the *Metaphysic of Ethics* Kant distinguished between *Wille* and *Willkür*. *Wille* is pure practical reason which, through its autonomous legislation, creates moral duty in a being who does not by nature adhere to the law. It is by *Willkür* that an action in accordance with, or opposed to, this law is undertaken. If one continues the political metaphor of autonomy, one can say that *Wille* is the autonomous legislative function and *Willkür* exercises the executive function. The freedoms of the two are therefore conceptually different. Kant even says: "*Wille*, which is concerned with nothing else than law, can not be called either free or not free, because it is not concerned with actions but directly concerned only with legislation for maxims... Only *Willkür* can be called free."[9] And in the *Critique of Judgement* he says: "Where the moral law speaks, objectively there is no further free choice with respect to what is to be done."[10] Consequently one must distinguish as follows:

(a) The moral autonomy of *Wille*, i.e., its independent authorship of law independent of motives and impulses of the empirical, sensible world; and

---

[5] *Ibid*, Section 5.

[6] *Ibid*, p. 4, note.

[7] *Ibid*, Sections 5,6.

[8] *Ibid*, Section 8.

[9] *Metaphysics of Morals*, Akademie ed. VI, p. 226.

[10] *Critique of Judgment*, Section 5 Akademie ed. V, p. 210.

(b) The moral freedom of *Willkür*, i.e., its capacity of spontaneously obeying the law as its maxim and thereby inserting a new link in the causal chain of events in the sensible world.

Before Kant explicitly drew this distinction, autonomy and freedom and *Wille* and *Willkür* were almost interchangeable terms, and he spoke not only of the freedom of *Wille* but even of the autonomy of *Willkür*.[11] In spite of these confusions I will speak of moral freedom simpliciter when I refer to the concept of freedom which is analytically connected with the concept of the pure moral law.   It is the kind of freedom manifest in and only in genuine moral action—not even in merely legal, unmoral, or immoral actions.[12]

3. The Concept of Freedom as Spontaneity

"Freedom as Spontaneity" is not entirely suitable as a title for this conception, since Kant uses "spontaneity" with respect to both moral and transcendental freedom, and he does not give a specific title to the broader, nonmoral conception to be described in this section.   I can, however, think of no other title which might not be as misleading as this.

The argument for moral freedom has as [its] premise the consciousness of the moral law and, more specifically, the moral law in its specifically Kantian formulation.   A free action and an action done out of respect for the law are the same.   Here arises an aporia.   An unmoral (legal) or immoral action is not done because of the law (even if, as legal, it conforms to the law), but is done on account of subjective, individual, empirical impulses.   A nonmoral or an immoral act is to be entered to the credit of the mechanism of nature and is therefore not morally imputable.   But to do justice to the ethical phenomenon, one must have a concept of freedom which permits the imputation of unmoral and immoral actions.   The criteriological or analytical connection between freedom and morality (positive moral value) must be loosened.

Accordingly, in *Religion within the Limits of Reason Alone* Kant argued as follows.   Since imputable but immoral (evil) actions occur,

---

[11] *Critique of Practical Reason*, p. 36.

[12] *Ibid*, Section 8 end.

Willkür must choose its guiding maxims freely and not from the necessity of nature. The "act of *Willkür*" must have two functions:

(a) "the use of freedom whereby the highest maxim (be it in accordance with, or opposed to, the law) is taken up into *Willkür*"; and

(b) the use of freedom "such that the action itself... is exercised according to that (freely chosen) maxim."[13]

Even if the maxim is opposed to the law, the action done under it can be free and imputable. This kind of freedom, unnamed by Kant, is unlike empirical freedom, because it is inexplicable by natural causality; and it is unlike moral freedom, because it is not a *sufficient* condition of positive moral worth. In fact, Kant does not use this concept of freedom exclusively in his treatment of morality at all. He does not systematically discuss the concept in this, its broader use, but I find two passages which concern this broader use.

The first passage is the familiar one at the beginning of Part III of the *Foundations of the Metaphysics of Morals*, and its position in that work may suggest that Kant is thinking about freedom in a moral context. But the argument is not limited to the ethical alone:

> Now I say that every rational being which cannot act otherwise than under the idea of freedom is thereby really free in a practical respect... Now I affirm that we must necessarily grant that every rational being who has a will also has the idea of freedom and that it acts only under this idea... Now we cannot conceive of a reason which consciously responds to a bidding from the outside with respect to its judgments, for then the subject would attribute the determination of its power of judgment not to reason but to an impulse. Reason must regard itself as the author of its principles, independently of foreign influences.[14]

The remainder of the paragraph, in speaking of practical reason, does integrate this consideration with moral philosophy; but enough has been said already to indicate that, even in thinking, reason must regard itself as autonomous and not as mechanically responding to natural causes. This is the explicit theme of the following passage: The philosopher who denies freedom "has deeply in his soul, although he does not want to confess it, presupposed that the understanding has the

---

[13] *Religion Within the Limits of Reason Alone*, Akademie ed. VI, p. 31.

[14] *Foundations of the Metaphysics of Morals*, Akademie ed. IV, p. 448.

faculty of determining his judgment according to objective grounds which are always valid, and that it does not stand under the mechanism of merely subjective determining causes which can vary in their consequences."[15] In this confrontation with the denier of freedom, Kant does not begin with the moral consciousness (though in earlier parts of his review he has repeated the more usual moral argument), which might conceivably be explained away on psychological grounds. Rather, he begins with the phenomenon of decision in general. One could almost speak of autonomy in a non-moral sense. Against Schulz, who denied freedom, Kant continued: "He always assumed freedom to think, without which there is no reason"—and this includes theoretical reason and our whole cognitive capacity, for thinking is also a kind of deciding and acting. Everyone who decides presupposes that his decision was not causally determined in advance.

After I have reached a decision, someone can explain to me the causal grounds on which he had already in advance foreseen what my decision was going to be, for my character traits and the relevant psychological and physiological laws made my decision and action causally necessary. Indeed I myself can subsequently sometimes explain my own actions in the same way; I regularly do so when I excuse myself, for, as Sartre says, "Psychological determinism is an attitude of excuse."[16] I say that I was not responsible, for my behavior had causes which did not lie within my power, which were at the time unknown to and therefore uncontrollable by me, and which reduced my "decision" to an illusory experience (like a "decision" made as a consequence of hypnotic suggestion). *Post facto* I can be a fatalist about what I have done; but if I did not in the moment of choosing have this experience of free choice, the phenomenon of choice would not merely be illusory—it would not even exist as an illusion. I experience no choice or decision (that is, I do not choose or decide) without believing that my decision or choice will make a difference,

---

[15] *Recension zu Schulz's Sittenlehre*, Akademie ed. VIII, p. 14. Körner, *Proceedings of the British Academy* LIII (1967), p. 203, finds a like thought in Kant's *Reflexion* 4904.

[16] *Being and Nothingness* (New York, 1956), p. 40. Kant accepts no excuse (*Critique of Pure Reason, A* 555/B 583; *Critique of Practical Reason*, p. 98). A more indulgent attitude to human weakness and the strength of nature is found in the note to *Critique of Pure Reason, A* 551/B 579.

that is, without believing that the outcome is not already causally fixed. My experience of freedom of choice—that the choice is "up to me" and makes a difference in the outcome—is *schlichtgegeben* and has a self-evidence greater than any possible causal law which would entail its necessary illusoriness.

I am not asserting that this phenomenon is *in every case* self-certifying; we do have the counter-example of post-hypnotic "decisions."[17] The mere experience of decision does not prove the reality of freedom, for it is a genuine experience of decision only when the decision itself is really free. A madman believes he decides something (i.e., he has the experience of deciding) when in fact he doesn't possess even *empirical* freedom. Mephistopheles says: "You believe you push, but you are pushed." Genuinely deciding means, analytically, freely deciding; but the question is still open whether genuine decisions do take place. According to Kant moral freedom, and presumably the freedom which has been analyzed in the present section of this paper, would be impossible, in spite of their *Schlichtgegebenheit*, if there were no freedom in the transcendental sense.[18]

4. The Concept of Transcendental Freedom

The concept of freedom discussed in the foregoing section might be called the *transcendental concept* of freedom, a "transcendental concept" being Kant's name for one which underlies the possibility of *a priori* cognition; for without that concept of freedom, Kant tells us that reason (both theoretical and practical) would be impossible. The concept we are now about to discuss is the one Kant calls the *concept of transcendental freedom* meaning, I think, a transcendental concept of a peculiar kind of freedom which in all strictness might better be called *transcendent freedom* because it deals with a matter which transcends the limits of possible experience and the knowledge of

---

[17] *In The Actor and the Spectator* I have argued that it is self-confirming only in the case of assent to an argument concerning the causation or reasons for this assent.

[18] *Critique of Pure Reason*, A 534/B 562; *Critique of Practical Reason*, *passim*.

theoretical reason.   But the name "transcendental freedom" is too deeply entrenched in Kant's writings to make such a revision feasible.

In his own words, which in this instance are not highly accurate, the *Critique of Pure Reason* attempted to show not the actuality but only the possibility of freedom.[19]   If freedom and the causality of nature were contradictory, there could be no freedom (except in the empirical sense).[20]   It was the task of the first *Critique* to show that they did not contradict each other; it was reserved for the second *Critique* to show that the freedom shown possible in the first (transcendental freedom) is actual (moral freedom).   So much for the formalities of the argument; in fact some of the first *Critique* is concerned with the reality of freedom, and some of the second with its possibility.

Kant's theory of transcendental freedom is so well known that it can be recapitulated with great brevity.   On purely epistemological grounds Kant showed that nature is a unitary causal system in which each state or event has a sufficient condition in preceding and simultaneous states or events.   The thesis of the Third Antinomy proved that natural causality is not the only causality, and that there is also a non-temporal cause, i.e., that there is a causality of a free cause which is not causally determined by antecedent or contemporaneous events.   The proof of the thesis is hardly more than a repetition of the Aristotelian-Thomistic proof of the reality of a primordial cause of the world, which is not a consequent of any antecedent condition and therefore not causally determined.   This thesis is opposed to the antithesis, which proves the universal validity of natural causality and excludes free causation from the course of nature and also a first cause.

Kant believed that he proved both.   The solution of the problem arising from proofs of the truth of two propositions which contradict each other he found in his famous "two-world theory."   According to this, there is a phenomenal world, wherein each change is determined by an earlier one in space and time; and a noumenal world, which is not spatial and temporal, and of which the phenomenal world is only an appearance to minds constituted like ours.   Free causality within the noumenal world and between the noumenal and the phenomenal can be *thought* without contradiction, but only the temporal causality relating

---

[19] Only the logical possibility, not the real possibility or the actuality, is established, according to *Critique of Pure Reason*, A 558/B 586.

[20] *Critique of Pure Reason*, B xxix.

events and states in the phenomenal world can be *known*. There is no contradiction, because free causation and natural causation are predicated of ontologically different kinds of beings. Consequently the causality of a thing in itself in the noumenal world can be thought of as free, while its appearance in the phenomenal world can be known (in principle) without exception as causally necessitated. One and the same action is to be regarded as free, inasmuch as it arises in the reality of the noumenal world, and as causally necessitated, since it occurs in the complex of phenomena of the spatio-temporal world of appearances.

The thesis of the Third Antinomy is explicitly concerned only with the question as to whether there was a (free) creation of the world. In showing (to his own satisfaction) that the thesis can be true without conflicting with the "reign of law" in nature, Kant says that he has only shown the *possibility* of freedom, and has given a sufficient answer to those who would argue against freedom on the ground that it is impossible because inconsistent with the mechanism of nature. If a philosopher finds good grounds for asserting the freedom of human action, the fatalist can no longer object that freedom is impossible because it would overthrow natural causality. But (except hardly as *obiter dicta*) the first *Critique* does not argue for the reality of transcendental freedom.

The *Critique of Practical Reason* finds in morality good grounds for the assertion of transcendental freedom by showing that moral freedom presupposes it (or is identical with it). But this redemption of freedom from the universal mechanism of nature proves both too much and too little. Too much: for according to it every phenomenon has its transcendental ground or noumenal causation. A proof which shows that if anything is free then everything is free proves too much. One wants to show that only the empirical, moral, or spontaneously free action is transcendentally free, and not that just any event, a bodily reflex or an apple falling off a tree, is free.

The theory proves also too little. Kant himself concedes that according to it, I judgments "at first appear to conflict with all equity."[21] But is this only *prima facie*? Why should one rue an unjust deed, when the deed was unavoidable? How can one maintain that a man is responsible for his actions, and at the same time assert: "Every

---

[21] *Critique of Practical Reason*, p. 99.

one of the voluntary actions is determined in advance in the empirical character, before it ever occurred"?[22] May one assert that a man is free after one has declared that if we knew all the empirical facts and the natural laws of their connection, we would be able "to compute his behavior with certainty, as we do an eclipse of the sun or moon"?[23]

If transcendental freedom means noumenal causality, the ubiquity of noumenal causality trivializes the concept of freedom. Since the noumena and their causality are unknowable, there is no possibility, in research into human phenomena, to determine why in some individual cases we should be allowed to apply the concept of moral freedom and in other cases forbidden to do so. The uniformity of human actions — including moral actions—is in principle as great as that of the solar system, according to Kant's theory of nature. Granted this and the ubiquity of noumenal causation there is no reason why assertions of the freedom of our actions should have any consequences different from denials of that freedom. (There will be consequences either way, which seem to "conflict with equity." We assume the freedom of the noumenal man, but we hang the phenomenal man.) If the faculty of transcendental freedom has any meaning for the course of nature and history—i.e., if free men act differently from unfree men by virtue of their freedom and not by virtue of different natural causes (education, environment, heredity, and the like) —then the uniformity of nature is abrogated. And if it has no consequences for the uniformity of nature, moral freedom, which Kant holds depends upon it, is an empty pretension.

5. The Concept of Postulated Freedom

To remove, or at least to ameliorate, these aporias we must investigate a passage in the first and one in the third *Critique*, where we find a sketch of a theory of freedom as a postulate or as a heuristic maxim, and revise the common interpretation of Kant's ontology as a "two-world theory."

When I speak here of freedom as a postulate, I am not referring to the "postulate theory" of the *Critique of Practical Reason*. According

---

[22] *Critique of Pure Reason*, A 553/B 581.

[23] *Critique of Practical Reason*, p. 99.

to it, a postulate of pure practical reason is an assumption inextricably connected with morality yet theoretically unprovable. In this sense Kant held the immortality of the soul and the existence of God to be postulates and in one place he counts the freedom of the will among the postulates.[24] There is (with respect to freedom) nothing new in this; it only makes explicit what had already been indicated in discussion of the concepts of freedom in the Analytic of Pure Practical Reason, namely, that one cannot act without presupposing a theoretically unprovable freedom.

Instead of to this well-known conception of postulates, I am referring here to a conception which Kant did not work out in full, and in the discussion of which he does not even use the word "postulate." In the *Critique of Pure Reason* Kant makes a remark which suggests not only the other theory of postulates but also a revision of the two-world theory. He says:

> As regards (man's) empirical character, there is no freedom, and yet it is only in the light of this character that man can be studied if, that is to say, we are simply *observing*, and in the manner of anthropology seeking to institute a physiological investigation into the motive causes of his actions. But when we consider these actions in their relations to reason—I do not mean speculative (i.e., theoretical) reason, by which we endeavour *to explain* their coming into being, but reason in so far as it is itself the cause *producing* them—if, that is to say, we compare them with (the standards of) reason in its *practical* bearing, we find a rule and order altogether different from the order of nature.[25]

Instead of thinking of two worlds, one noumenal and one phenomenal, Kant is here thinking of one world under two aspects. There is not one *homo noumenon*, who is free, and a *homo phaenomenon* who is not. The noumenal and the phenomenal are not ontologically distinct (like an object and a picture of it) but are aspects determined by methodological procedures chosen with regard to the

---

[24] *Critique of Practical Reason*, p. 132. The three postulates are not cognate. Those of immortality and the existence of God are necessary for the *summum bonum*, while that of freedom is necessary for morality itself. See my *Commentary*, ch.14.

[25] *Critique of Pure Reason*, A 550/B 578.

divergent purposes of two kinds of inquiry.[26] Each of these aspects is determined by what I shall call its respective postulate. The postulate theory of freedom, and the double-aspect theory of noumenon and phenomenon, are two expressions of the same fundamental theory. From the scientific point of view of the observer, causal conditions are sought and (in principle) found. From the practical point of view of the acting man (or the man who is normatively judging another's actions), the reasons for decisions and actions are sought and evaluated. It is only from the second standpoint that an action can be interpreted as free and imputable.[27]

It is not until the *Critique of Judgment* that Kant gives much help in developing this postulate theory of freedom. There he presents an

---

[26] This is not the place to reconstruct the theory of the thing in itself and the noumenon along the lines presupposed in the present discussion. Though Kant often writes almost as if the thing in itself were a Lockean substance (an "unknown cause of my sensations") and as if the phenomena and things in themselves were numerically different things of different ontological kinds, he also writes as if the thing perceived can be thought (not known) as existing in itself without regard to the forms under which it is known. Regarded in this way the very thing perceived is the thing in itself. We perceive the thing itself but not as it is in itself. As an object of thought but not of knowledge, it is properly called noumenon; as an object of perceptual knowledge, it is properly called phenomenon. The denial of the two-world theory in favor of a two-aspect theory (the phenomenal and noumenal character of a single thing) was undertaken in my Commentary on *Kant's Critique of Practical Reason*, pp. 192 ff, and has been ably supported by Gerold Prauss, *Erscheinung bei Kant* (Berlin, 1971) and *Kant und das Problem der Dinge an sich* (Bonn, 1974); and by Henry E. Allison "Things in Themselves, Noumena and the Transcendental Object," *Dialectica* 32 (1978), pp. 41-76.

[27] The previous footnote has pointed out the relation between thing in itself and noumenon. These terms may have the same denotation, but their connotations are quite different. If we do not identify them, and if we deny ontological dualism between either of them and a phenomenal object, and if we think with Kant of reason (as "the higher faculty of desire") as especially concerned with morals and of understanding as exclusively a cognitive faculty, then it makes perfectly good sense to say that a human being as an object of ethical judgment, and thus as a free agent, is a *homo noumenon*. This does not mean that he is a ghostly non-temporal, non-spatial unknowable *Ding an sich*. This accords with Kant's own usage in the *Rechtslehre* (Akademie ed. VI, p. 335). Thus, after all, it is the noumenal man who gets hanged.

antimony between teleological and mechanical explanation which readily suggests by analogy the theory of freedom and natural cause as postulates. The Antinomy of Teleological Judgment is analogous to the Third Antinomy of the first *Critique*, but its solution is wholly different. The analogy is between natural law and moral law (in the first *Critique*) and mechanical law and teleological law (in the third). The solution of the Antinomy in the first *Critique* is, as we have seen, ontological (the two-world theory); the solution of the Antinomy in the third *Critique* is purely methodological and postulational. In consequence, the Second Analogy of Experience in the first *Critique*, which gives rise to the antithesis of the Third Antinomy, is interpreted by Kant himself, in the third *Critique*, as a methodological maxim or postulate. The effect of this reinterpretation upon the ontology of the first *Critique* is a profound one. It is no longer the case that one of the laws (the law of natural causality) is given a pejorative standing as a law of appearance only of what is ultimately real and true. This is evident in the third *Critique's* reformulation of the Second Analogy, which is now read as a methodological rule: "All production of material things and their forms must be held to be possible according to purely mechanical laws." As a maxim it does not contradict the other maxim of judgment: in the explanation of organic forms seek the purpose of each member.[28] Nor does it contradict the postulate underlying action and the judgment of actions, which is that actions must be imputed to free agents.

Had Kant explained in his solution of the Third Antinomy that the antithesis is not a constitutive principle of nature but only a regulative idea or methodological maxim—a conclusion he reached only in 1790[29]—he would not have found it necessary to defend two opposed philosophical theorems by the desperate ontology of the two-world theory. He could have lived happily with two postulates which do not conflict because they are not used at the same time or for the same purpose. They are:

---

[28] *Critique of Judgment*, Sections 70-76.

[29] Once (*Critique of Pure Reason*, A 798/B 826) he called the antithesis of the Third Antinomy a maxim, but he did not exploit this meaning. The word "regulative" as applied to the Analogies of Experience is stated (A180-B223) not to have the significance which later the *Critique of Judgment* ascribed to it.

(a) *Postulate for the scientific explanation of human actions*: In natural sciences always seek natural causes, and do not admit nonnatural causes in the explanation of natural phenomena (including human actions).

(b) *Postulate for ethical and practical decisions*: Act as if the maxim of your will were a sufficient determining ground for the action undertaken.

(Corollary: *Postulate for the normative evaluation of another's action*: Judge as if the maxim of the will were a sufficient determining ground for the action in question.)

None of these postulates makes an ontological claim. Rather, they tell us what we must do in order to execute the function of a scientific observer, an agent, or a judge.

In spite of the words "as if" in the formula of the second postulate and its corollary, the theory I am proposing here is not a form of a dogmatic fictionalism which asserts that men are not free, but that in practice one must think and act as if they were free. Such fictionalism presupposes mechanical determinism as a metaphysical truth, in comparison with which freedom is only a fiction. The view I find in Kant and am here defending holds that there is as much—and as little—ground to hold all the postulates as fictions. They are on an equal footing and, in different spheres of experience, equally inescapable. Their truth is not absolute, for they limit each other; their truth is in the context of their respective employment definite and justified; outside the respective contexts there are no criteria for their correct application.

In this conception we are no longer, as in orthodox Kantianism, forced to assign to the sciences the realm of the appearances (in an ontologically pejorative sense) and to ethics the realm of noumena (in an epistemologically pejorative sense.) The *a priori* structures of each context remain intact, and each claims to govern the entire relevant experience of its realm.

When we accept this revision of Kantian transcendental theory, we may regard the realm of practice as one aspect of the scope of our experience in general, which, under other postulates and concepts, appears as the realm of nature. It is almost the same to hold the causal concept of the Second Analogy as regulative for the investigation of nature, and to hold the practical concept of freedom to be constitutive for the realm of human actions, as it is to hold with Kant in the

Methodology of the first *Critique* that natural causality is a constitutive concept and free causality a regulative Idea. The more mature theory, towards which I think he was moving even before the *Critique of Judgment*, holds that each is regulative, or each is constitutive of its own realm. According to Kant we know that a change is an objective event only under the condition that we know it to have a cause; analogously, we know that a human event is an action only under the condition that we know it to have reasons and not merely causes. Each of these definitional conditions depends upon the methodological postulates in use.

6. The Complementarity of Freedom and Natural Necessity

There is an analogy between the theory outlined here and the principle of complementarity in physics. In physics one and the same thing must be described sometimes as a wave and sometimes as a particle. Which description fits is dependent upon the conditions of its observation, which cannot be simultaneously fulfilled. The question of what the thing itself is, irrespective of the conditions of its observation, is unanswerable; but it is a question that need never arise. Similarly here. One cannot give a context-free answer to the question: Is this man, or this piece of behavior, free? Nor can one, like Kant, ascribe both freedom and natural necessity to the same action. *But one does not ever need to do so, either for the sake of science or of morals.* The remainder of this paper will discuss the reasons for this.

Looked at abstractly and schematically, freedom and natural necessity appear to exclude one another. Accordingly, Kant's version of compatibilism, his two-world theory, has the appearance of a paradox, since it asserts both at the same time of the same action. Just so, "the wave theory of the electron" and "the particle theory of the electron," taken abstractly and schematically, appear to contradict each other.

Looked at concretely and empirically, however, no occasion for contradiction arises in either case. In practice, one never has occasion to say of an electron that it is acting like a wave and acting like a particle at the same time in the same observational field; nor does one ever have occasion in a situation calling for decision or evaluation to affirm both the thesis and the antithesis of the Third Antinomy or of the Antinomy of Teleological Judgment. In practice, one chooses between them. In no single case does one say: "The criminal behavior of the defendant was caused by a specific brain injury (or a specific physiological state, or the like) and therefore was as unavoidable as an eclipse of the sun; *nevertheless* the defendant acted freely and is therefore responsible for his action." If I did not, as a Kantian philosopher, hold *a priori* that any action whatsoever was causally determined, but rather as a forensic expert concretely and empirically did know precisely what empirical cause produced the action under investigation, then I would no longer say (with Kant) that this action was a free one and the defendant was responsible for it. In a court of law opposing counsel dispute whether the behavior in question was necessitated (or at least made highly probable) by definite, precise, perhaps pathological conditions; and for this they have criteria of empirical freedom more sophisticated than those of Aristotle and common sense. But whether the causally necessitated action was *also* a free action—outside the philosophical seminar and lecture hall that is never the question.[30]

The theory of freedom as a postulate for practical and moral life and of natural necessity as postulate for research into nature and human nature enables us to draw from empirical observation the practical conclusion as to whether in a specific case a specific human being behaved freely or not. We have gained a position from which empirical freedom can be taken with conceptual seriousness. If we do not assume, merely schematically and *a priori*, that every action has a

---

[30] I do not speak contemptuously of the seminar room and the lecture hall, but the kinds of investigations which go on in them are not designed to discover actual causes of behavior, and my argument is that when we are convinced that we know the actual causes we must rescind the imputation of freedom, whereas in the philosophical lecture hall we can entertain a schematic, abstract, compatibilism, which Körner (*op. cit.*, p. 209) wittily compares to eating one's cake and having it too. In *The Actor and the Spectator* (pp. 105-107) I pushed the analogy with the principle of complementarity to the point of showing that the conditions under which a specific, concrete causal explanation of an action is given prevent its being a free action, and not merely add another conceptual determination which prevent its being interpreted as a free action.

natural cause, but discover empirically under the governance of this postulate natural causes sufficient to explain it, the postulate of natural causality is [thereby] confirmed, and we rescind the imputation of freedom and responsibility. Since in most cases we are not capable of perfecting such causal explanations, the question often remains unanswered whether a specific man in a specific situation acted freely or not. But according to this theory that question is answerable in principle, whereas a practical, contingent answer could not be supported by a theory of transcendental freedom based upon the two-world theory ordinarily associated with Kant's name.

Kant said that the theory of transcendental freedom appeared *prima facie* to conflict with equity. It must be granted here, too, that if we act on the theory of freedom as a practical postulate we may sometimes unjustly impute to a man an action which he could not have left undone. In this case, we commit an error and do an injustice. It may also happen that we abstractly and schematically explain an action causally for which no *sufficient* causal explanation can in fact be given. In this case we do not accord the man the dignity which belongs to him. Since we cannot empirically determine the limits of our explanatory schemata, such scientific dogmatism, and such injustice, are perhaps unavoidable.

In both cases we judge unjustly, sometimes imputing unfree actions, sometimes denying responsibility where it actually exists. But the alternative to sometimes making such mistakes is—always making such mistakes. If we assume the two-world theory of transcendental freedom and phenomenal necessity, I think we *always* judge wrongly when we hold a man responsible for any of his actions, since, according to the first and second *Critiques*, his action could not have remained undone. I believe that if Kant had rewritten the *Critique of Practical Reason* in the light of the *Critique of (Teleological) Judgment* he would have been better able to avoid moral judgments "which appear to conflict with equity."

It is gratifying to find that, following a very different path, I have come to conclusions so consonant with those of Stephan Körner in his British Academy lecture, "Kant's Conception of Freedom" (1967). The alternative standpoints and postulates in my account correspond very closely to the alternative categorial schemata (p. 195) and ideal concepts (p. 212) in his revision of Kant. I hope that my formulation of the principal conclusion is as acceptable to him as his is to me; for, as he says, unless one denies the uniqueness of the Kantian categorial schema of nature, "effective freedom can only be saved in Kantian fashion by being located in the noumenal world" (p. 210), but the rejection of its uniqueness "removes (freedom) from the noumenal world and places it firmly into nature" (p. 214). I would venture to disagree only with the very last word, "nature." What I conceive of as nature is under categorial schemata which exclude freedom. I would substitute for "nature" his expression "world of experience" (p. 211, last line). It is the world of (precategorial) experience which provides material for a diversity of categorial schemata, including those of nature, morality, and culture.

12. What Have We Learned from Kant? *

The publication of Immanuel Kant's *Critique of Pure Reason* two centuries ago concerns a wider public than the professional philosophical community. Although the *Critique of Pure Reason* was written almost exclusively for the professional philosopher, it was nonetheless the foundation for most of Kant's other writings, nearly half of which were addressed to the general learned public.

Great philosophers such as Kant speak not just to the professoriate, but to all who agree with Socrates that the unexamined life is not worth living. Accordingly, in his own work Kant explicitly distinguished between the "interests of the school" and the "interests of humanity." The interests of the school are those of professional philosophers. Kant believed that the interests of the school were subordinate to the interests of humanity though, in the long run, important to them. As a young man Kant wrote in a private jotting:

> By inclination I am an enquirer. I feel a consuming thirst for knowledge, the unrest which goes with the desire to progress in it, and the satisfaction which comes with every advance in knowledge. There was a time when I believed that this constituted the honor of humanity, and I despised the people, who know nothing.. . . [But] I have learned to honor man, and would find myself more useless than the common laborer if I did not believe that this attitude of mine [as an enquirer] can give a worth to all others, in establishing the rights of mankind.[1]

Kant openly sympathized with both the French and the American revolutions, at a time when expressions of such sympathy were in Germany personally hazardous. When he wrote of "the rights of mankind," he certainly meant political and legal rights of the kind that

---

* Reprinted with permission from *Self and Nature in Kant's Philosophy* ed. A. Wood, pp. 17-30. Ithaca: Cornell University Press, 1984.
[1] Akademie ed. XX, p. 44

those revolutions were meant to secure. But Kant's conception of rights was much more than political. Political rights were, he thought, essential to all others; they were conditions for the exercise of other rights—the rights of people to enlighten themselves, to use their talents freely in the discovery of truth, and to develop their moral character. All of these constitute the calling *(Bestimmung)* of man.

To determine the calling of man, philosophy is needed. Around the time Kant wrote the note just quoted, he also remarked, "If there is any science which man stands in need of, it is one which teaches him to occupy properly the place assigned to him in creation, and one from which he can learn what he must be, in order to be a man."[2] *But what is man?* This is the principal question of philosophy, and it epitomizes three preliminary questions: What can I know? What ought I to do? What may I hope?[3] To each of these questions a great *Critique* is devoted, but only the entire corpus is adequate to answer the principal question. The three preliminary questions have definite answers in their respective *Critiques;* nowhere is there a simple, explicit answer to the principal question. Yet Kant's answers to the first three queries point unmistakably to an answer to the ultimate question, for there is a single common theme running through all the *Critiques* that leads always to the same reply to the question, What is man?

Philosophy of Science

In the philosophy of science Kant effected what has been called (though not by him) the Copernican Revolution. Copernicus found that the phenomena of planetary astronomy can best be understood by taking into account the movements of the earth. The real motion of the astronomer who observes the skies introduces an order into the observations that would not be there if the earth itself stood still, or if the astronomer denied its motion. The movement of every perceiving subject must be reckoned in with the movements observed, in order to discover the real motion of the object one is observing.

Kant drew a fruitful analogy between terrestrial motion and other factors which, from the side of the observer, determine in part both the

----

[2] *Ibid.*, p. 45.
[3] *Lectures on Logic*, Akademie ed. IX, p. 25; cf. A 805/B 833.

subjective and the objective (that is, the intersubjective) aspects of what is observed. The knowing subject can understand any phenomenon of the world (whether or not it involves motion) only if he takes account of his own contribution (whether the parallax of his own motion, or some other factor). The observer's contribution is not just the relatively unimportant, that is, nonexplanatory secondary qualities, but the most objective of all properties and structures, the formal characteristics of experience and its underlying laws. These are, as it were, read into experience by the intellectual and operational acts of the observing and explaining mind. Therefore, Kant says, "The understanding derives its laws (*a priori*) not from nature, but rather prescribes them to nature."[4] By subsequent experience we are instructed as to what specific generalizations and laws obtain, as specifications of a priori concepts such as cause, substance, magnitude, and position. Nature, says Kant, is "the existence of things so far as it is determined by universal laws;"[5] accordingly, the human mind can be regarded not only as the legislator or the lawgiver of nature, but as the creator of nature—not of the stuff of nature, of course, for the human mind is finite and must work with material supplied by some unknown source—but of nature considered as a system existing under laws the knowledge of which gives nature whatever intelligibility it exhibits. (When the German idealists denied the limitations Kant placed on our cognitive capacity, they thought of the mind as being the creator of nature in a much more extravagant sense. Kant should not be blamed for their excesses, which in fact he tried to prevent.) Kant stands between the doctrine of Nicolas of Cusa and Vico that *verum et factum convertuntur* (truth is what is made, we can know only what we can make), and Nietzsche's profound aphorism, "*Bevor 'gedacht' wurde, muss schon gedichtet worden sein*" (Before something is 'thought' it must first be *composed*).[6]

---

[4] *Prolegomena*, Section 36.

[5] *Ibid.*, section 14.

[6] On the equivalence of *verum* and *factum*, see Isaiah Berlin, *Vico and Herder* (London, 1976), pp. 21 and 142n. The aphorism is in Nietzsche's *Gesammelte Werke*, Musarion Ausgabe (Munich, 1925), vol. 16, p. 115. All quotations in the text, except those from the *Critique of Pure Reason*, are translated by me; those from the first *Critique* are from the Kemp Smith translation.

The only science Kant knew was Newtonian; the only geometry, Euclidean; the only logic, Aristotelian. Because all of these have been superseded or revised, it is sometimes said that the *Critique of Pure Reason,* which supported them, was a defense of lost causes. Nevertheless, the epistemological foundations Kant supplied to Newtonian physics and Euclidean geometry are reminders that non-Newtonian physics and non-Euclidean geometries also stand on epistemological foundations. The latter are not self-explanatory and self-justifying; they must be, in Kant's language, transcendentally deduced. It is a point of dispute in modern philosophy of science whether the foundations needed for these new disciplines are more like or more unlike those of the Kantian model of classical physics. Whether like or unlike, a treatise analogous to the *Critique of Pure Reason* needs to be written after every scientific revolution. The resemblances between the *Critique of Pure Reason* and modern positivistic, operationalistic, and model theories are striking, for all these contemporary theories emphasize one Kantian theme: the ways in which the mind's own activities in inquiry are projected into and reflected back by nature. Naturally this Kantian theme has been modified, and most of these modifications move in the same direction; that is, away from what Stephan Körner has called Kant's uniqueness-thesis, in other words, the doctrine that there is only one way of organizing experience so that we can make any knowledge-claims, even false ones.[7] No doubt the rigidity of the Kantian transcendental apparatus must be relaxed, alternative category systems must be conceded, knowledge itself must be relativized according to changing cultural systems. The creative activity of minds—the central thought in the *Critique of Pure Reason*—is made perhaps even more pervasive by those who undertake these revisions than it was by Kant himself: whereas the creativity in Kant's account is somewhat abstract and transcendental, modern studies of conceptual change emphasize the actual historical, social, and personal factors, and give empirical meaning to the notion of cognitive creations. These changes do not evade the issue that led Kant to write the *Critique,* namely, How can free creations of the mind have objective validity? This question remains, even when the concepts Kant thought of as

---

[7] Stephan Körner, "The Impossibility of Transcendental Deductions," *Kant Studies Today,* ed. L. W. Beck (La Salle, Ill., 1969), p. 233.

unique creations of the mind have long since been shown to have alternatives or, indeed, have been replaced by others in the progress of science. Contemporary sociology of knowledge emphasizes cultural factors in the creation and acceptance of alternative portrayals of the world. Kant, on the other hand, was aware of only one system of grammar. He also thought—perhaps in part for that reason—that there was only one type of cognizing mind, only one system of scientific knowledge. He overlooked the variable social dimensions of thought and was little interested in the philosophy of language (in fact, little interested in language itself, which he seems to have regarded as hardly more than a transparent medium). Because he presented his categorial system as a "transcendental grammar,"[8] Kant appears to belong to the tradition Noam Chomsky has called "Cartesian linguistics."

But anti-Cartesian linguistics also may have Kantian sources, as seen originally in the work of Kant's disciples Herder and Humboldt and in this century in that of the neo-Kantians Georg Simmel and Ernst Cassirer. Alternative pictures of the universe and of society depend upon the symbol systems in use, which determine the a priori features of experiences accepted into the communication network. Whether or not a single universal grammar exists, the linguistic turn in philosophy a generation ago was an analogue of the Copernican Revolution, with or without the uniqueness-thesis. Whether the epistemological center (like the sun in Copernican astronomy) is a single universal grammar or whether there are at the ultimate depths diverse and irreducible systems of semiotic rules, the a priori forms of experience of the world correspond to the forms in which this experience is articulated and communicated. We see only what we can say.

Each culture, each scientific paradigm, each linguistic system requires something analogous to a *Critique of Pure Reason* in order to understand how its principles and rules are projected into its cosmological and cultural conceptions. It was no surprise to me, therefore, when Ernest Gellner recently counted Kant as chief among the ancestors of structuralism.[9]

---

[8] *Prolegomena*, section 39.

[9] Ernest Gellner, "What Is Structuralism?," *Times Literary Supplement*, July 31, 1981, p. 881.

Morality And Politics

Just as Kant's Copernican Revolution taught that the scientific thinker gives the form of lawfulness to the events in nature, reads the law into nature, as it were, and then specifies the variables by empirical research, an analogous revolution occurs in Kant's moral philosophy, which I call the Rousseauistic Revolution. Rousseau, Kant's favorite modern author, wrote: "Freedom is obedience to a law which man gives to himself."[10] Rousseau meant this primarily in a political sense, and the idea was the basis of his theory of self-government. Only by participation in government and not by mere tacit consent is political authority justified. Kant developed this political theory further than Rousseau did, and he also developed it into a philosophy of morals.

The moral law, which philosophers before Kant had found in what they considered to be the will of God, or the law of nature, or the human desire for happiness, he found (using a political metaphor) in autonomy. Perhaps for the first time, a clear conceptual distinction was drawn between morality and prudence raised to an almost transcendental elevation. Prudence is reasonable adherence to policies for reaching desired and desirable ends; morality is adherence to a maxim out of respect for its status as a law for rational beings. Respect is a unique feeling evoked only by a law which, having no prudential sanctions, is an expression of one's rational capacity shown both in making and judging knowledge-claims and in reaching and justifying practical decisions. I can *obey* laws out of concern with reward and punishment, and if I am prudent I usually do so; but I can *respect* them only if their origin in my own rational lawgiving capacity humbles my merely prudential concerns.

There is an analogy between moral principles and the categorial principles in the first *Critique*. The only theoretical law or principle I can acknowledge as a priori necessary is one my understanding prescribes to nature. 'Acknowledge as necessary' is the first *Critique's* epistemological analogue of moral 'respect' in the second *Critique*. Autonomy is a fundamental condition of both cognitive and practical activity; because the *word* did not come into Kant's vocabulary until after 1781, many readers have missed the *thing* in the first *Critique*.

---

[10] Rousseau, *Social Contract*, 1:8 (Everyman ed., London, 1946), p. 16.

Yet the analogies are vivid. Pure practical reason stands in the same relation to the moral realm (the realm of ends) as pure understanding does to the realm of nature. Both are sources of a priori laws. One exacts our obedience in interpreting nature, which we regard as equivalent to nature's own obedience to law. The other exacts our obedience in the pursuit of happiness, human rights, and virtue, regardless of whether nature responds favorably to our efforts, or thwarts them. Whether virtue is rewarded with happiness is something that does not lie with man; what is within his power, and what he ought to undertake, is to be *worthy* of happiness. Obedience to a law given by one's rational nature is a necessary condition of such worthiness, but it is neither necessary nor sufficient for the attainment of other human goals.

Many have objected that Kant held obedience to be so high a virtue—indeed the only virtue—that he regarded the origin and consequences of a law as morally irrelevant. Therefore, it has been held, he could not distinguish between legitimate and illegitimate laws, could not condemn fanaticism devoted to some immoral goal, and could not morally criticize any actual government or resist any actual tyranny. Paradoxically, the friend of the American and French revolutions has been seen as a defender of political absolutism.

I must grant that there are paradoxes in Kant's political philosophy, especially in his adherence to the Lutheran position on the unrighteousness of rebellion, which led him into some not very edifying casuistry. Nevertheless, Kant always clearly distinguished between the moral law, which derives from reason, and the positive law, which arises from empirically determined power relations. Even in his casuistical accounts of the misadventures of the French Revolution he never failed to give priority to the moral: "Politics," he says, "must always bend its knee to morality."[11] The law we respect is no arbitrary edict with sanctions of reward and punishment; rather, it is a law of a kind we as impartial lawgivers prescribe, or at least could prescribe, for ourselves. It is a maxim made under the veil of empirical ignorance, with the moral innocence of the dove instead of the political wisdom of the serpent. A law of this kind arises, and is valid, only insofar as it is reasonable. 'Reasonable' here means far more than merely self-consistent; it means constrained by the universal rights and

---

[11] "Perpetual Peace," Akademie ed. VIII, p. 380.

serviceable to the universal interests of mankind. The moral law, then, is not an absolutized positive law, but rather a rational criterion of the legitimacy of statute law. Moral law is the rationalized and secularized form of the law of God or the law of nature, and fulfills much the same functions that these venerable concepts had served as constraints on arbitrary political power.

I have just compared Kant's theory to the traditional doctrines of the law of nature or the law of God, but one might better ask, What is *living* in Kant's moral philosophy? Indeed, there has been a revolution in the moral life just as great as the revolution in the scientific world-picture, and one may well believe that Kant's humanistic ethic with its Jewish, Christian, and Stoic components and Protestant Prussian coloration is as antiquated as the Euclidean geometry and Newtonian physics to which Kant adhered. Nowadays we do not have his faith in the rationality and universality of morality. The very word "rationalization" expresses psychoanalytic suspicions, and the Kantian equation of moral actions with actions done out a punctilious sense of duty or out of pure reason is hardly persuasive today. We see many factors as limitations on human freedom that were morally irrelevant for Kant.

Such reservations appear to me to be legitimate and important, and yet are somewhat superficial, because they misread Kant as a casuist and do not touch the principal points of his moral philosophy. After every moral revolution a new *Critique of Practical Reason* ought to be written, or at least Kant's own ought to be reread. Our present-day ethical views, however far from Kant's they may be, need philosophical foundations not found in clinical psychology or modes and fashions; they need what Kant perhaps misleadingly called a "metaphysics of morals." The foundations of every ethics are to be found in conceptions of an ideal human nature. It is possible that Kant conceived this nature too rationalistically in trying to establish an ethics valid for all rational beings and not for human beings alone, but the metaethical structure of ethical systems based upon quite different ideals of human nature may well be Kantian.

People often indignantly contrast *Kantian* ethics with *human* ethics and say of the former, "It may be right in theory, but will not hold in practice."[12] Against this objection, recall Kant's rejoinder to those who presumed to criticize Plato on the sorry pretext of the impracticality or unfeasibility of his political theory: "Nothing indeed can be more injurious or more unworthy of a philosopher than the vulgar appeal to so-called adverse experience. Such experience would never have existed at all, had history followed the prescriptions of Plato" (A 316-17/B 373). Per corollary, one ought not object to the Kantian moral philosophy on grounds of its impracticality, but rather one ought to use it as an admonition against actual tendencies that do not aim to establish the kingdom of God on earth (or, in Kantian language, the realm of ends), in which rational beings will be treated as ends in themselves, and not as means only.

Philosophy of Art

One of the strangest phenomena in the history of thought is that Kant led a revolution in our conception of art. It is strange because it was so unlikely: in his entire life, Kant probably never had an opportunity to see a fine painting or hear a good performance of great music. His Copernican and Rousseauistic revolutions were historically conservative; they did not revolutionize science or morals but provided new and revolutionary foundations for the science and the moral ideals already current. His aesthetic revolution, on the other hand, was a renunciation of the critical standards of his time. It prepared the way for artistic developments that occurred after he wrote, and, in the case of German romanticism, in part *because* of what he wrote.

Here again we meet with an analogue of the Copernican Revolution. M.H. Abrams, writing of Wordsworth, says that "the Copernican revolution in epistemology—...the general concept that the perceiving mind discovers what it has itself partly made was effected in England by poets and critics before it manifested itself in academic philosophy."[13] But in Germany the revolution in aesthetics came first, in Kant's academic philosophy.

---

[12] See, for example, F. Sartiaux, *Morale kantienne et morale humaine* (Paris, 1917).

[13] M.H. Abrams, *The Mirror and the Lamp* (New York, 1953), p. 58.

Kant turned against two dominant aesthetic principles that had governed European thought on art, if not art itself: that art is the imitation of nature (*ut pictura poesis*) and that the purpose of art is moral edification. Kant rejected both principles because they confined art and made it parasitic upon either knowledge or morals. Kant is clear and convincing in his rejection of theories that the aesthetic response is a response to the information content of a work of art. He saw that aesthetic value is attached to the syntactic, not the semantic, dimension of meaning. Only in that way is the artist free to create something "purposive, [but] without purpose."[14]

One cannot maintain that Kant was completely successful in separating moral from aesthetic interests. Perhaps he was not sufficiently independent of the critical thought of his time to have made a clean break between them. It is not clear whether, given the rest of his theory, he should have, or could have, done so. Historically, however, the principal thrust of Kant's arguments has been in the direction of the emancipation of art from extra-artistic criteria, whether of factual truth or moral value.

Kant replaced the two standard critical principles of his time—the imitation of nature, and the moral edification of the audience—with his theory of genius. Genius is a law unto itself, and it creates a second nature, not just a copy of a first nature. The German romantic movement developed its program from Kant's philosophical emancipation of art through genius. Because the excesses of romantic genius were distasteful to Kant, some may believe that the romantic and other later anticlassical movements in art have made his aesthetic theory as obsolete as they view his defense of Newtonian physics, Christian ethics, and Roman law. After all, Kant's taste was for tulips and arabesques; what could he have seen in Duchamp's *Nude Descending a Staircase*?

Nineteenth- and twentieth-century revolutions of thought about art (perhaps with the exception of the Marxist) appear to be pushing to an extreme what was implicit in Kant's own theory; that is, the doctrine of the autonomy of art, its freedom from nonartistic concerns, or art for art's sake. The creativity of the artist, not the contingent occurrence of beautiful objects and the talent to reproduce them faithfully on canvas, is the decisive condition of aesthetic excellence. If we imagine Kant

---

[14] *Critique of Judgment*, Akademie ed. V, p. 241.

coming back to life and visiting our museums and laboratories, I suspect that, after an initial shock and a little time to get his bearings, he might be as much at home in the one as in the other. And I even suspect that in the art gallery he would be more comfortable with *Nude Descending a Staircase* than with Titian's nudes, because his theory of human beauty is not, at least in any obvious way, consistent with his formalistic analyses, which apparently fit arabesques better than they do human portraits.[15] Designs, without representational content or moral message, which present or stimulate the free play of imagination, were the paradigms of Kant's aesthetic theory, and are especially characteristic of much post-Kantian art.

The Promethean Revolution

From the foregoing, a common theme may be seen in Kant's work in science, morals, and art. The same theme underlies his theories of mathematics, history, religion, and politics. All his works lead to the same answer to the question, What is man? That answer is, man is creator. To Kant's Copernican and Rousseauistic revolutions, therefore, I would add a third: his work also represents a Promethean Revolution in philosophy. It was Prometheus who seized the prerogative of the gods and gave it to humankind. Through possession of fire, everything else could be created. Certainly the Prometheus role is not without its mortal danger; the ancient hero suffered martyrdom, and Prometheanism leads to the vice of hubris. Kant avoided both the fate and the vice by never forgetting that man is a finite-all-too-finite being, and that the world created by man is a human-all-too-human world—indeed, a world of appearance, the basic conditions and materials of which lie beyond the limits of human knowledge and power. Man is no god, but in his creativity he may be godlike, and

---

[15] Paul Guyer in "Formalism and the Theory of Expression in Kant's Aesthetics," *Kant-Studien* LXVIII (1977), pp. 46-70, argues very effectively that the limitation to formal (geometric) elements is not inherent in Kant's theory. "Nothing in this doctrine," Guyer says, "need be seen as excluding concepts, symbols and the like from being *part of the manifold of imagination* which the mind ranges over in its free play" (p. 55).

many of the tasks previously assigned to god in the creation and governance of the world are reassigned by Kant to man.

The world man orders, or seeks to order, is only the known part of the unknown all. Kant was the anthropologist of a race that dwelt in "the land of truth"—"the land of truth" is man's realm, man is the lawgiver in it. But the "land of truth" is only an island, surrounded by "a wide and stormy ocean, the native home of illusion, where many a fog-bank and many a swiftly melting iceberg give the deceptive appearance of farther shores, deluding the adventurous seafarer ever anew with empty hopes, and engaging him in enterprises which he can never abandon and yet is unable to carry to completion" (A 235-36/B 294-95).

The cultivation of this island and the exploration of this ocean is the calling of man. In these dual efforts of *Aufklärung,* the human race stands alone and independent: "Nature has willed that man, by himself, should produce everything that goes beyond the mechanical ordering of his animal existence, and that he should partake of no other happiness or perfection than that which he himself, independently of instinct, has created by his own reason."[16]

Were it not for the words "happiness" and "reason" in this quotation, you might have thought that I was quoting a rather prosaic Sartre. The autonomy of the individual in creating out of chaos the world in which one is to live is as characteristic of Kant's teaching as it is of that of the modern existentialist thinker. But "happiness" and "reason" cannot be left out of the quotation. For Kant, only reasonable human beings, in spite of all their errors, can create a world in which there is some chance for well-being and happiness, and only the criticism and discipline of reason can lead toward the requisite wisdom.

Like the present, the Age of Reason had its irrationalists. The German Enlightenment had its Counter-Enlightenment just as we have a counterculture. Kant lived in an age that was changing just as rapidly and violently as ours, in which tradition was under as serious a challenge as now, in which it was just as questionable as it is now what should be saved in established institutions and practices and what should be changed or rejected. There were those in his day, as in our own, who were brought to skepticism by the knowledge explosion and by conflicts in values. There were people, even in Königsberg, who

---

[16] "Idea for a Universal History," Akademie ed. VIII, p. 19.

had no faith in the life of reason and took refuge in irrationalistic enthusiasms and superstitions. The Germans had a name for this rebellion: *Sturm und Drang.* (The very name sounds frightening.) Kant saw Storm and Stress as a threat to the progress of knowledge and to civilized life, which depends upon that progress. What Kant said in 1786 is as portentous now, because something like *Sturm und Drang* is still with us. These words were addressed to the people of Storm and Stress, but they may be meant also for us:

> Friends of the human race, and of that which is holiest to it! ... Do not wrench from reason what makes it the highest good on earth, the prerogative of being the final touchstone of truth. If you do this, you will become unworthy of freedom, and lose it, and bring misfortune to those who want to use freedom in a lawful manner to secure the good of mankind.[17]

---

[17] "What is Orientation in Thinking," Akademie ed. VIII, pp. 146-7.

Appendix 1:

How I Became Almost a Philosopher[*]

Nietzsche draws a distinction between philosophers and philosophic workmen. I am among the latter.

In 1925, I was awakened from my dogmatic slumber by newspaper accounts of the "Monkey Trial." John T. Scopes was found guilty of breaking a law of the state of Tennessee prohibiting the teaching of the theory of evolution. Reading accounts of both sides of the trial made me admit that Mr. Scopes was indeed guilty-there was no question about that-but made me see that the law itself was foolish. I bought and read *The Origin of Species*, which confirmed what became a new dogmatism for me. An uncle-a businessman with the heart of a scholar-had told me that there was some hot stuff in the infamous fifteenth chapter of Gibbon, and reading that planted some new doubts and new convictions in me. By the age of twelve, my education as the village atheist was essentially complete.

Two years later my sister gave me a copy of Will Durant's *The Story of Philosophy*. I cannot say how much I learned from and how much I delighted in that book; sixty years later I still remember it with pleasure. What was most important to me was discovering that there had been others before me who had had the kind of thoughts and had asked the kind of questions that had bothered me during and since the Scopes trial. What I had thought an idiosyncrasy to be hidden from others turned out to be a healthy and traditional exercise of thought. I discovered that I was not alone, and not the first to ask questions most of my fellows thought silly. Even then, however, I did not know that there was still extant a craft of philosophers and philosophic workmen

---

[*] Reprinted with permission from *Falling in Love with Wisdom: American Philosophers Talk about Their Calling* ed. D.D. Karnos and R.G. Shoemaker, pp. 13-15. New York: Oxford University Press, 1993.

with living practitioners. I wrote a few articles for our high school newspaper on topics vaguely philosophical, with purple passages taken from Thomas Henry Huxley. But it was Huxley's science, not his philosophy, that I studied, for I had by that time made up my mind to become a scientist.

I worked summers at the Agricultural Experiment Station near our town. At twelve-and-a-half cents an hour I was employed in the botany and entomology laboratories. This experience got me a very informal job during the school year as "lab assistant" in the high school chemistry and physic laboratories. For setting up demonstrations and helping my classmates with their laboratory exercises, I was allowed to play in the laboratories after school hours, without supervision. My passion was for doing organic syntheses, for which I used to bring buckets of tar from the gasworks. The messes I made in the laboratory were never cleaned up, but my teachers were so relieved that I had not blown up the building when synthesizing TNT that they did not loudly complain about the odor and smudges of tar.

When I went to college (Emory), I was permitted to skip the ordinary introductory chemistry courses and to begin with organic chemistry. This was a mistake. I did not know as much inorganic as the professor thought, and my grounding was not sufficient for more advanced organic. In addition, I was overshooting end points and getting grotesquely wrong results in the quantitative lab. Thus I discovered (but kept to myself) that I was color blind. In those days, before much laboratory work was electronically instrumented, this was like a sentence of professional death. By some fancy use of the slide rule, however, I kept my secret so successfully that at the end of my junior year I was elected to an honorary fraternity for chemists, an honor not previously given to an undergraduate. To me, though, it was an empty honor because I knew I would never become a chemist, and I had no idea what other career would be open to me.

The investiture, or whatever it might be called, fell on a day when my laboratory work had been unusually frustrating. I had never heard of *Gedankenexperimente*, of course, but I must have wished for some discipline in which experiments could be performed in the armchair instead of in a hood, and at 6:00 P.M. on that day I did not know such a discipline existed.

To initiate the new members, there was a dinner followed by a talk by the professor of philosophy entitled "The Limits of Scientific

Concepts." He spoke to me directly and almost personally. He dealt with the values and disvalues of science that had underlain my awareness of the science-religion dispute. I remember the lecture well (for I gave much the same lecture innumerable times later on!) It was based on Heinrich Rickert's *Die Grenzen der naturwissenschaftlichen Begriffsbildungen* and Cassirer's *Substance and Function*. Here I listened to a real, living philosopher, and I instantly saw that this was what I wanted to become. After a night sleepless from intellectual excitement, I went to his office and asked if I could change my major from chemistry to philosophy. It took some hurried scurrying since I had only one year to complete my undergraduate work. But he did cut the red tape and take on the extra burden of tutoring me and of having me live in his house during the vacation so that I could use his library under his guidance. One year later I entered graduate school in philosophy.

The man who made this possible, whom I remember with gratitude, admiration, and love, was Leroy Loemker.

Appendix 2:

Bibliography of Lewis White Beck's Publications

1937

"A Neglected Aspect of Butler's Ethics." *Sophia* (Napoli) V: 11-15.

1938

"The Method of Personalism." *The Personalist* XIX: 368-378.

1939

"The Synoptic Method." *Journal of Philosophy* XXXVI: 337-345.

Reviews of:
> C.C. Pratt: The Logic of Modern Psychology. *Philosophy and Phenomenological Research* I: 240-243.

> Eugen Huess: Rationale Biologie und ihre Kritik. *Philosophical Review* XLVIII: 446.

1940

"The Psychophysical as a Pseudo-Problem." *Journal of Philosophy* XXXVII: 561-571.

Reviews of:
> Paul Weiss: Reality. *Philosophy and Phenomenological Research* I: 114-119.

Hugo Dingler: Die Methode der Physik. *Philosophical Review* XLIX: 473-474.

Erich Heintel: Nietzsches System in seinen Grundbegriffen. *Philosophical Review* XLIX: 595-596.

1941

"The Formal Properties of Ethical Wholes." *Journal of Philosophy* XXXVIII: 5-15.

"The Concept of Wholeness in Ethics" (abstract). *Psychological Bulletin* XXXVI: 592.

"William Stern's Philosophy of Value." *The Personalist* XXII: 353-363.

Reviews of:
> W.L. Bryan: Wars of Families of Minds. *Philosophy and Phenomenological Research* II: 126-127.
>
> W.H. Werkmeister: Philosophy of Science. *Philosophy and Phenomenological Research* II: 242-245.
>
> Kurt Goldstein: Human Nature in the Light of Psychopathology. *Philosophy and Phenomenological Research* II: 245-249.
>
> P. Mason: The X of Psychology. *Philosophy and Phenomenological Research* II: 386-389.
>
> Otto Kein: Schellings Kategorienlehre. *Philosophical Review* L: 96.

1942

"Nicolai Hartmann's Criticism of Kant's Theory of Knowledge." *Philosophy and Phenomenological Research* II: 472-500. [Reprinted in

Studies in the Philosophy of Kant, 1965. Revised version in *Nicolai Hartmann 1882-1982*, ed. A.J. Buch, 46-58. Bonn, Bouvier, 1982.]

"Philosophy in War-Time." *Journal of Philosophy* XXXIX: 71-75.

Reviews of:
Ledger Wood: The Analysis of Knowledge. *Philosophical Review* LI: 415-417.

O.L. Reiser: A New Earth and a New Humanity. *Philosophical Review* LI: 534-535.

Louis Finkelstein and Lyman Bryson: Science, Philosophy and Religion. *Philosophy and Phenomenological Research* III: 249-254.

1943

"The Principle of Parsimony in Empirical Science." *Journal of Philosophy* XL: 617-633.

"Art Criticism and Semantic Discipline." *Delaware Notes* XVI: 31-63.

Reviews of:
Helmut Kuhn: Freedom Forgotten and Remembered. *Philosophy and Phenomenological Research* IV: 101-104.

E.G. Boring: Sensation and Perception in the History of Experimental Psychology [with Harlow W. Ades]. *Philosophy and Phenomenological Research* IV: 104-106.

1944

"Character and Deed." *Philosophy and Phenomenological Research* IV: 547-553.

"Concerning Landmann's 'Nicolai Hartmann and Phenomenology'." *Philosophy and Phenomenological Research* IV: 592-594.

"Judgments of Meaning in Art." *Journal of Philosophy* XLI: 169-178. [Reprinted in *Contemporary Aesthetics*, ed. Mathew Lipman, 183-191. Allyn & Bacon, 1973.]

"Reply to Mrs. Hess" and "Remarks on Mrs. Hess's 'One Word More to Mr. Beck'." *Journal of Philosophy* XLI: 516-518, 520-521.

"Opportunities for Chemists in Literature Service Work." *Journal of Chemical Education* XXI: 315-318.

Reviews of:
> Louis Finkelstein and Lyman Bryson: Science, Philosophy and Religion, Third Symposium. *Philosophical Review* LIII: 90-91.

> E.J. Koehle: Personality: A Study in the Philosophy of Scheler and Hartmann. *Philosophy and Phenomenological Research* IV:582-584.

1945

"A Bibliography of Kant's Ethics." *Delaware Notes* XVIII: 23-43.

"Electronic Tools in Chemical Research" (with Robert H. Osborn). *Electronic Industries* IV: 82-85, 142, 148.

"Editorial Aids to Technical Writers" [with Lura Shorb]. *Special Libraries*: 311-314.

Review of:
> Aron Gurwitsch: La science biologique d'après Kurt Goldstein. *Philosophy and Phenomenological Research* V: 434-435.

1946

"Secondary Quality." *Journal of Philosophy* XLIII: 599-610.

"What Can We Learn from Kant?" *Emory University Quarterly* II: 137-144.

Review of:
William S. Quillian: The Moral Theory of Evolutionary Naturalism. *Philosophy and Phenomenological Research* VII: 179-181.

1947

"Potentiality, Property, and Accident." *Philosophical Review* LVI: 613-630.

"The Distinctive Traits of an Empirical Method." *Journal of Philosophy* XLIV: 337-344.

"Remarks on A. Gurwitsch's 'The Object of Thought'." *Philosophy and Phenomenological Research* VII: 353-355.

"The Primary and Secondary Qualities of Time" [abstract]. *The American Psychologist* II: 402.

"Report of the [Chairman of the] Committee on Information Service." *Proceedings and Addresses of the American Philosophical Association* XX: 546-547.

Reviews of:
J.R. Kantor: Psychology and Logic, vol. I. *Philosophy and Phenomenological Research* VII: 466-470.

Henri Bergson: The Creative Mind. *Philosophy and Phenomenological Research* VII: 659-661.

Arthur Pap: The A Priori in Physical Theory. *Philosophy and Phenomenological Research* VII: 661-662.

1949

Translation of Kant, *Critique of Practical Reason and Other Writings in Moral Philosophy*. Chicago: University of Chicago Press.

"Intelligence and the Crisis of Our Culture." *The Georgia Review* II: 248-259.

"Self-Justification in Epistemology." *Journal of Philosophy* XLV: 253-260.

"A Redefinition of Primary and Secondary Quality" [abstract]. *The American Psychologist* III: 326-327.

"Report[s] of the [Chairman of the] Committee on Information Service." *Proceedings and Addresses of the American Philosophical Association* XXI: 375-376; XXII: 469-470.

"Remarks on the Distinction between the Analytic and the Synthetic." *Philosophy and Phenomenological Research* IX: 720-729. [Reprinted in *Studies in the Philosophy of Kant*, 1965.]

"The Natural Science Ideal in the Social Sciences." *Scientific Monthly* LXVIII: 386-394. [Reprinted in *Theory in Anthropology*, ed. R.A. Manners and D. Kaplan. Aldine Press, 1968.]

1950

"Constructions and Inferred Entities." *Philosophy of Science* XVII: 74-86. [Reprinted in *Readings in the Philosophy of Science*, ed. Herbert Feigl and May Brodbeck. Appleton Century, 1953.]

"Medicine and the Natural Sciences." *The Scalpel of Alpha Epsilon Delta* XX: 47-50.

Translation of Kant, *Foundations of the Metaphysics of Morals*. Chicago: University of Chicago Press. [Reprinted from *Critique of Practical Reason and Other Writings in Moral Philosophy*, with new Introduction.]

"The Limits of Skepticism in History." *South Atlantic Quarterly* XLIX: 461-468.

"Report of [the Chairman of] the Committee on Information Service." *Proceedings and Addresses of the American Philosophical Association* XXIII: 84-86.

Reviews of:
"Four new translations of Kant's works." *Journal of Philosophy* XLVII: 269-270.

Virgilius Ferm: A History of Philosophical Systems. *The New Leader*, December 4, 23-24.

1951

"On Professor Margenau's Kantianism." *Philosophy and Phenomenological Research* XI: 568-573. [Reprinted in *Studies in the Philosophy of Kant*, 1965.]

"Report of [the Chairman of] Information Service Committee." *Proceedings and Addresses of the American Philosophical Association* XXIV: 62-63.

1952

Philosophic Inquiry: An Introduction to Philosophy. New York: Prentice-Hall.

"Strategy in Social Science Research." *The Georgia Review* VI: 322-341.

"The Strife of the Faculties." *The Key Reporter of Phi Beta Kappa* XVII: 2-3, 7.

Review of:
Gottfried Martin: Immanuel Kant. Ontologie und Wissenschaftslehre. *Journal of Philosophy* XLIX: 424-425.

1953

Reviews of:

Wolfgang Ritzel: Studien zum Wandeln der Kantauffassung. *Philosophical Review* LXII: 640-641.

E.M. Butler: The Fortunes of Faust. *Philosophical Review* LXII: 304-305.

H.H. Price: Thinking and Experience. *Journal of Philosophy* L: 558-561.

1954

"Die Kantkritik von C.I. Lewis und der analytischen Schule." *Kant-Studien* XLV: 3-20.

"Psychology and the Norms of Knowledge." *Philosophy and Phenomenological Research* XIV: 494-506.

"Philosophy" in Symposium: "The American Mind, 1929-1954." *Emory University Quarterly* X: 112-121.

Review of:

E.C. Mossner: The Life of David Hume. *The Humanist* XV: 193.

1955

"Sir David Ross on Duty and Purpose in Kant." *Philosophy and Phenomenological Research* XVI: 98-107. [Reprinted in *Studies in the Philosophy of Kant*, 1965.]

"Can Kant's Synthetic Judgments be Made Analytic?" *Kant-Studien* XLVII: 168-181. [Reprinted in *Studies in the Philosophy of Kant*, 1965; in *Kant: A Collection of Critical Essays*, ed. R. Wolff, Doubleday, 1967; in *Kant: Disputed Questions* ed. M.S. Gram, Quadrangle Books, 1967; and in German translation in *Kant: Zur*

Deutung seiner Theorie von Erkennen und Handeln, ed. Gerold Prauss, Köln, 1973.]

"Kant's Letter to Marcus Herz, February 21, 1772. Introduction." *The Philosophical Forum* XIII: 96-102. [Reprinted in *Studies in the Philosophy of Kant*, 1965.]

Reviews of:
    H.W. Cassirer: Kant's First Critique. *Philosophy and Phenomenological Research* XVI: 248-252.

    Sverre Klausen: Kants Ethik und ihre Kritiker. *Journal of Philosophy* LII: 526-527.

1956

Translation of Kant, *Critique of Practical Reason*. New York: Liberal Arts Press. [Revised, with new Introduction, from 1949 edition.]

"Kant's Theory of Definition." *Philosophical Review* LXV: 179-191. [Reprinted in *Studies in the Philosophy of Kant*, 1965; in Wolff, *Kant: A Collection of Critical Essays*; and in Gram, *Kant: Disputed Questions*.]

"Nicolai Hartmann," in *Encyclopedia of Morals*, ed. Vergilius Ferm, 200-207. New York: Philosophical Library.

Review of:
    Leibniz's Philosophical Papers and Letters, translated by L.E. Loemker. *Emory University Quarterly* XII: 187-189.

1957

"Apodictic Imperatives." *Kant-Studien* XLIX: 7-24. [Reprinted in *Studies in the Philosophy of Kant*, 1965; and in R. Wolff, ed., *Kant: Foundations of the Metaphysics of Morals, Text and Critical Essays*, Bobbs Merrill, 1969.]

"On the Meta-Semantics of the Problem of the Synthetic A Priori."
Mind LXVI: 228-232. [Reprinted in *Studies in the Philosophy of Kant*,
1965.]

Translation of Kant, *Perpetual Peace*. New York: Liberal Arts Press.
[A reprint, with a new introduction, of the translation in *Critique of
Practical Reason and Other Writings in Moral Philosophy*, 1949, and
reprinted in *Kant on History*, 1963.]

Review of:
    Heinz Heimsoeth: Studien zur Philosophie Immanuel Kants.
    Philosophical Review LXVI: 405-409.

1959

Translation of Kant, *Foundations of the Metaphysics of Morals*. Liberal
Arts Press. [Revised from 1950 Chicago edition, and reprinted in *Kant:
Foundations of the Metaphysics of Morals, Text and Critical Essays*,
ed. R. Wolff.]

Reviews of:
    A.R.C. Duncan: Practical Reason and Morality. *Philosophical
    Review* LXVIII: 400-402.

    Schopenhauer: The World as Will and Idea, transl. E.F.J.
    Payne. *Philosophy and Phenomenological Research* XX: 279-
    280.

1960

A Commentary on Kant's Critique of Practical Reason. Chicago:
University of Chicago Press. [German translation of K.-H. Ilting,
München: Wilhelm Fink Verlag, 1975.]

Six Secular Philosophers. New York: Harper & Brothers. [Re-issue
Collier, 1966.]

[Report on the] "Hauptversammlung of the Kant-Gesellschaft."
Philosophy and Phenomenological Research XXI: 286-287.

Reviews of:
Helmut Stoffer: Aufgabe und Gestaltung des
Philosophieunterrichts. *Philosophy and Phenomenological
Research* XXI: 284-285.

D. Runes: Pictorial History of Philosophy. *Philosophy and
Phenomenological Research* XXI: 274.

1961

"Das Faktum der Vernunft. Zur Rechtfertigungsproblematik in der
Ethik." *Kant-Studien* LII: 271-282. [English translation in *Studies in
the Philosophy of Kant,* 1965.]

Articles on *The American People's Encyclopedia*: Descartes, Kant,
Leibniz.

Reviews of:
K.M. Wolff: Georg Simmel. *Philosophy and
Phenomenological Research* XXI: 422.

A.J. Ayer: Logical Positivism. *Philosophy and
Phenomenological Research* XXI: 423.

Mariano Campo: Schizzo storico della esegesi e critica
kantiana. *Philosophy and Phenomenological Research* XXII:
132-133.

J.O. Urmson: The Concise Encyclopedia of Western
Philosophy and Philosophers. *Philosophy and
Phenomenological Research* XXII: 121-122.

A. Schil: Kant's Pre-Critical Ethics. *The New Scholasticism*
XXXV: 410-412.

J.W. Wiggens and H. Schoeck: Relativism and the Study of
Man. *Emory University Quarterly* XVII: 248-249.

1962

"Les deux concepts kantiens du vouloir dans leur contexte politique." *Annales de philosohie politique* IV: 119-137. [English translation in *Studies in the Philosophy of Kant*, 1965. Reprinted as "Kant's Two Conceptions of Will in Their Political Context," in *Kant and Political Philosophy*, eds. R. Beiner and W. Booth. New Haven: Yale University Press, 1993.]

"Report on Grant no. 2684 (1959): History of Neo-Kantianism." *American Philosophical Society Year Book*: 462-463.

Editor of *The Monist*, Vol. 47, no. 1: "Philosophical Implications of the New Cosmology."

Review of:
B.K. Milmed: Kant and Current Philosophical Issues. *Philosophy and Phenomenological Research* XXII: 426-427.

1963

[Editor] *Kant on History*. Bobbs Merrill Co. [Contains Introduction and the following translations by L.W. B.: "What is Enlightenment?," "Idea for a Universal History" and "Perpetual Peace."]

"Introduction" to Kant, *Lectures on Ethics*, transl. Louis Infield. New York: Harper and Row. [Reprinted 1980 by Hackett Publishing Co.]

Articles in the *Encyclopedia International* [formerly *Grolier Encyclopedia*]: Agnosticism, Kant, Phenomenon, Transcendental.

Review of:
Martin Heidegger: Kant and the Problem of Metaphysics. *Philosophical Review* LXXII: 396-398.

1965

Studies in the Philosophy of Kant. New York: Bobbs Merrill Co.

"Agent, Actor, Spectator, and Critic." *The Monist* XLIX: 167-182.

Principal editor of *The Monist*, Vol. 49, no. 2: "Agent and Spectator."

1966

[Editor] *Philosophy of the Eighteenth Century.* New York: The Free Press.

"Conscious and Unconscious Motives." *Mind* LXXV: 155-179. [German translation in *Gründe und Ursache gesellschaftlichen Handelns,* ed. Jürgen Ritsert, 165-195. Frankfurt, Campus Verlag, 1975.]

"Is There Intelligent Extra-Terrestrial Life?" *The Rochester Review*, Autumn number, 12-14, 27.

"Comments" [on Nicholas Rescher, "Evaluative Metaphysics"] in *Metaphysics and Explanation*, ed. W.H. Capitan and K.R. Merrill. Pittsburgh: University of Pittsburgh Press.

"The Second Analogy and the Principle of Indeterminacy." *Kant-Studien* LVII: 199-205. [Reprinted in *Einheit und Sein* - Festschrift für Gottfried Martin, Bonn, 1966; in *The First Critique*, ed. T. Penelhum and J.J. MacIntosh, Wadsworth, 1970; in *Essays on Kant and Hume*, 1978; German translation in *Kant: Zur Deutung seiner Theorie von Erkennen und Handeln*, ed. G. Prauss, 1973.]

"Report of [chairman of the] Committee on Publication." *Proceedings and Addresses of the American Philosophical Association* XXXIX: 77.

Reviews of:
   M.J. Gregor: Laws of Freedom. *Philosophical Review* LXXV: 254-258.

   Samuel Atlas: From Critical to Speculative Idealism. *Philosophical Quarterly* XVI: 281-283.

H. Delius and G. Patzig: Argumentationen. *Philosophical Quarterly* XVI: 186.

1967

"Kant's Strategy." *Journal of the History of Ideas* XXVIII: 224-236. [Reprinted in Penelhum and MacIntosh, *The First Critique*, 1970, and in *Essays on Kant and Hume*, 1978; Serbian translation by P. Cicovacki, in *Gledista* XXVIII (1987): 175-188.]

"Once More Unto the Breach. Kant's Answer to Hume, Again." *Ratio* IX: 33-37. [Reprinted in *Essays on Kant and Hume*, 1978; German translation by Wolfgang Farr, *Hume and Kant: Studien zum Erkenntnisproblem*, Freiburg, 1981.]

"German Philosophy," "Neo-Kantianism," and "William Stern." Articles in *Encyclopedia of Philosophy* III: 291-309; V: 468-473; VIII: 15. New York: Macmillan.

"Report of [Chairman of] the committee on Publication." *Proceedings and Addresses of American Philosophical Association* XL: 72.

[Editor] *The Monist* LI: nos. 3 and 4: "Kant Today, I and II."

Review of:
D.P. Dryer: Kant's Solution for Verification in Metaphysics. *Journal of Value Inquiry* I: 153-155.

1968

Philosophic Inquiry, second edition [with Robert L. Holmes]. New York: Prentice-Hall.

"Critique of Pure Reason." *The Encyclopedia Americana* VIII: 224.

Alban Gregory Widgery [obituary]. *Proceedings and Addresses of the American Philosophical Association* XLI: 138-140.

1969

Early German Philosophy. Kant and His Predecessors. Cambridge, Mass.,: Harvard University Press, Belknap Press.

[Editor] *Kant Studies Today.* Open Court Publishing Company.

"Reply to Professors Murphy and Williams." *Ratio* XI: 82-87.

"Lambert und Hume in Kants Entwicklung von 1769-1772." *Kant-Studien* LX: 123-130. [English translation in *Essays on Kant and Hume*, 1978.]

"The Kantianism of Lewis." in *The Philosophy of C.I. Lewis* (The Library of Living Philosophy, Open Court Publishing Company), 271-288. [Reprinted from *Studies in the Philosophy of Kant*, 1965.]

"Report of the Delegate to ACLS" and "Report of the [Chairman of the] Committee on Publication." *Proceedings and Addresses of the American Philosophical Association* XLII: 108-110, 113.

Review of:
Kant: Philosophical Correspondence, 1759-1799, ed. and transl. Arunulf Zweig. *Philosophical Review* LXXVIII: 557-559.

1970

"Professions, Ethics, and Professional Ethics," in *Ethics and the School Administrator,* ed. G.L. Immengart and J.M. Burroughs, 43-56. Danville, IL: Interstate Printers and Publishers.

"Introduction and Bibliography [to the Philosophy of the History of Philosophy]." *The Monist* LIII: 523-531.

"Report of the Delegate of Learned Societies." *Proceedings and Addresses of the American Philosophical Association* XLIII: 120-121.

Review of:

Gottfried Martin: Immanuel Kant, Ontologie und Wissenschaftstheorie, 4. Aufl. *Kant-Studien* LXI: 273-274.

1971

"Kant and the Right of Revolution." *Journal of the History of Ideas* XXXII: 411-422. [Reprinted in *Essays on Kant and Hume*, 1978.]

"Mrs. Foot on the Sufficiency of Hypothetical Imperatives." *Philosophical Exchange* I: 147-152.

1972

"Lovejoy as a Critic of Kant." *Journal of the History of Ideas* XXXIII: 471-484. [Reprinted in *Essays on Kant and Hume*, 1978.]

[Editor] *Proceedings of the Third International Kant Congress*, Rochester, 1970. Dordrecht: Reidel.

"Immanuel Kant." In *The Horizon Book of Makers of Modern Thought*, ed. B. Mazlish, 220-235. New York: American Heritage Publishing Company.

1973

"Antimony of Pure Reason." In *Dictionary of the History of Ideas*, ed. P.P. Wiener, I: 91-93. New York: Charles Scribner.

"Extraterrestrial Intelligent Life." *Proceedings and Addresses of the American Philosophical Association* XLV (1971-72): 5-21. [Danish translation, "Intelligent liv uden for Jorden." *UFO-Kontakt*, 1973, 96-99, 119-122, 156-160. Reprinted in E. Regis, ed., *Extraterrestrials*, Cambridge University Press, 1988.]

[Editor.] "Philosophy of War." *The Monist* LVII: no. 4.

1974

[Editor] *Kant's Theory of Knowledge. Selected Papers from the Third International Kant Congress.* Dordrecht: Reidel.

"The Fourth International Kant Congress." *Philosophie* (Zurich) II: no. 3 (May, June 1974), 8.

"'Was-Must Be' and 'Is-Ought' in Hume." *Philosophical Studies* XXVI: 219-228. [Reprinted in *Essays on Kant and Hume*, 1978.]

1975

The Actor and the Spectator. Cassirer Lectures. New Haven: Yale University Press. [German translation by K.-H. Ilting, *Aketur und Betrachter: Zur Grundlegung der Handlungstheorie*, Freiburg, 1976.]

"Bringing Philosophy outside the Classroom." *Rochester Times Union*, September 18.

"Kritische Bemerkungen zur vermeintlichen Apriorität der Geschmacksurteile." In *Bewusstsein, Festschrift für Gerhard Funke*, ed. A.J. Bucher *et al.* , 369-373. Bonn, Bouvier. [English translation in *Essays on Kant and Hume*, 1978.]

"Hatte denn der Philosoph von Königsberg keine Träume?" *Akten des IV. Kant Kongresses*, III: 26-43. Berlin, Walter de Gruyter. [English translation in *Essays on Kant and Hume*, 1978.]

"Analytic and Synthetic Judgments before Kant." In *Reflections on Kant's Philosophy*, ed. W.H. Werkmeister, 7-27. Gainesville: University Presses of Florida. [Reprinted in *Essays on Kant and Hume*, 1978.]

"What Can We Learn from Kant?" *Proceedings of the Heracleitean Society* (Western Michigan University) I: no. 4, 242-253.

1976

"Reformation, Revolution, and Restoration in Hegel's Political Philosophy." *Journal of the History of Philosophy* XIV: 51-62.

"Is there a Non Sequitur in Kant's Proof of the Principle of Causation?" *Kant-Studien* LXVII: 385-389. [Reprinted in *Essays on Kant and Hume*, 1978.]

"Report of the Acting Delegate to the American Council of Learned Societies." *Proceedings and Addresses of the American Philosophical Association* XLIX: 66-67.

"Towards a Meta-Critique of Pure Reason." In *Proceedings of the Ottawa Kant Congress*, 182-198. Ottawa: University of Ottawa Press. [Reprinted in *Essays on Kant and Hume*, 1978.]

1978

Essays on Kant and Hume. New Haven: Yale University Press.

[Editor] "The Philosophy of Thomas Reid." *The Monist* LXI: no. 2.

1979

"World Enough, and Time." In *Probability, Time, and Space in Eighteenth-century Literature*, ed. Paula Backscheider, 113-140. New York: AMS Press.

"Kant on Education." In *Education in the Eighteenth Century*, ed. John Browning. Studies in the Eighteenth Century VII: 10-24. New York: Garland.

"A Prussian Hume and a Scottish Kant." *McGill Hume Studies*, ed. David F. Norton, N. Capaldi and W.L. Robison, 63-79. San Diego. [Included also in *Essays on Kant and Hume*, 1978; German translation by Wolgang Farr, *Hume und Kant: Studien zum Erkenntnisproblem*, Freiburg, 1981. Reprinted in *Prolegomena in Focus*, ed. B. Logan, 139-155. Oxford: Routledge, 1996.]

[Anonymous.] *Mr. Boswell Dines with Professor Kant*. Edinburgh, Tragara Press.

1980

"Philosophy as Literature." In *Philosophical Style*, ed. Berel Lang, 234-258. Chicago: Nelson Hall.

1981

"Was Haben Wir von Kant Gelernt?" *Kant-Studien* LXXII: 1-10. [English translation in *Self and Nature in Kant's Philosophy*, ed. A. Wood. Cornell University Press, 1984.]

"Über die Regelmässigkeit der Natur bei Kant." *Dialectica* XXXV: 43-56. [English translation in *Synthese* XLVII: 449-64.]

Review of:
Ernst Cassirer: Symbol, Myth, and Culture. *Archiv für Geschichte der Philosophie* LXIII: 111-112.

1982

"Doctoral Dissertations on Kant Accepted by Universities in the United States and Canada 1879-1980." *Kant-Studien* LXXIII: 96-113.

1983

Review of:
Peter Heintel und Ludwig Nagl: Zur Kantforschung der Gegenwart. *Idealistic Studies* XIII: 74-76.

1984

"The Philosophical Implications of Establishing Permanent Human Presence in Space." *Office of Technology Assessment*, U.S. Congress, Appendix, 22-37.

Review of:
S.J. Dick: Plurality of Worlds. *Journal of the History of Philosophy* XXII: 365-366.

1985

Japanese translation of *Commentary on Critique of Practical Reason*, by Shogo Fujita. Osaka.

Reviews of:
J.P. Wright: The Sceptical Realism of David Hume. *Eighteenth-Century Studies* XVIII: 254-257.

K.L. Reinhold: Korrespondenz. *Journal of the History of Philosophy* XXIII: 596-597.

1986

Kant's Latin Writings: Translations, Commentaries, and Notes. New York and Bern: Peter Lang.

"Kant on Faith and Reason." *TLS* June 20, 679. [Letter]

Reviews of:
Karl Ameriks: Kant's Theory of Mind. *Eighteenth-Century Bibliography* VIII: 168

Roger Scruton: *Kant. Eighteenth-Century Bibliography* VIII: 476.

Obituary for W.H. Walsh. *NAKS Newsletter*, June. [Reprinted in *Kant-Studien* LXXVII: 271-272.]

1987

"Five Conceptions of Freedom in Kant." In *Stephen Körner - Philosophical Analysis and Reconstruction*, ed. J.T.J. Srzednicki, 35-51. Dordrecht, Martinus Nijhoff.

Foreword to Manfred Kuehn's *Scottish Common Sense in Germany*, ix-xi. Montreal: McGill Queens University.

"Science and the Belief in Extraterrestrials." *Research Review* (University of Rochester), Summer 1987, 17.

Obituary for Maurice Mandelbaum. *Proceedings and Addresses of the American Philosophical Association* LX: 858-859.

Review of :
   Hegel: The Letters, ed. Butler and Seidler. *Journal of the History of Philosophy* XXV: 456-458.

1988

Kant Selections, New York: Macmillan 1988.

"Pursuing an Advanced Degree in Philosophy" *Proceedings and Addresses of the American Philosophical Association* LXII: Supplement 1, 264-266.

Reviews of:
   Ernst Behler, ed.: Immanuel Kant: Philosophical Writings;
   Frederick C. Beiser: The Fate of Reason;
   G. di Giovanni and H.S. Harris: Between Kant and Hegel.
   Eighteenth-Century Studies XXI: 250-253.

   Gawlik and Kreimendahl: Hume in der deutschen Aufklärung.
   Eighteenth-Century Studies XXI: 405-408.

   Crowe: The Extraterrestrial Life Debate. *Journal of the History of Philosophy* XXVI: 324-326.

1989

"Two Ways of Reading Kant's Letter to Herz: Comments on Carl." In *Kant's Transcendental Deductions*, ed. Eckart Förster, 21-26. Palo Alto, Stanford University Press.

Reviews of:
   S. Palmquist: Complete Index to Kemp Smith's Translation of *Critique of Pure Reason*. *Kant Studien* LXXX: 121-122.

Delfosse, *et al*: Wolff-Index. *Lessing Yearbook* XXI: 264-265.

1990

Second and revised edition of Kant's *Foundations of the Metaphysics of Morals*. New York: Macmillan, Library of Liberal Arts.

1992

Second and revised edition of *Kant's Latin Writings: Translations, Commentaries, and Notes*. New York and Bern: Peter Lang. (The first edition was published in 1986.)

"Goethe and Nietzsche on Time and Eternity." *Lonergan Review*, 1991-92.

Foreword to Klaus Reich's *The Completeness of Kant's Table of Judgments*, trans. J. Kneller and M. Losonsky, xi-xx. Stanford, Stanford University Press.

1993

"How I Became Almost a Philosopher." In *Falling in Love with Wisdom*, ed. D.D. Karnos and R.G. Shoemaker, 13-15. New York, Oxford University Press.

"From Leibniz to Kant." *Routledge History of Philosophy*, Vol. VI: *The Age of German Idealism*, ed. R.C. Salomon and K.M. Higgins, 5-39. New York, Routledge.

Review of:
    John Zammito: The Genesis of Kant's Critique of Judgment. *Eighteenth-Century Studies* XXVII: 135-138.

1994

Kant's Three Critiques, Introduced by Prof. Lewis White Beck. Bristol: Thoemmes Press.

Vol. 1 *Critik der Reinen Vernunft,* First Edition 1781.

Vol. 2 *Critik der Reinen Vernunft,* Second Edition 1787.

Vol. 3 *Critik der Practischen Vernunft,* First edition 1788.

Vol. 4 *Critik der Urtheilskraft,* First Edition 1790.

Vol. 5 *Critik der Urtheilskraft,* Second Edition 1793.

Index